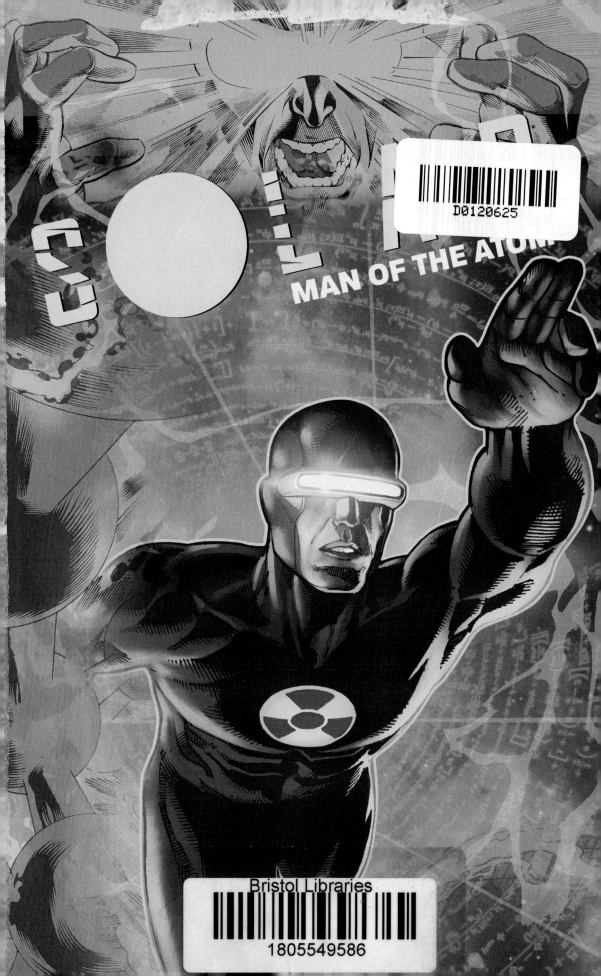

MAN OF THE ATOM

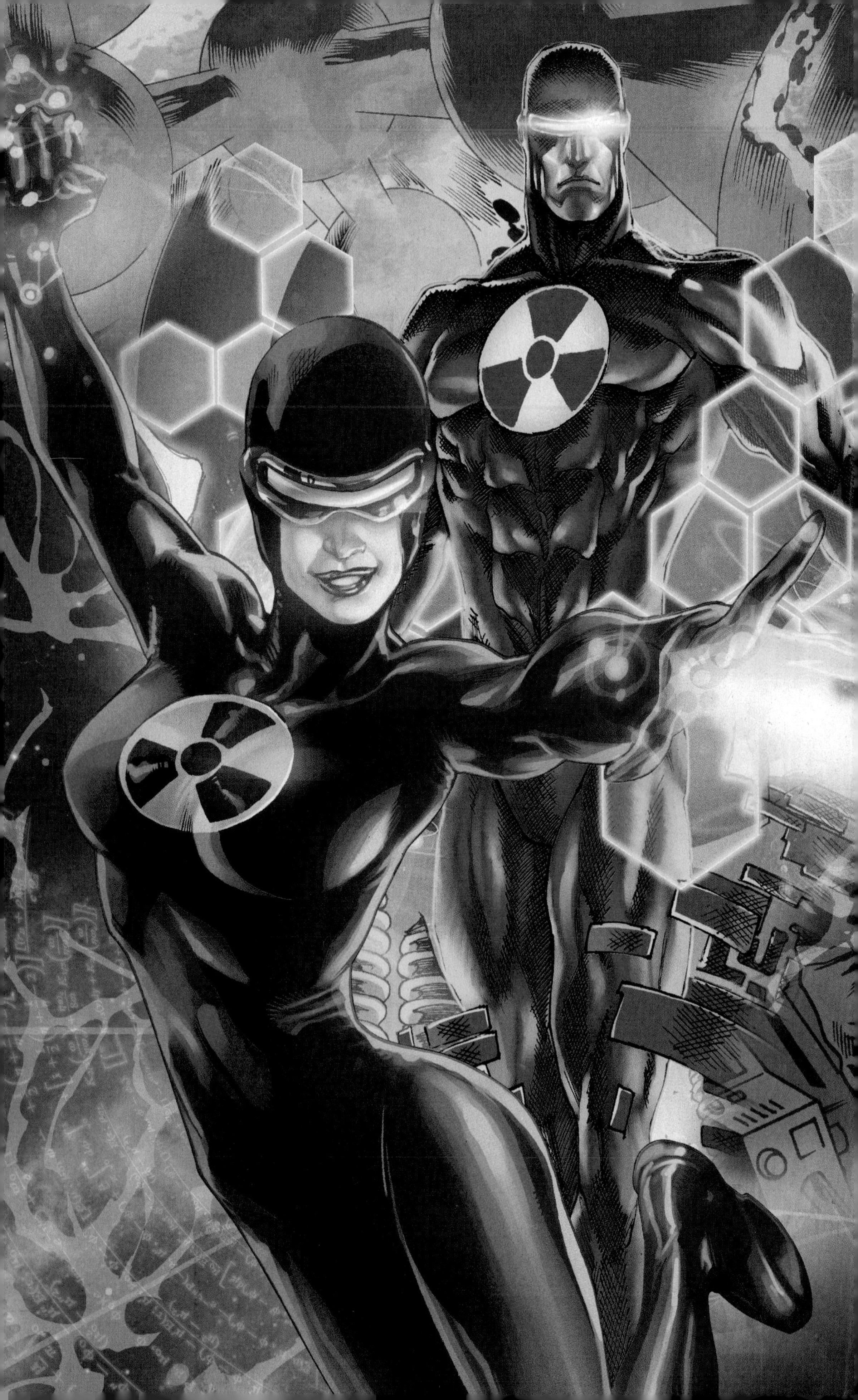

SOLAR®
MAN OF THE ATOM
NUCLEAR FAMILY

WRITTEN & LETTERED BY
FRANK J. BARBIERE

ART BY
JOE BENNETT
RICHARD CASE
ROGER ROBINSON
MATTHEW MARKS
SANDY JARRELL
JONATHAN LAU

COLORS BY
LAUREN AFFE
KELLY FITZPATRICK
MAURÎCIO WALLACE
LUIGI ANDERSON

COLLECTION COVER BY
JUAN DOE

COLLECTION DESIGN BY
KATIE HIDALGO

SPECIAL THANKS TO **TOM ENGLEMAN**, **BEN CAWOOD**,
NICOLE BLAKE, AND **COLIN MCLAUGHLIN**

PACKAGED AND EDITED BY **NATE COSBY**
OF COSBY AND SONS PRODUCTIONS

THIS VOLUME COLLECTS ISSUES 1-4 OF SOLAR
MAN OF THE ATOM BY DYNAMITE ENTERTAINMENT

DYNAMITE®

Nick Barrucci, CEO / Publisher
Juan Collado, President / COO
Rich Young, Director Business Development
Keith Davidsen, Marketing Manager

Joe Rybandt, Senior Editor
Hannah Elder, Associate Editor
Molly Mahan, Associate Editor

Jason Ullmeyer, Design Director
Katie Hidalgo, Graphic Designer
Chris Caniano, Digital Associate
Rachel Kilbury, Digital Assistant

ISBN-10: 1-60690-542-2   ISBN-13: 978-1-60690-542-5   First Printing   10 9 8 7 6 5 4 3 2

Visit us online at **www.DYNAMITE.com**
Follow us on Twitter **@dynamitecomics**
 Like us on Facebook **/Dynamitecomics**

For information regarding press, media rights, foreign rights, licensing, promotions, and advertising e-mail:

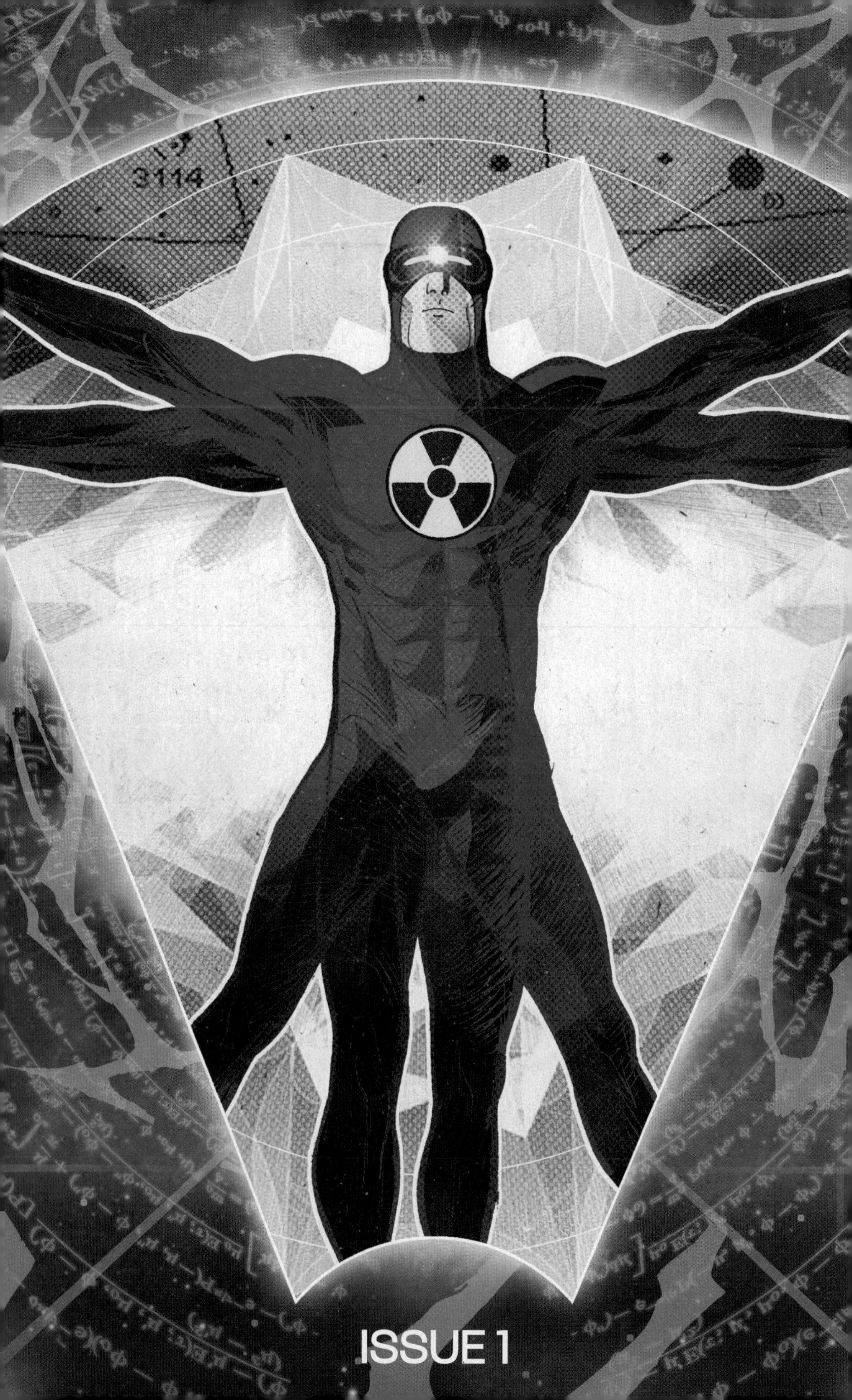
3114
ISSUE 1

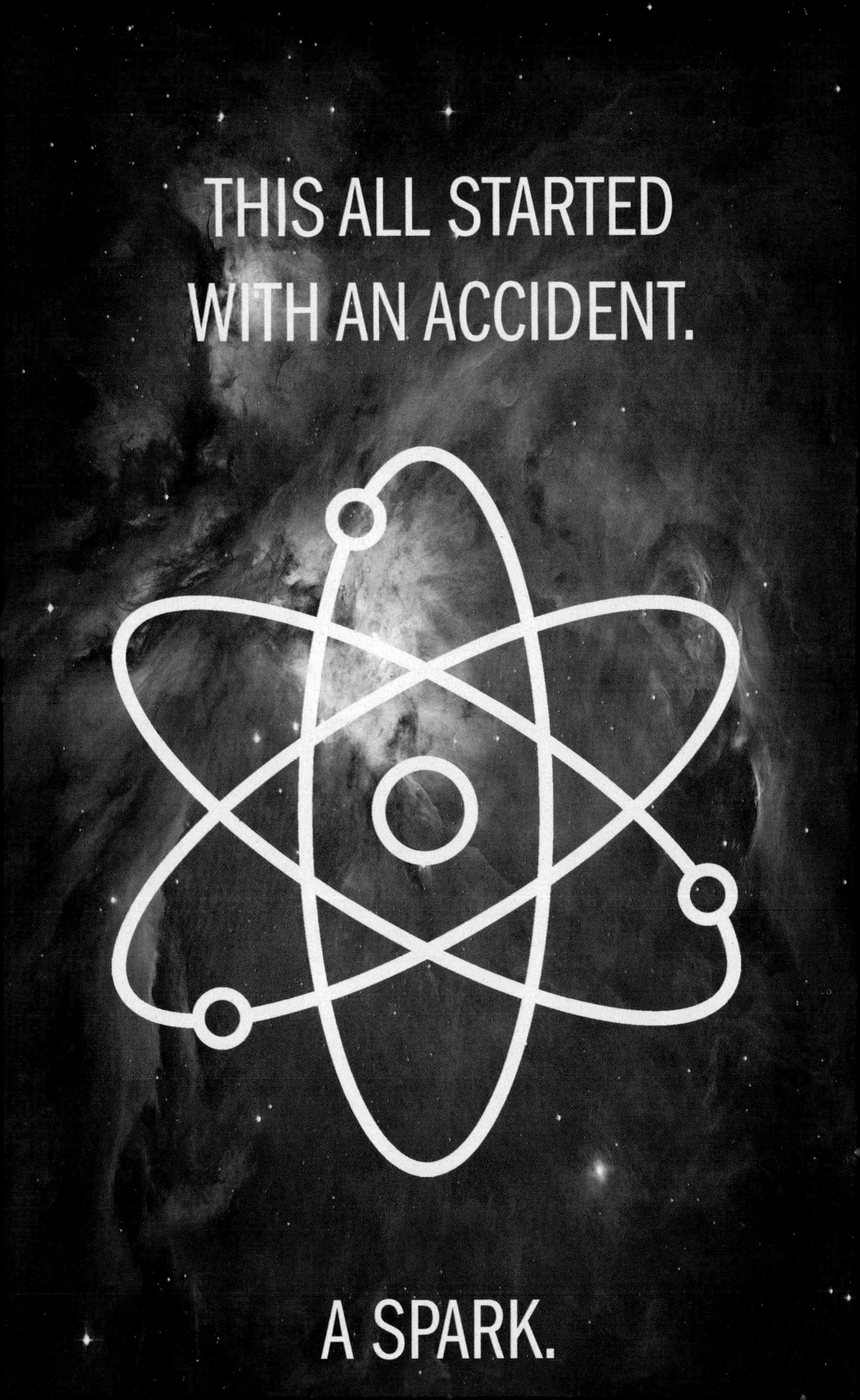
THIS ALL STARTED
WITH AN ACCIDENT.
A SPARK.

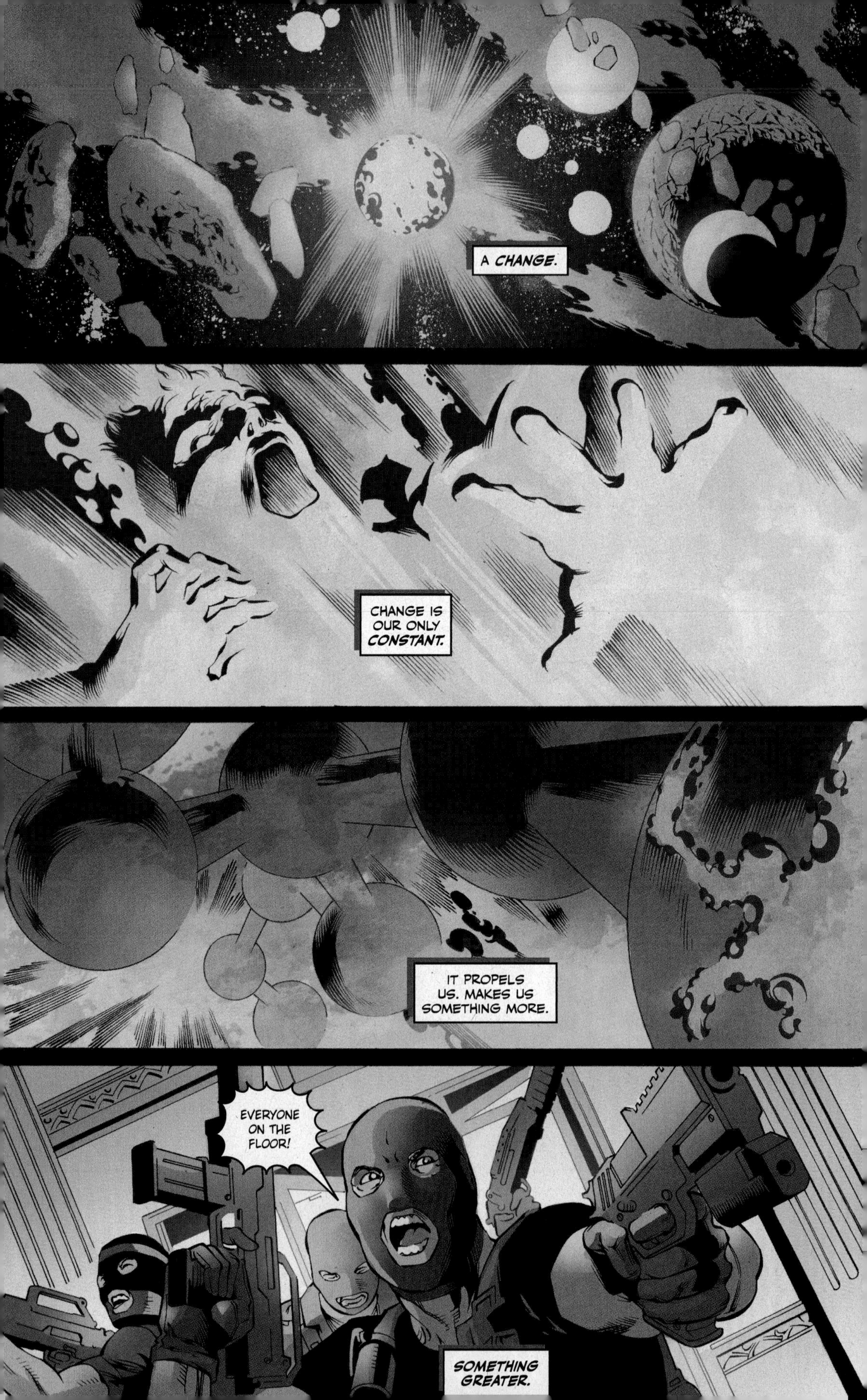
A CHANGE.
CHANGE IS OUR ONLY CONSTANT.
IT PROPELS US. MAKES US SOMETHING MORE.
EVERYONE ON THE FLOOR!
SOMETHING GREATER.

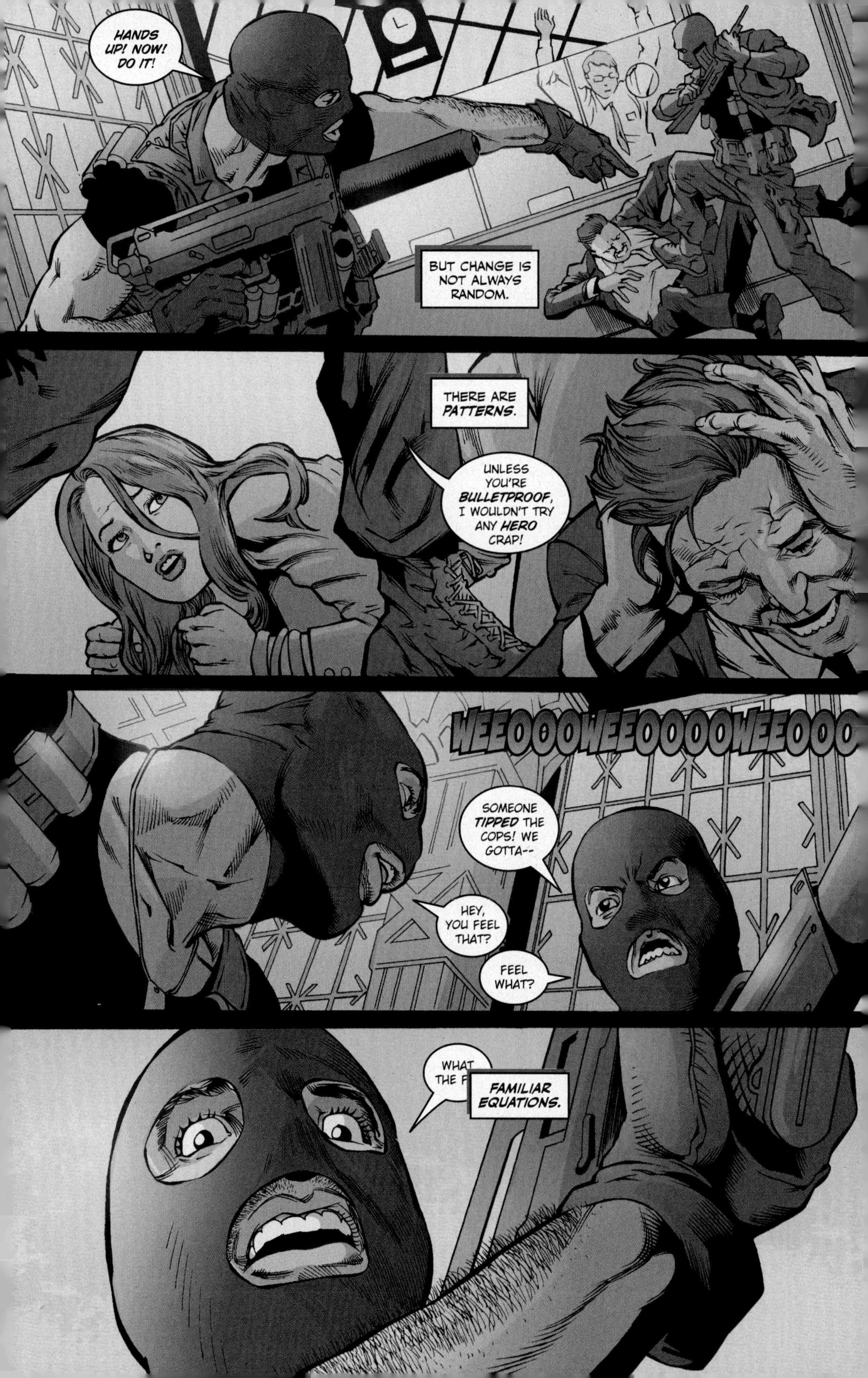
HANDS UP! NOW! DO IT!
BUT CHANGE IS NOT ALWAYS RANDOM.
THERE ARE PATTERNS.
UNLESS YOU'RE BULLETPROOF, I WOULDN'T TRY ANY HERO CRAP!
WEEOOOWEEOOOOWEEOOO
SOMEONE TIPPED THE COPS! WE GOTTA--
HEY, YOU FEEL THAT?
FEEL WHAT?
WHAT THE F
FAMILIAR EQUATIONS.

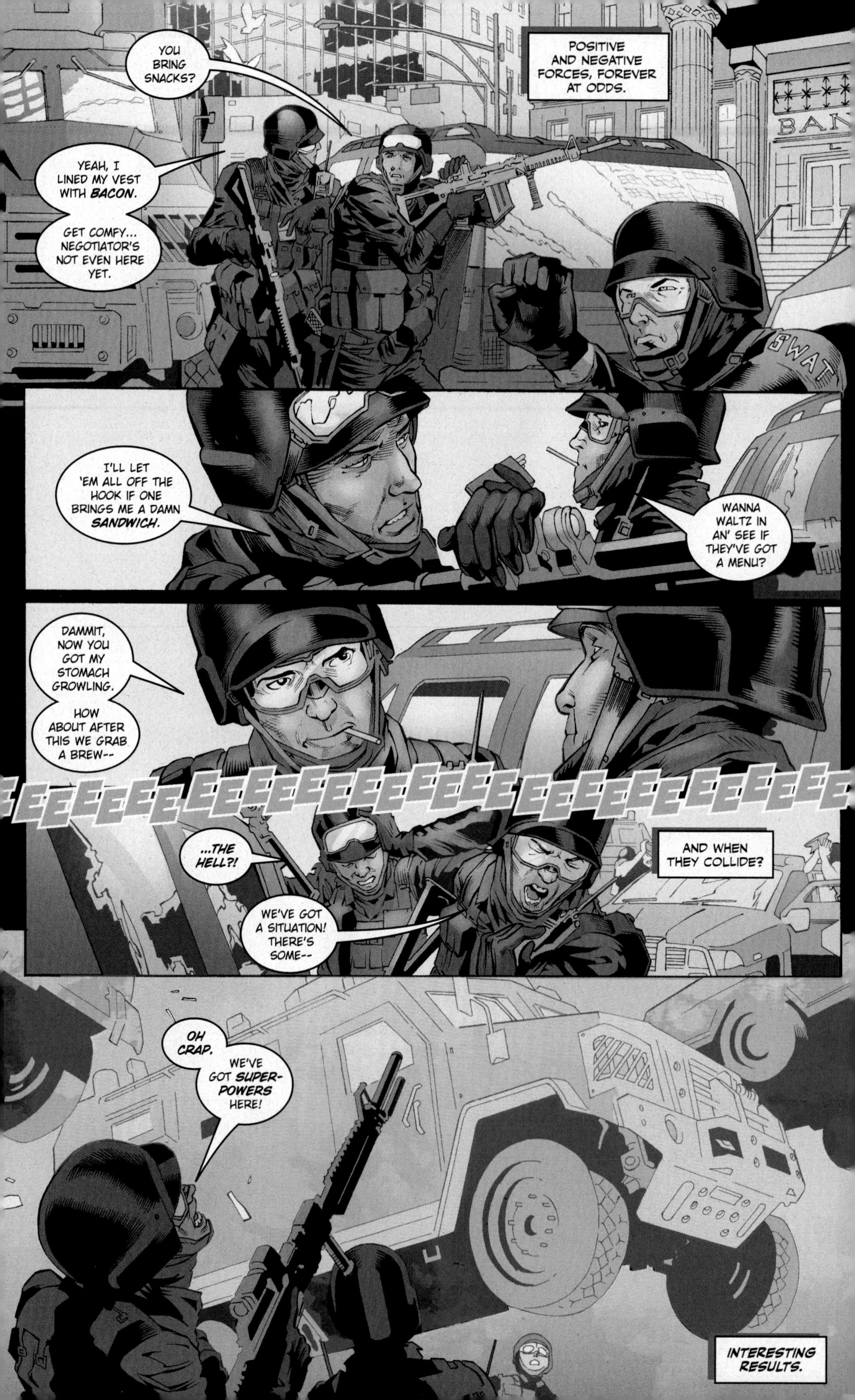
POSITIVE AND NEGATIVE FORCES, FOREVER AT ODDS.
YOU BRING SNACKS?
YEAH, I LINED MY VEST WITH BACON.
GET COMFY... NEGOTIATOR'S NOT EVEN HERE YET.
I'LL LET 'EM ALL OFF THE HOOK IF ONE BRINGS ME A DAMN SANDWICH.
WANNA WALTZ IN AN' SEE IF THEY'VE GOT A MENU?
DAMMIT, NOW YOU GOT MY STOMACH GROWLING.
HOW ABOUT AFTER THIS WE GRAB A BREW--
EEEEEEEEEEEEEEEEEEEEEEEEEEEEEEEEEE
...THE HELL?!
WE'VE GOT A SITUATION! THERE'S SOME--
AND WHEN THEY COLLIDE?
OH CRAP.
WE'VE GOT SUPER-POWERS HERE!
INTERESTING RESULTS.

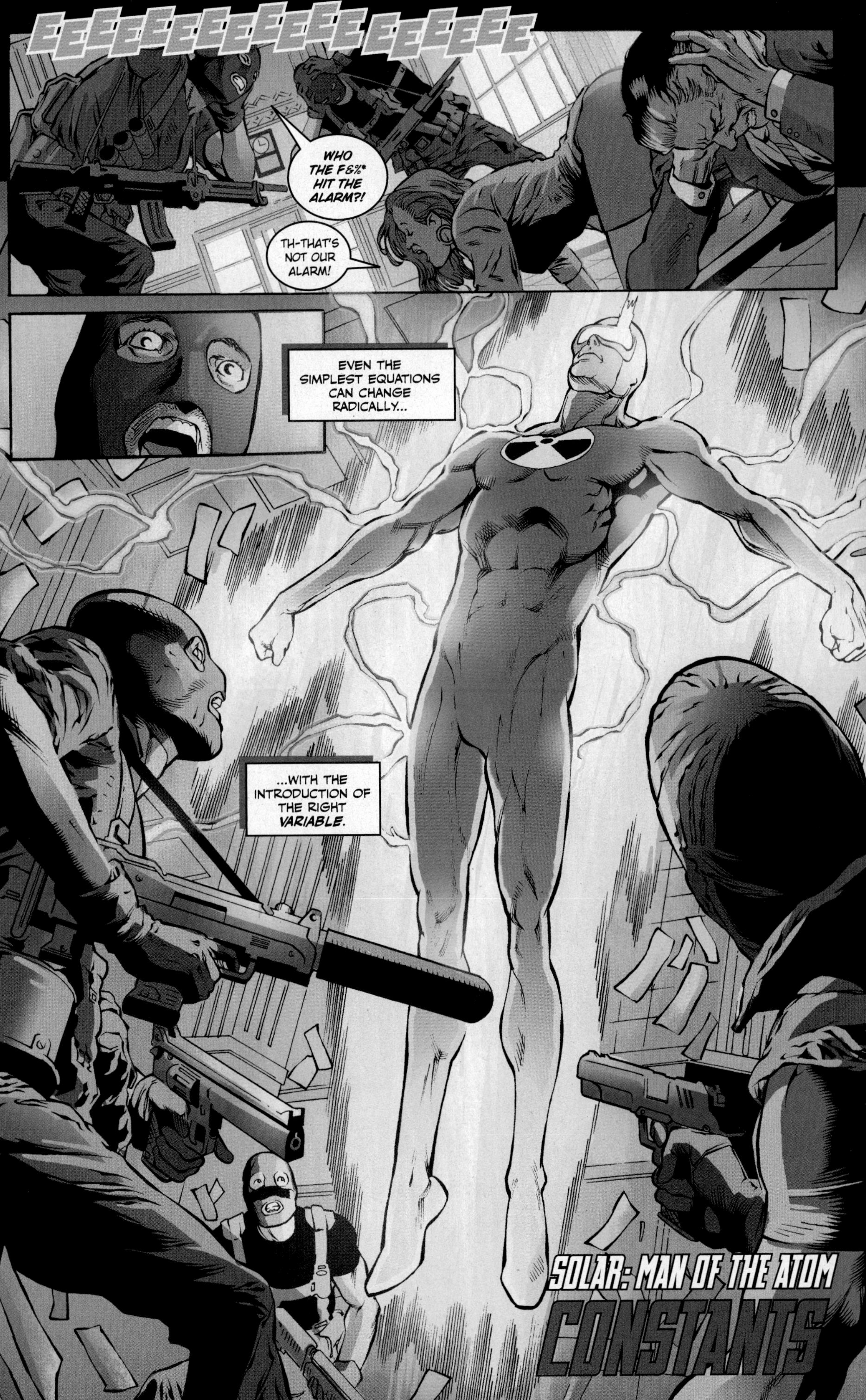
EEEEEEEEEEEEEEEEEEE
WHO THE F&%* HIT THE ALARM?!
TH-THAT'S NOT OUR ALARM!
EVEN THE SIMPLEST EQUATIONS CAN CHANGE RADICALLY...
...WITH THE INTRODUCTION OF THE RIGHT VARIABLE.
SOLAR: MAN OF THE ATOM
CONSTANTS

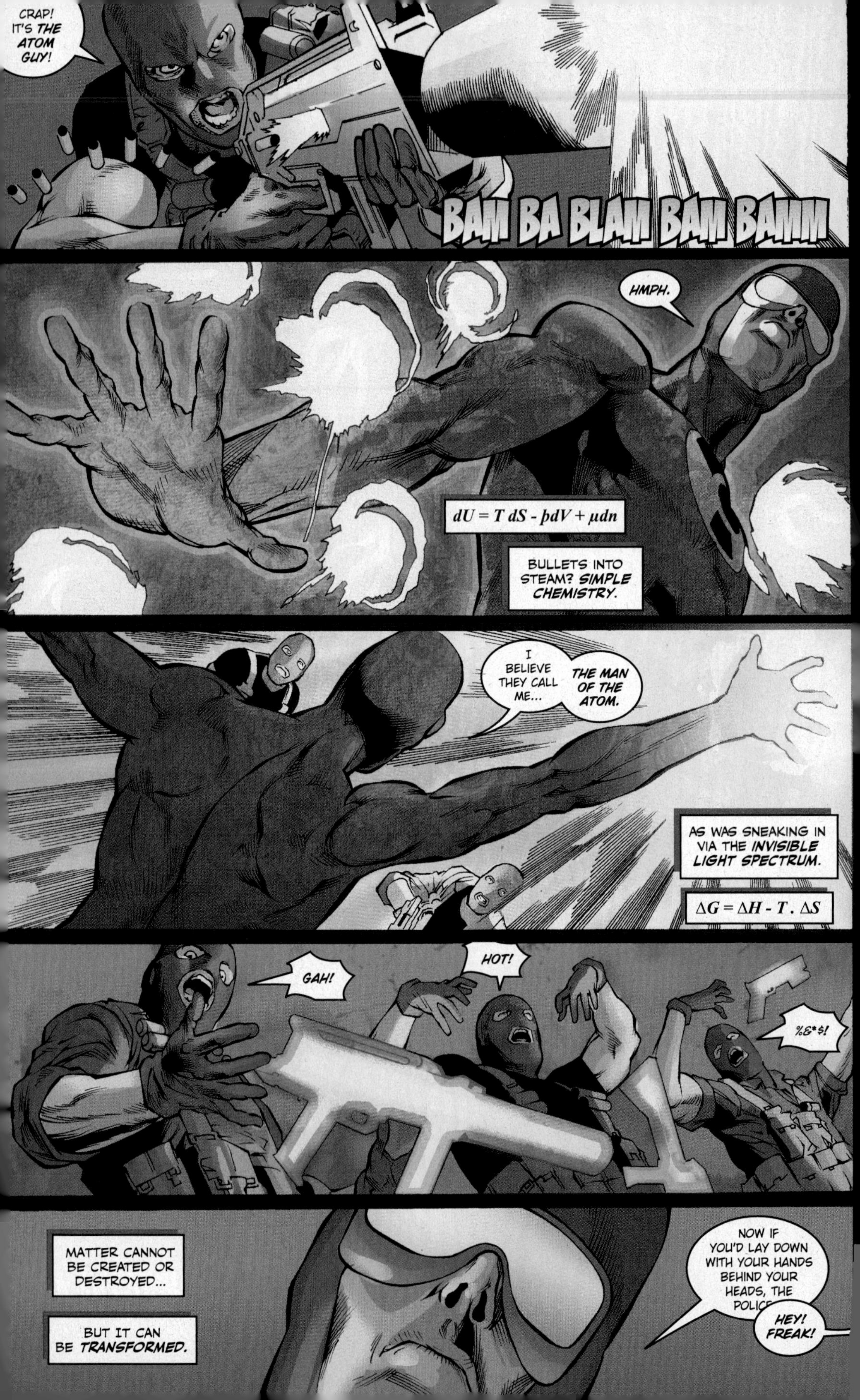
CRAP! IT'S THE ATOM GUY!
BAM BA BLAM BAM BAMM
HMPH.
$dU = T\,dS - p\,dV + \mu dn$
BULLETS INTO STEAM? SIMPLE CHEMISTRY.
I BELIEVE THEY CALL ME...
THE MAN OF THE ATOM.
AS WAS SNEAKING IN VIA THE INVISIBLE LIGHT SPECTRUM.
$\Delta G = \Delta H - T . \Delta S$
GAH!
HOT!
%&*$!
MATTER CANNOT BE CREATED OR DESTROYED...
BUT IT CAN BE TRANSFORMED.
NOW IF YOU'D LAY DOWN WITH YOUR HANDS BEHIND YOUR HEADS, THE POLICE
HEY! FREAK!

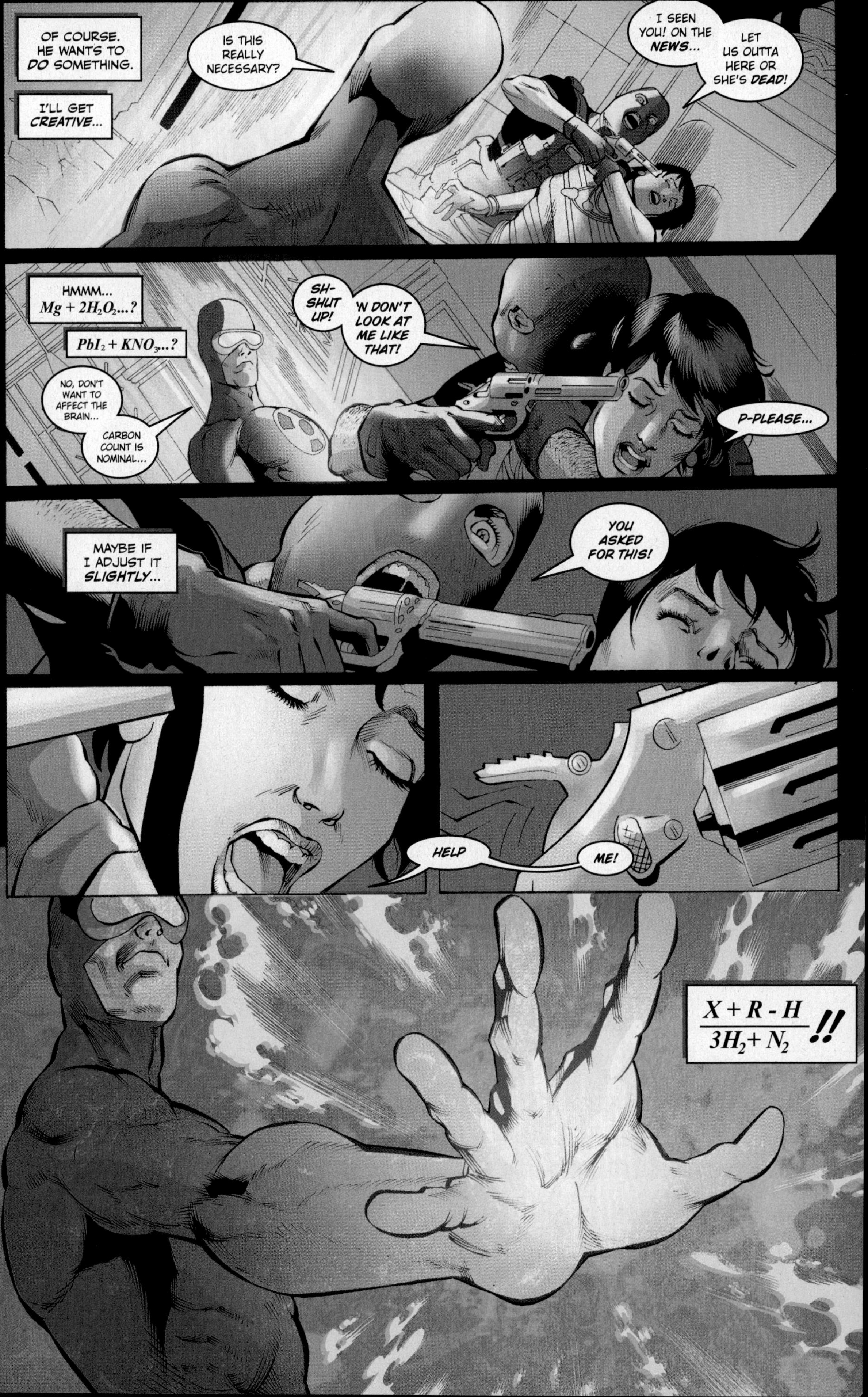
OF COURSE. HE WANTS TO DO SOMETHING.
I'LL GET CREATIVE...
IS THIS REALLY NECESSARY?
I SEEN YOU! ON THE NEWS...
LET US OUTTA HERE OR SHE'S DEAD!
HMMM... $Mg + 2H_2O_2$...?
$PbI_2 + KNO_3$...?
NO, DON'T WANT TO AFFECT THE BRAIN...
CARBON COUNT IS NOMINAL...
SH-SHUT UP!
'N DON'T LOOK AT ME LIKE THAT!
P-PLEASE...
MAYBE IF I ADJUST IT SLIGHTLY...
YOU ASKED FOR THIS!
HELP
ME!
$\frac{X + R - H}{3H_2 + N_2}$!!

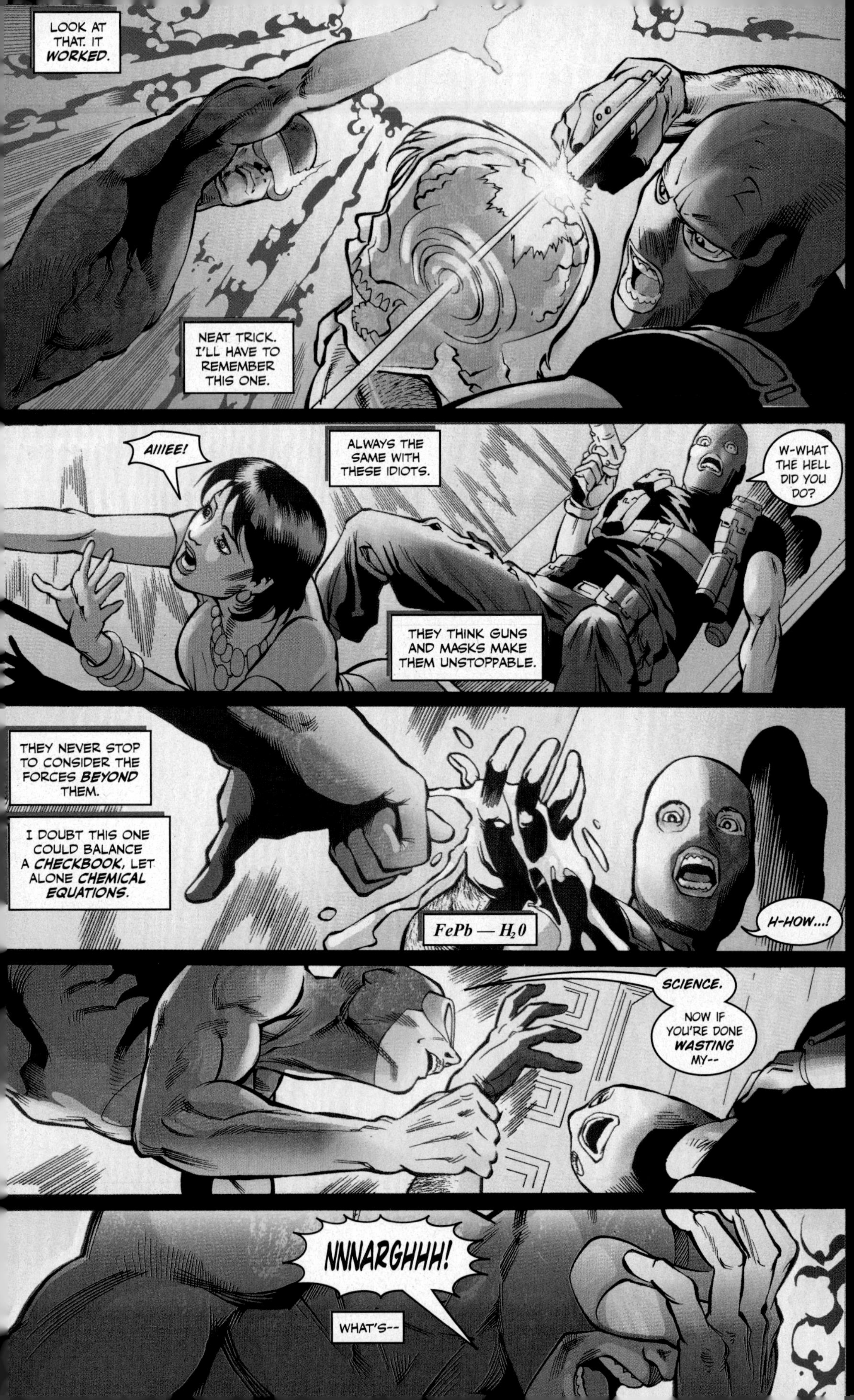
LOOK AT THAT. IT WORKED.
NEAT TRICK. I'LL HAVE TO REMEMBER THIS ONE.
AIIIEE!
ALWAYS THE SAME WITH THESE IDIOTS.
W-WHAT THE HELL DID YOU DO?
THEY THINK GUNS AND MASKS MAKE THEM UNSTOPPABLE.
THEY NEVER STOP TO CONSIDER THE FORCES BEYOND THEM.
I DOUBT THIS ONE COULD BALANCE A CHECKBOOK, LET ALONE CHEMICAL EQUATIONS.
FePb — H2O
H-HOW...!
SCIENCE.
NOW IF YOU'RE DONE WASTING MY--
NNNARGHHH!
WHAT'S--

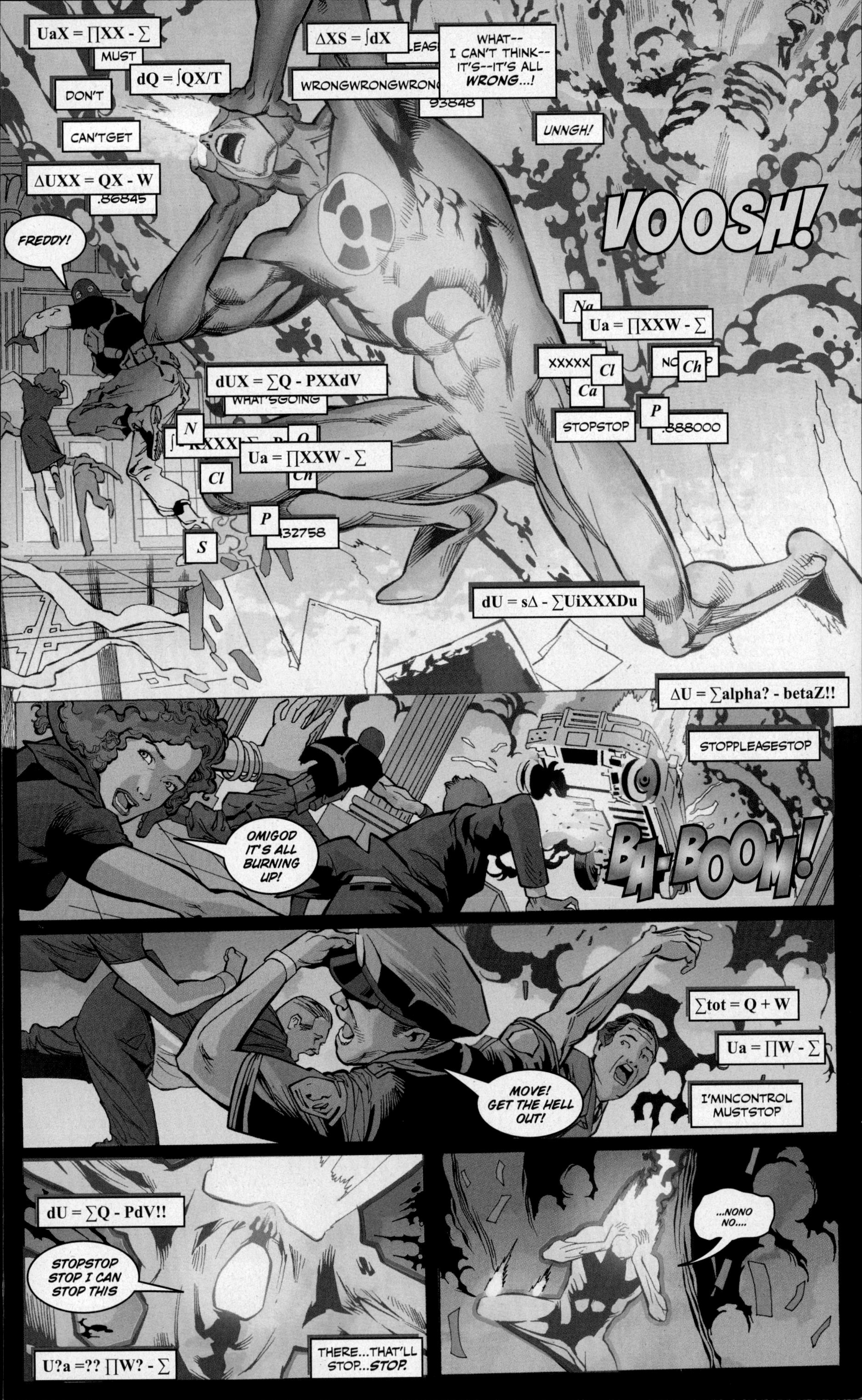
UaX = ∏XX - ∑
MUST
dQ = ∫QX/T
DON'T
CAN'TGET
ΔUXX = QX - W
.86845
FREDDY!
ΔXS = ∫dX
WRONGWRONGWRONG
93848
WHAT-- I CAN'T THINK-- IT'S--IT'S ALL WRONG...!
UNNGH!
VOOSH!
Ua = ∏XXW - ∑
XXXXX
Cl
Ca
Ch
STOPSTOP
P
.888000
dUX = ∑Q - PXXdV
WHAT'SGOING
N
Ua = ∏XXW - ∑
Cl
P
S
dU = sΔ - ∑UiXXXDu
ΔU = ∑alpha? - betaZ!!
OMIGOD IT'S ALL BURNING UP!
STOPPLEASESTOP
BA-BOOM!
∑tot = Q + W
Ua = ∏W - ∑
MOVE! GET THE HELL OUT!
I'MINCONTROL MUSTSTOP
dU = ∑Q - PdV!!
STOPSTOP STOP I CAN STOP THIS
U?a =?? ∏W? - ∑
THERE...THAT'LL STOP...STOP.
...NONO NO....

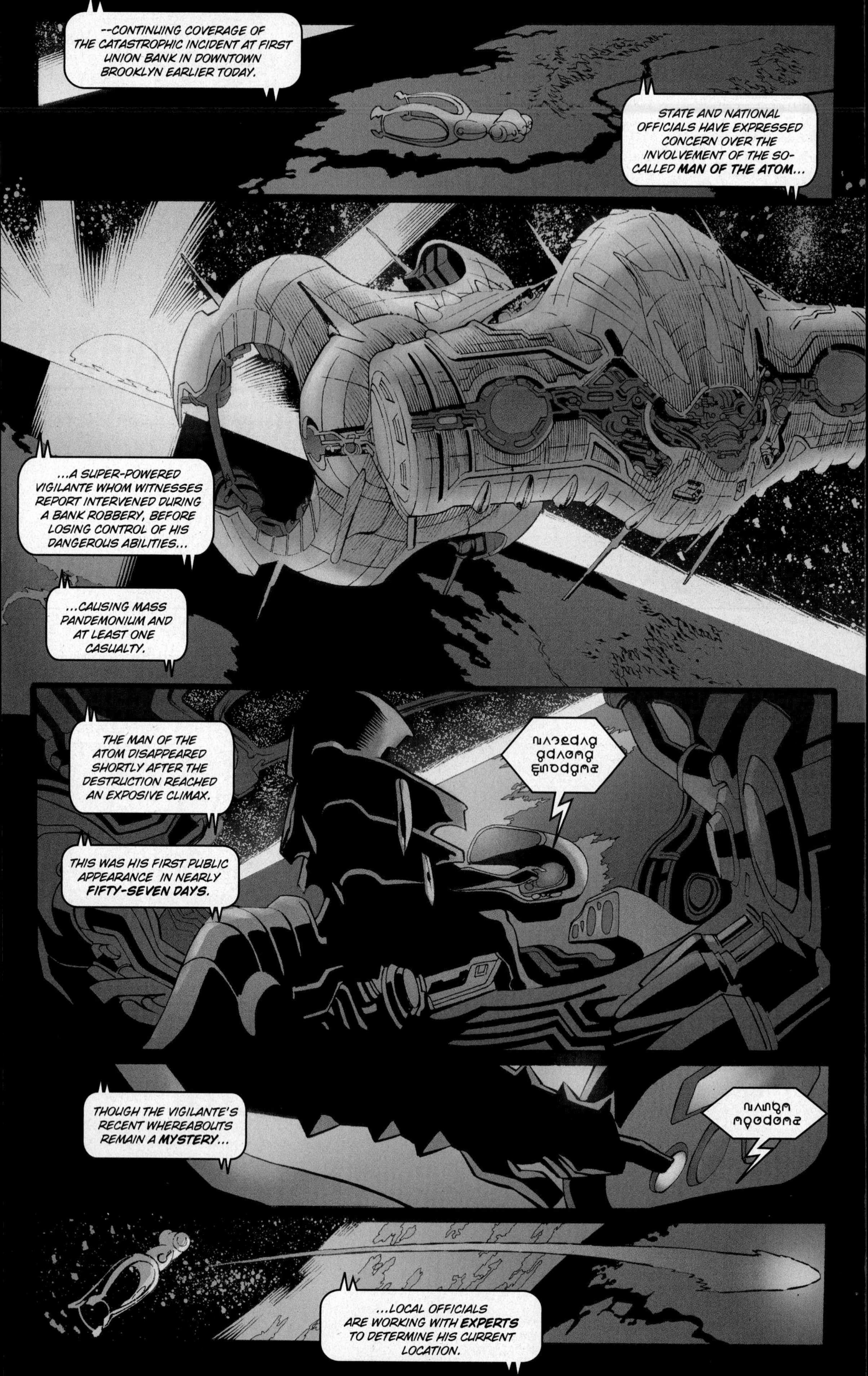
--CONTINUING COVERAGE OF THE CATASTROPHIC INCIDENT AT FIRST UNION BANK IN DOWNTOWN BROOKLYN EARLIER TODAY.
STATE AND NATIONAL OFFICIALS HAVE EXPRESSED CONCERN OVER THE INVOLVEMENT OF THE SO-CALLED **MAN OF THE ATOM**...
...A SUPER-POWERED VIGILANTE WHOM WITNESSES REPORT INTERVENED DURING A BANK ROBBERY, BEFORE LOSING CONTROL OF HIS DANGEROUS ABILITIES...
...CAUSING MASS PANDEMONIUM AND AT LEAST ONE CASUALTY.
THE MAN OF THE ATOM DISAPPEARED SHORTLY AFTER THE DESTRUCTION REACHED AN EXPOSIVE CLIMAX.
THIS WAS HIS FIRST PUBLIC APPEARANCE IN NEARLY **FIFTY-SEVEN DAYS**.
THOUGH THE VIGILANTE'S RECENT WHEREABOUTS REMAIN A **MYSTERY**...
...LOCAL OFFICIALS ARE WORKING WITH **EXPERTS** TO DETERMINE HIS CURRENT LOCATION.

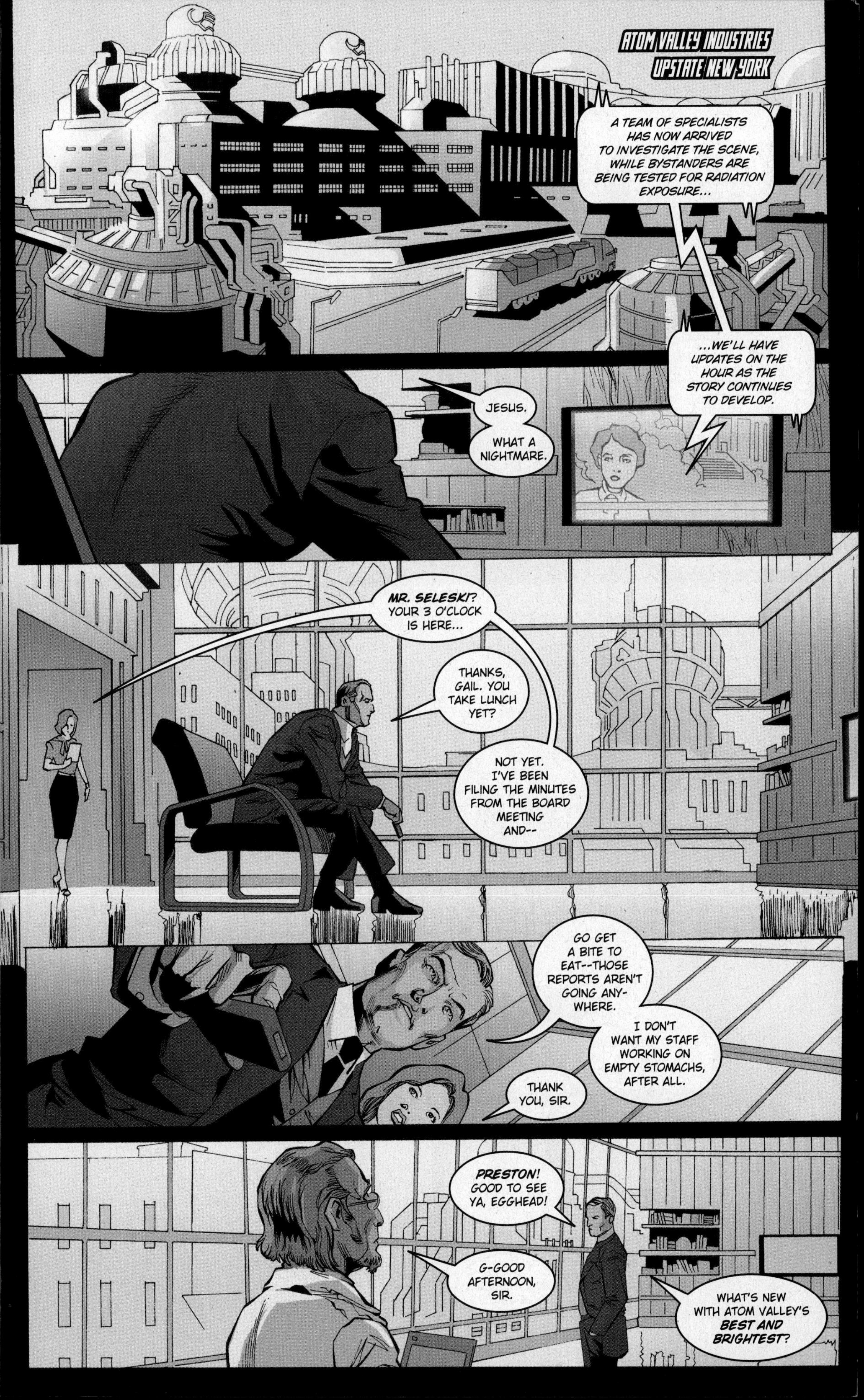
ATOM VALLEY INDUSTRIES
UPSTATE NEW YORK
A TEAM OF SPECIALISTS HAS NOW ARRIVED TO INVESTIGATE THE SCENE, WHILE BYSTANDERS ARE BEING TESTED FOR RADIATION EXPOSURE...
...WE'LL HAVE UPDATES ON THE HOUR AS THE STORY CONTINUES TO DEVELOP.
JESUS.
WHAT A NIGHTMARE.
MR. SELESKI? YOUR 3 O'CLOCK IS HERE...
THANKS, GAIL. YOU TAKE LUNCH YET?
NOT YET. I'VE BEEN FILING THE MINUTES FROM THE BOARD MEETING AND--
GO GET A BITE TO EAT--THOSE REPORTS AREN'T GOING ANYWHERE.
I DON'T WANT MY STAFF WORKING ON EMPTY STOMACHS, AFTER ALL.
THANK YOU, SIR.
PRESTON! GOOD TO SEE YA, EGGHEAD!
G-GOOD AFTERNOON, SIR.
WHAT'S NEW WITH ATOM VALLEY'S BEST AND BRIGHTEST?

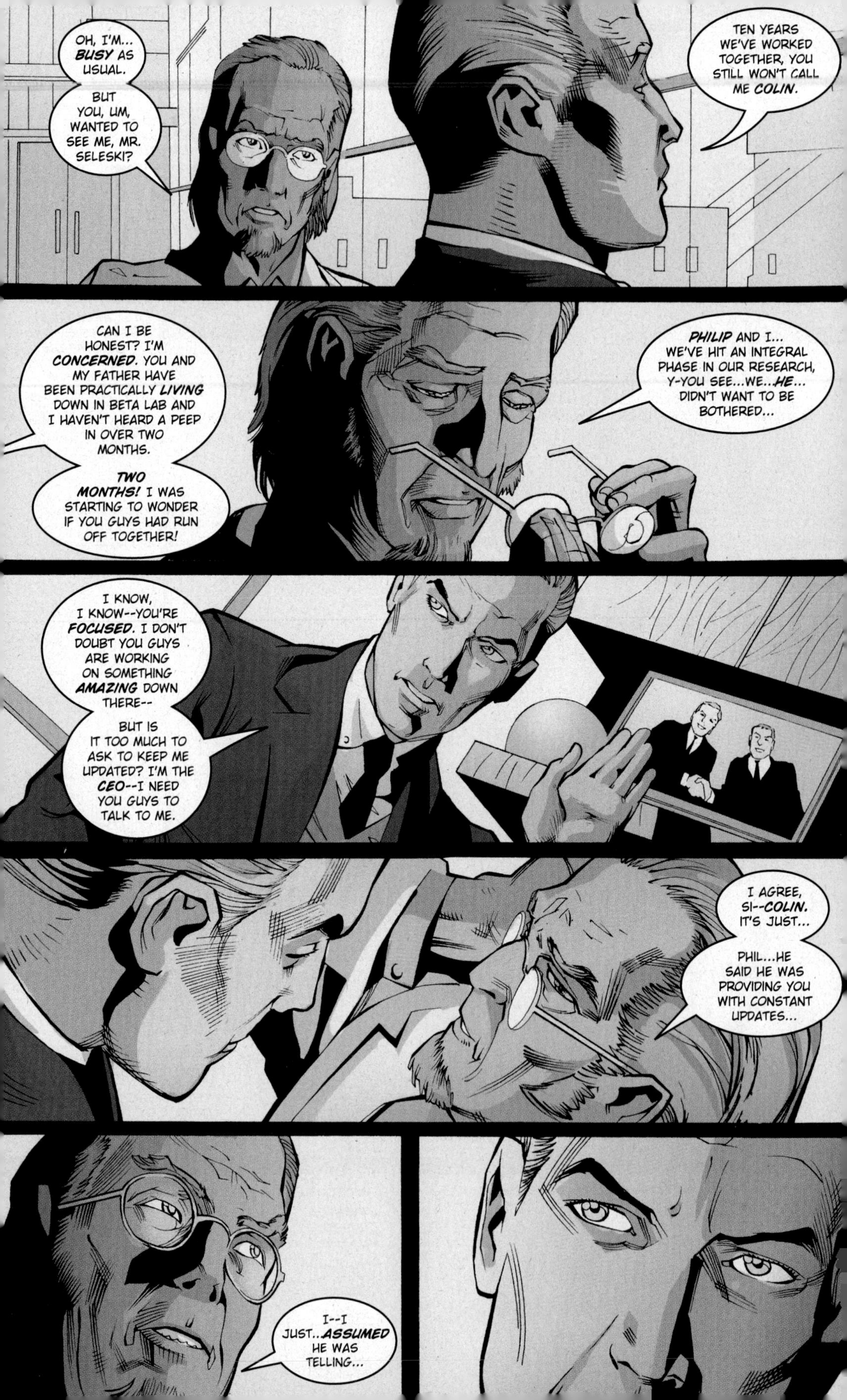
OH, I'M... BUSY AS USUAL.
BUT YOU, UM, WANTED TO SEE ME, MR. SELESKI?
TEN YEARS WE'VE WORKED TOGETHER, YOU STILL WON'T CALL ME COLIN.
CAN I BE HONEST? I'M CONCERNED. YOU AND MY FATHER HAVE BEEN PRACTICALLY LIVING DOWN IN BETA LAB AND I HAVEN'T HEARD A PEEP IN OVER TWO MONTHS.
TWO MONTHS! I WAS STARTING TO WONDER IF YOU GUYS HAD RUN OFF TOGETHER!
PHILIP AND I... WE'VE HIT AN INTEGRAL PHASE IN OUR RESEARCH, Y-YOU SEE...WE...HE... DIDN'T WANT TO BE BOTHERED...
I KNOW, I KNOW--YOU'RE FOCUSED. I DON'T DOUBT YOU GUYS ARE WORKING ON SOMETHING AMAZING DOWN THERE--
BUT IS IT TOO MUCH TO ASK TO KEEP ME UPDATED? I'M THE CEO--I NEED YOU GUYS TO TALK TO ME.
I AGREE, SI--COLIN. IT'S JUST...
PHIL...HE SAID HE WAS PROVIDING YOU WITH CONSTANT UPDATES...
I--I JUST...ASSUMED HE WAS TELLING...

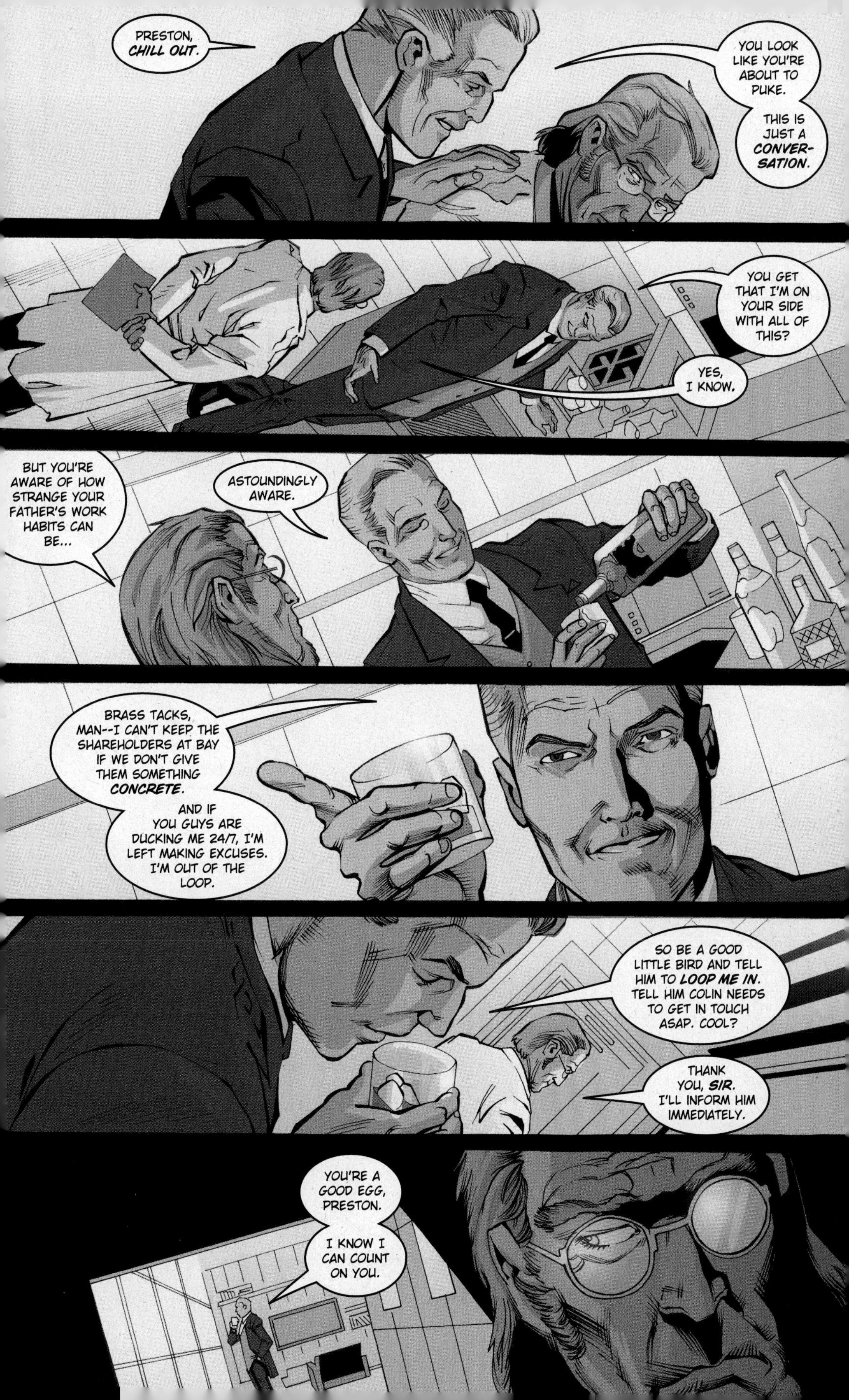
PRESTON, *CHILL OUT*.
YOU LOOK LIKE YOU'RE ABOUT TO PUKE.
THIS IS JUST A *CONVERSATION*.
YOU GET THAT I'M ON YOUR SIDE WITH ALL OF THIS?
YES, I KNOW.
BUT YOU'RE AWARE OF HOW STRANGE YOUR FATHER'S WORK HABITS CAN BE...
ASTOUNDINGLY AWARE.
BRASS TACKS, MAN--I CAN'T KEEP THE SHAREHOLDERS AT BAY IF WE DON'T GIVE THEM SOMETHING *CONCRETE*.
AND IF YOU GUYS ARE DUCKING ME 24/7, I'M LEFT MAKING EXCUSES. I'M OUT OF THE LOOP.
SO BE A GOOD LITTLE BIRD AND TELL HIM TO *LOOP ME IN*. TELL HIM COLIN NEEDS TO GET IN TOUCH ASAP. COOL?
THANK YOU, *SIR*. I'LL INFORM HIM IMMEDIATELY.
YOU'RE A GOOD EGG, PRESTON.
I KNOW I CAN COUNT ON YOU.

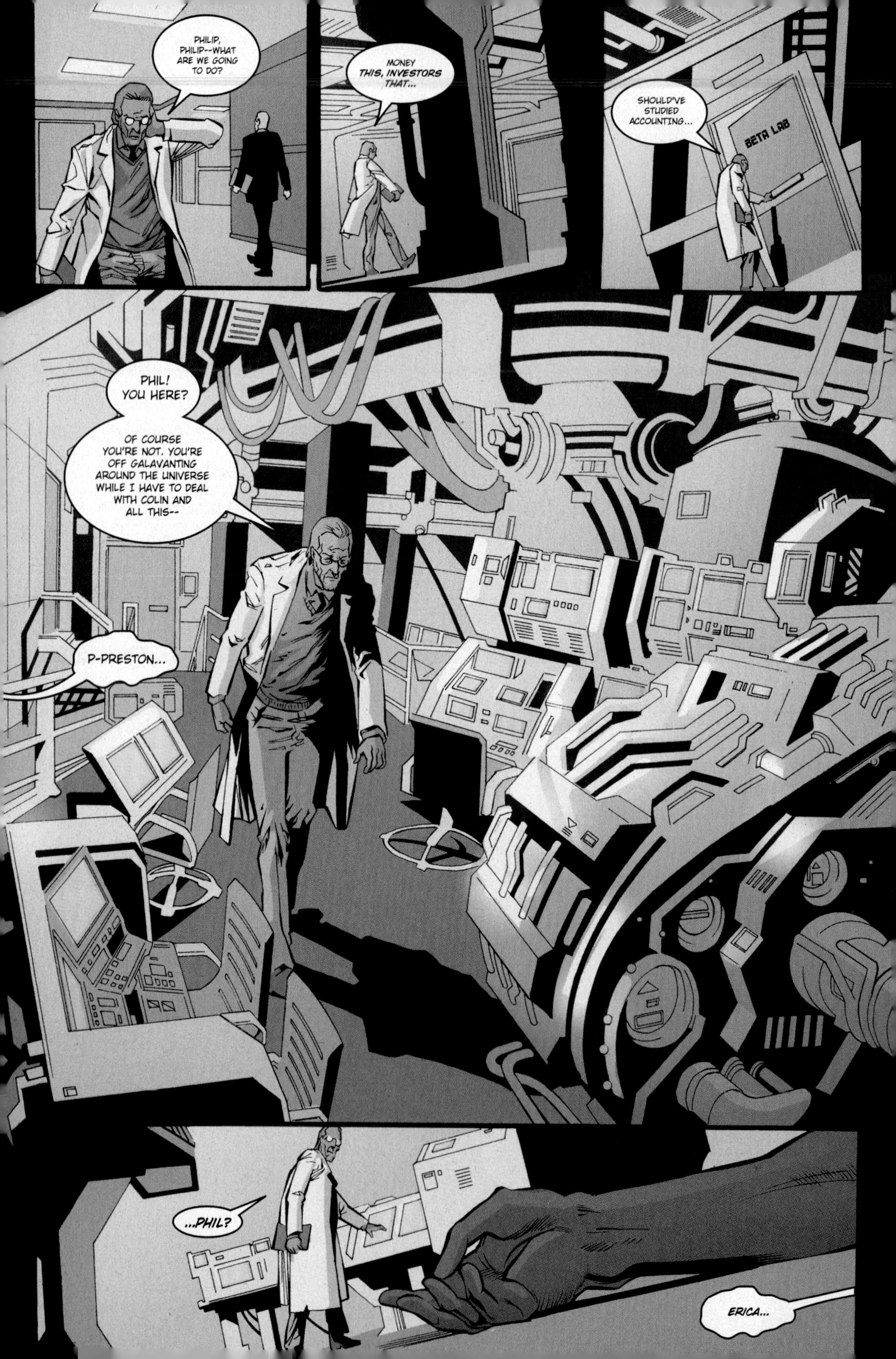
PHILIP, PHILIP--WHAT ARE WE GOING TO DO?
MONEY THIS, INVESTORS THAT...
SHOULD'VE STUDIED ACCOUNTING...
BETA LAB
PHIL! YOU HERE?
OF COURSE YOU'RE NOT. YOU'RE OFF GALAVANTING AROUND THE UNIVERSE WHILE I HAVE TO DEAL WITH COLIN AND ALL THIS--
P-PRESTON...
...PHIL?
ERICA...

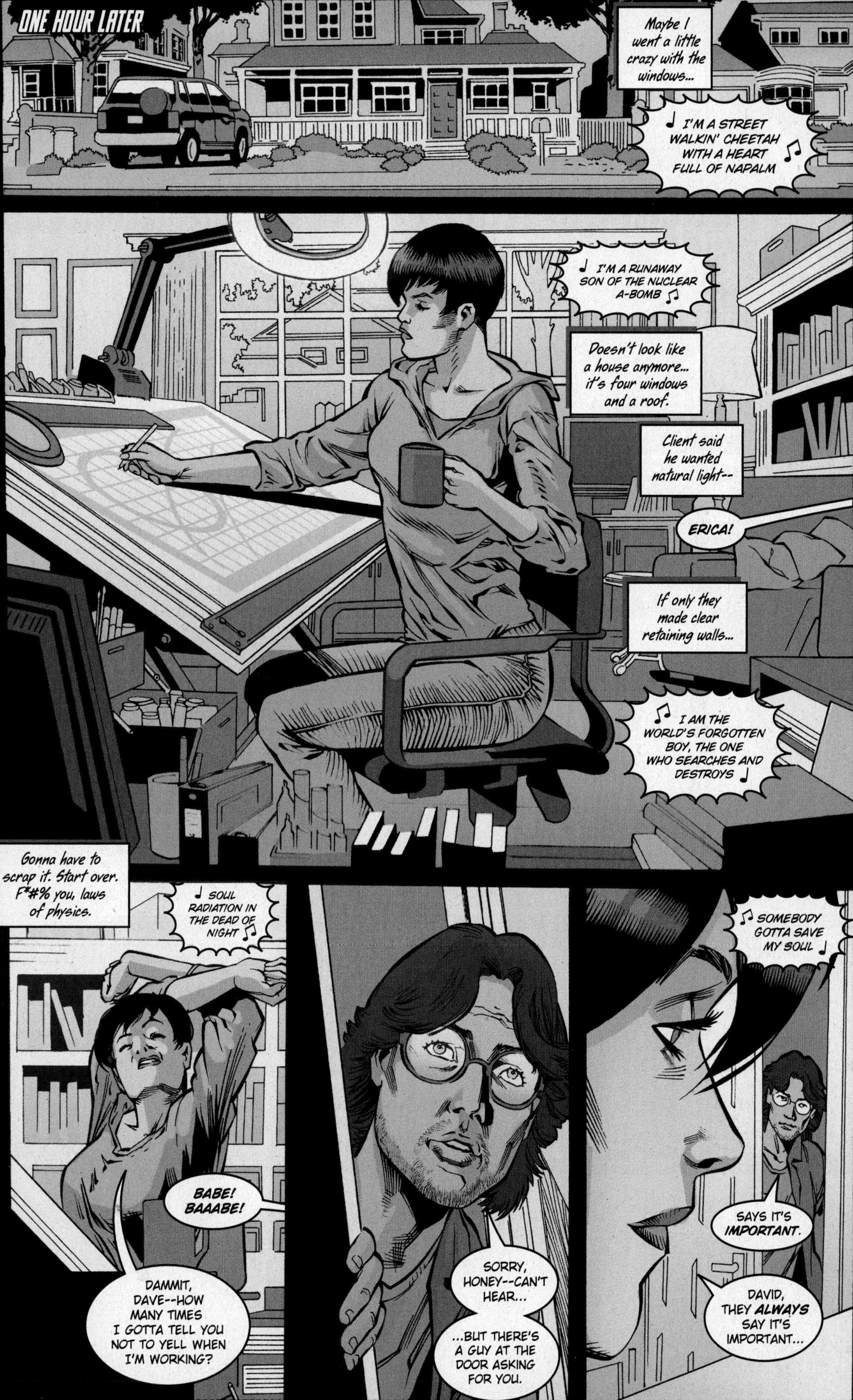
ONE HOUR LATER
Maybe I went a little crazy with the windows...
♩ I'M A STREET WALKIN' CHEETAH WITH A HEART FULL OF NAPALM ♫
♩ I'M A RUNAWAY SON OF THE NUCLEAR A-BOMB ♫
Doesn't look like a house anymore... it's four windows and a roof.
Client said he wanted natural light--
ERICA!
If only they made clear retaining walls...
♫ I AM THE WORLD'S FORGOTTEN BOY, THE ONE WHO SEARCHES AND DESTROYS ♩
Gonna have to scrap it. Start over. F*#% you, laws of physics.
♩ SOUL RADIATION IN THE DEAD OF NIGHT ♫
BABE! BAAABE!
DAMMIT, DAVE--HOW MANY TIMES I GOTTA TELL YOU NOT TO YELL WHEN I'M WORKING?
SORRY, HONEY--CAN'T HEAR...
...BUT THERE'S A GUY AT THE DOOR ASKING FOR YOU.
♫ SOMEBODY GOTTA SAVE MY SOUL ♩
SAYS IT'S IMPORTANT.
DAVID, THEY ALWAYS SAY IT'S IMPORTANT...

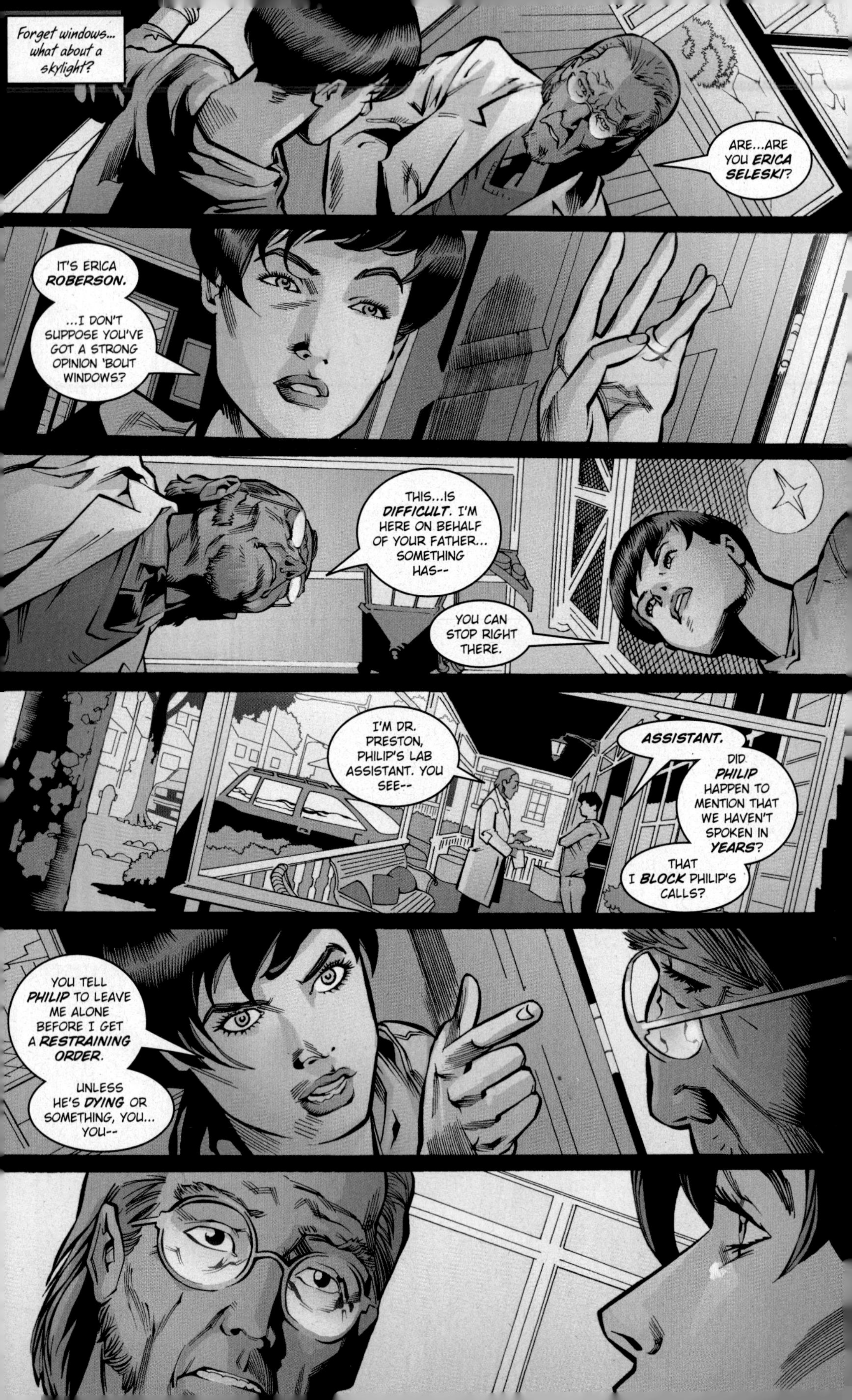
Forget windows... what about a skylight?
ARE...ARE YOU ERICA SELESKI?
IT'S ERICA ROBERSON.
...I DON'T SUPPOSE YOU'VE GOT A STRONG OPINION 'BOUT WINDOWS?
THIS...IS DIFFICULT. I'M HERE ON BEHALF OF YOUR FATHER... SOMETHING HAS--
YOU CAN STOP RIGHT THERE.
I'M DR. PRESTON, PHILIP'S LAB ASSISTANT. YOU SEE--
ASSISTANT.
DID PHILIP HAPPEN TO MENTION THAT WE HAVEN'T SPOKEN IN YEARS?
THAT I BLOCK PHILIP'S CALLS?
YOU TELL PHILIP TO LEAVE ME ALONE BEFORE I GET A RESTRAINING ORDER.
UNLESS HE'S DYING OR SOMETHING, YOU... YOU--

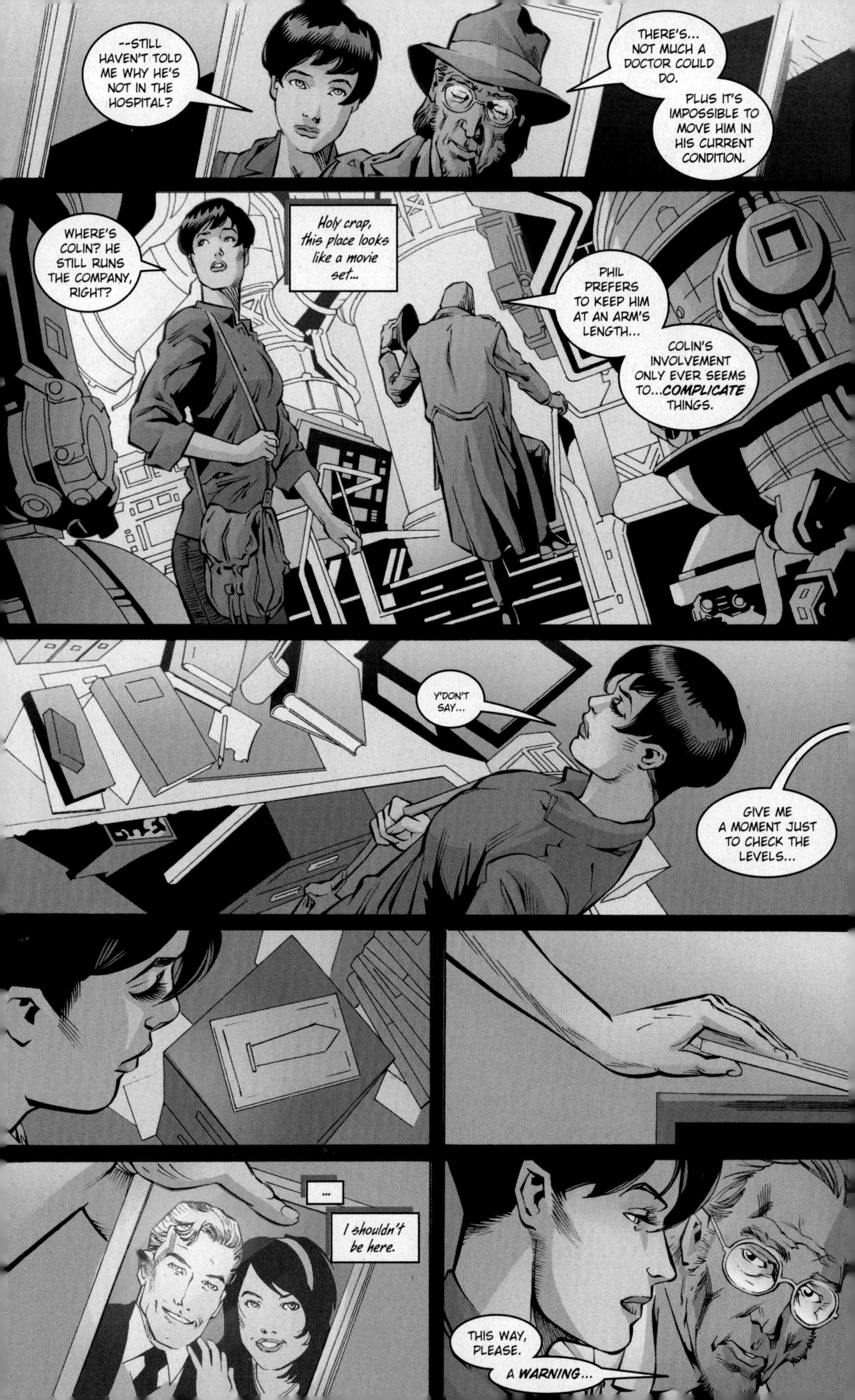
--STILL HAVEN'T TOLD ME WHY HE'S NOT IN THE HOSPITAL?
THERE'S... NOT MUCH A DOCTOR COULD DO.
PLUS IT'S IMPOSSIBLE TO MOVE HIM IN HIS CURRENT CONDITION.
WHERE'S COLIN? HE STILL RUNS THE COMPANY, RIGHT?
Holy crap, this place looks like a movie set...
PHIL PREFERS TO KEEP HIM AT AN ARM'S LENGTH...
COLIN'S INVOLVEMENT ONLY EVER SEEMS TO...COMPLICATE THINGS.
Y'DON'T SAY...
GIVE ME A MOMENT JUST TO CHECK THE LEVELS...
...
I shouldn't be here.
THIS WAY, PLEASE.
A WARNING...

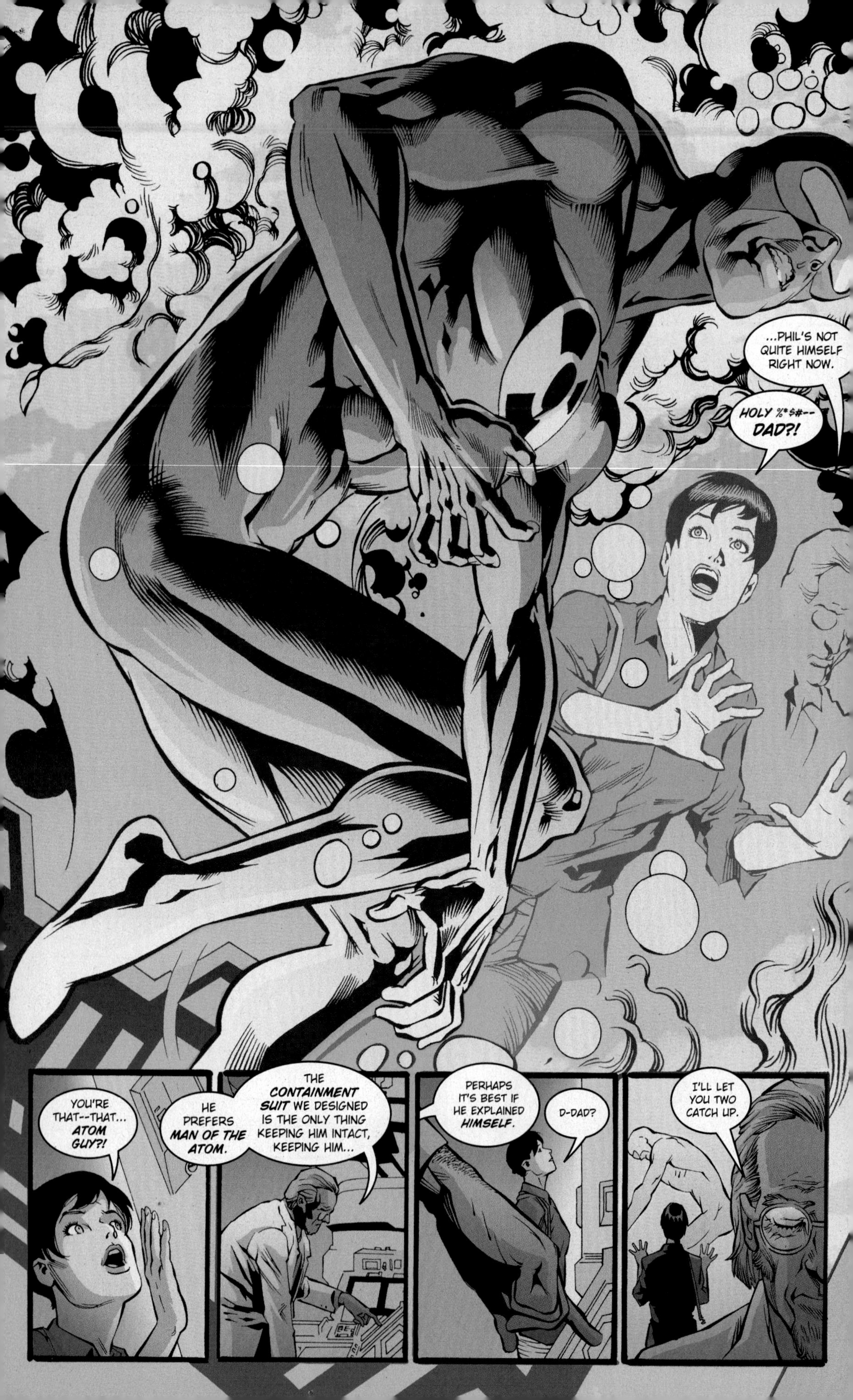
...PHIL'S NOT QUITE HIMSELF RIGHT NOW.
HOLY %*$#-- DAD?!
YOU'RE THAT--THAT... ATOM GUY?!
HE PREFERS MAN OF THE ATOM.
THE CONTAINMENT SUIT WE DESIGNED IS THE ONLY THING KEEPING HIM INTACT, KEEPING HIM...
PERHAPS IT'S BEST IF HE EXPLAINED HIMSELF.
D-DAD?
I'LL LET YOU TWO CATCH UP.

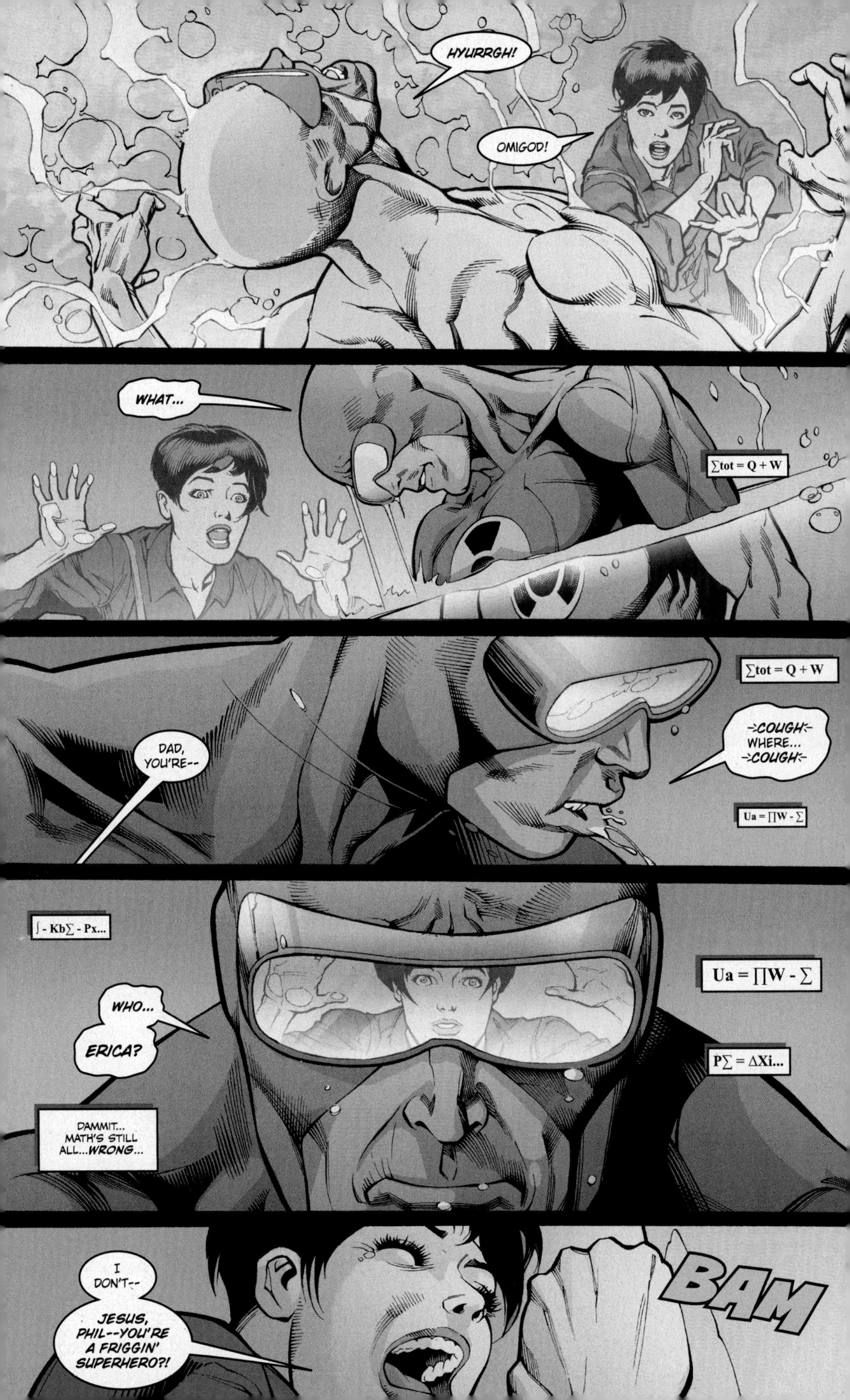

HYURRGH!
OMIGOD!
WHAT...
∑tot = Q + W
∑tot = Q + W
DAD, YOU'RE--
-COUGH- WHERE... -COUGH-
Ua = ∏W - ∑
∫ - Kb∑ - Px...
Ua = ∏W - ∑
WHO... ERICA?
P∑ = ΔXi...
DAMMIT... MATH'S STILL ALL...WRONG...
I DON'T--
JESUS, PHIL--YOU'RE A FRIGGIN' SUPERHERO?!
BAM

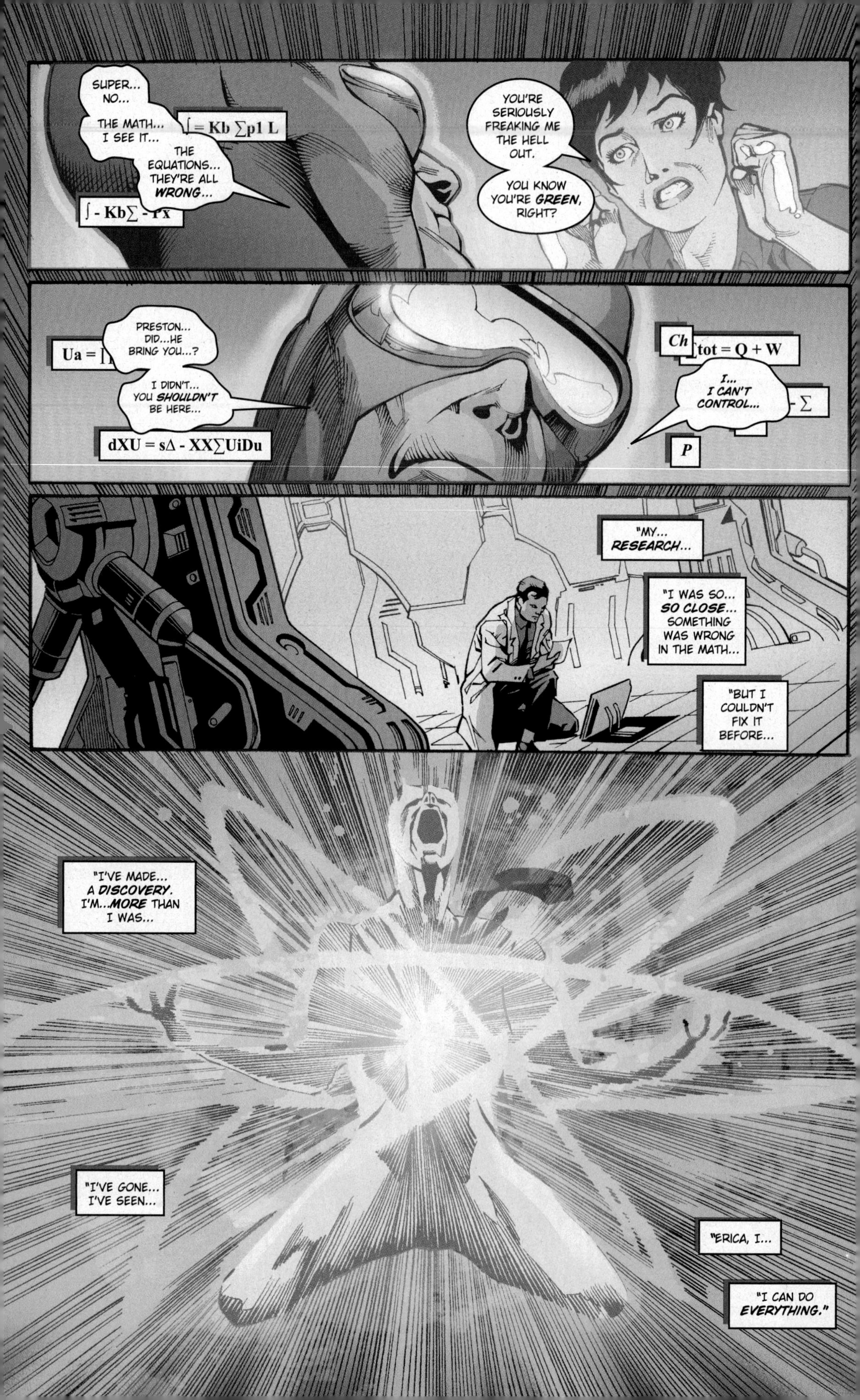
SUPER... NO...
THE MATH... I SEE IT...
∫ = Kb ∑p1 L
THE EQUATIONS... THEY'RE ALL WRONG...
∫ - Kb∑ - Px
YOU'RE SERIOUSLY FREAKING ME THE HELL OUT.
YOU KNOW YOU'RE GREEN, RIGHT?
Ua =
PRESTON... DID...HE BRING YOU...?
I DIDN'T... YOU SHOULDN'T BE HERE...
dXU = sΔ - XX∑UiDu
Ch
tot = Q + W
I... I CAN'T CONTROL...
- ∑
P
"MY... RESEARCH...
"I WAS SO... SO CLOSE... SOMETHING WAS WRONG IN THE MATH...
"BUT I COULDN'T FIX IT BEFORE...
"I'VE MADE... A DISCOVERY. I'M...MORE THAN I WAS...
"I'VE GONE... I'VE SEEN...
"ERICA, I...
"I CAN DO EVERYTHING."

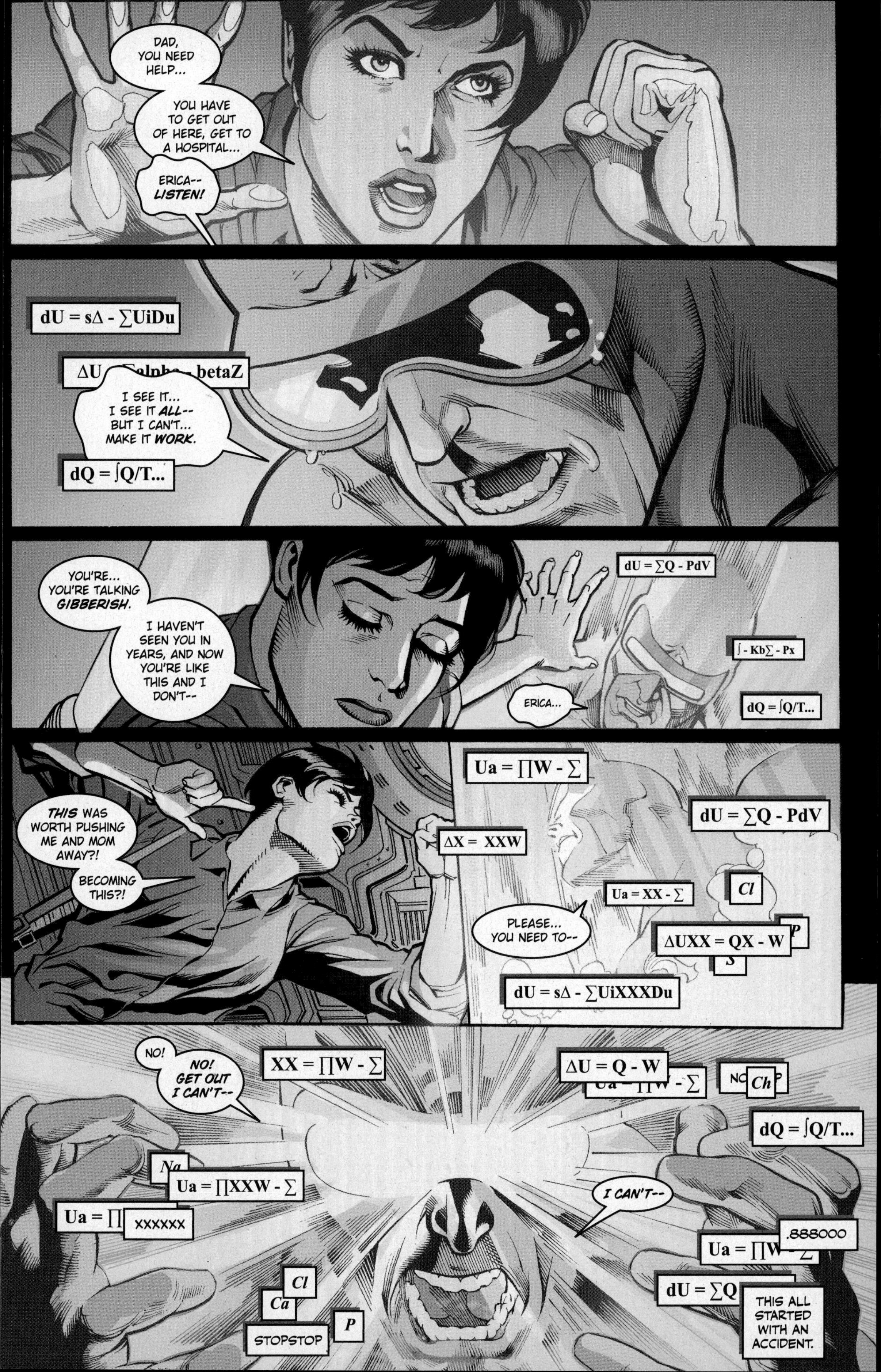
DAD, YOU NEED HELP...
YOU HAVE TO GET OUT OF HERE, GET TO A HOSPITAL...
ERICA-- *LISTEN!*
dU = sΔ - ∑UiDu
ΔU
betaZ
I SEE IT... I SEE IT *ALL*-- BUT I CAN'T... MAKE IT *WORK*.
dQ = ∫Q/T...
YOU'RE... YOU'RE TALKING *GIBBERISH*.
I HAVEN'T SEEN YOU IN YEARS, AND NOW YOU'RE LIKE THIS AND I DON'T--
dU = ∑Q - PdV
∫ - Kb∑ - Px
ERICA...
dQ = ∫Q/T...
THIS WAS WORTH PUSHING ME AND MOM AWAY?!
BECOMING THIS?!
Ua = ∏W - ∑
dU = ∑Q - PdV
ΔX = XXW
Cl
Ua = XX - ∑
PLEASE... YOU NEED TO--
ΔUXX = QX - W
dU = sΔ - ∑UiXXXDu
NO!
NO! GET OUT I CAN'T--
XX = ∏W - ∑
ΔU = Q - W
Ch
dQ = ∫Q/T...
Na
Ua = ∏XXW - ∑
XXXXXX
I CAN'T--
.888000
dU = ∑Q
Cl
Ca
P
STOPSTOP
THIS ALL STARTED WITH AN ACCIDENT.

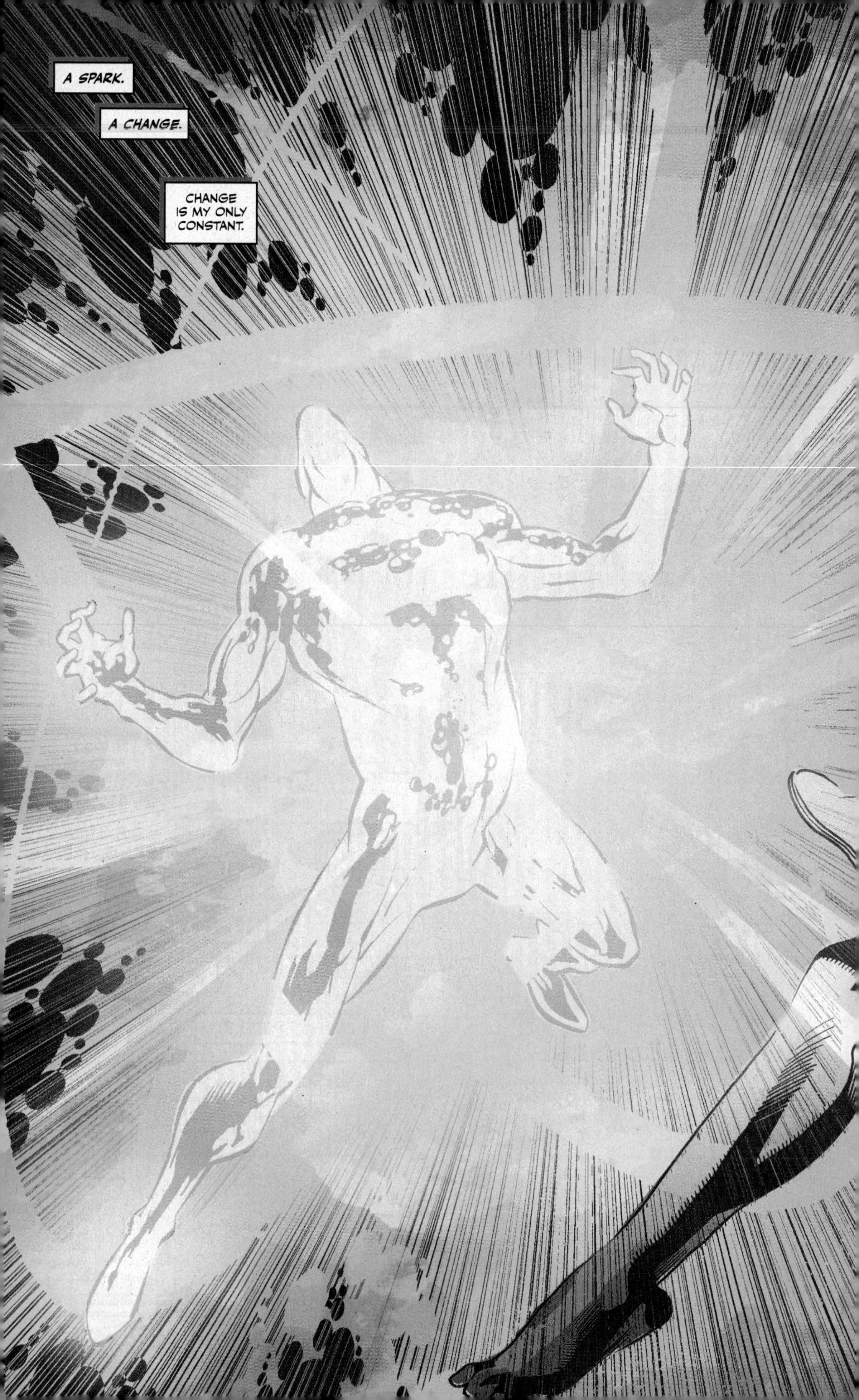
A SPARK.
A CHANGE.
CHANGE IS MY ONLY CONSTANT.

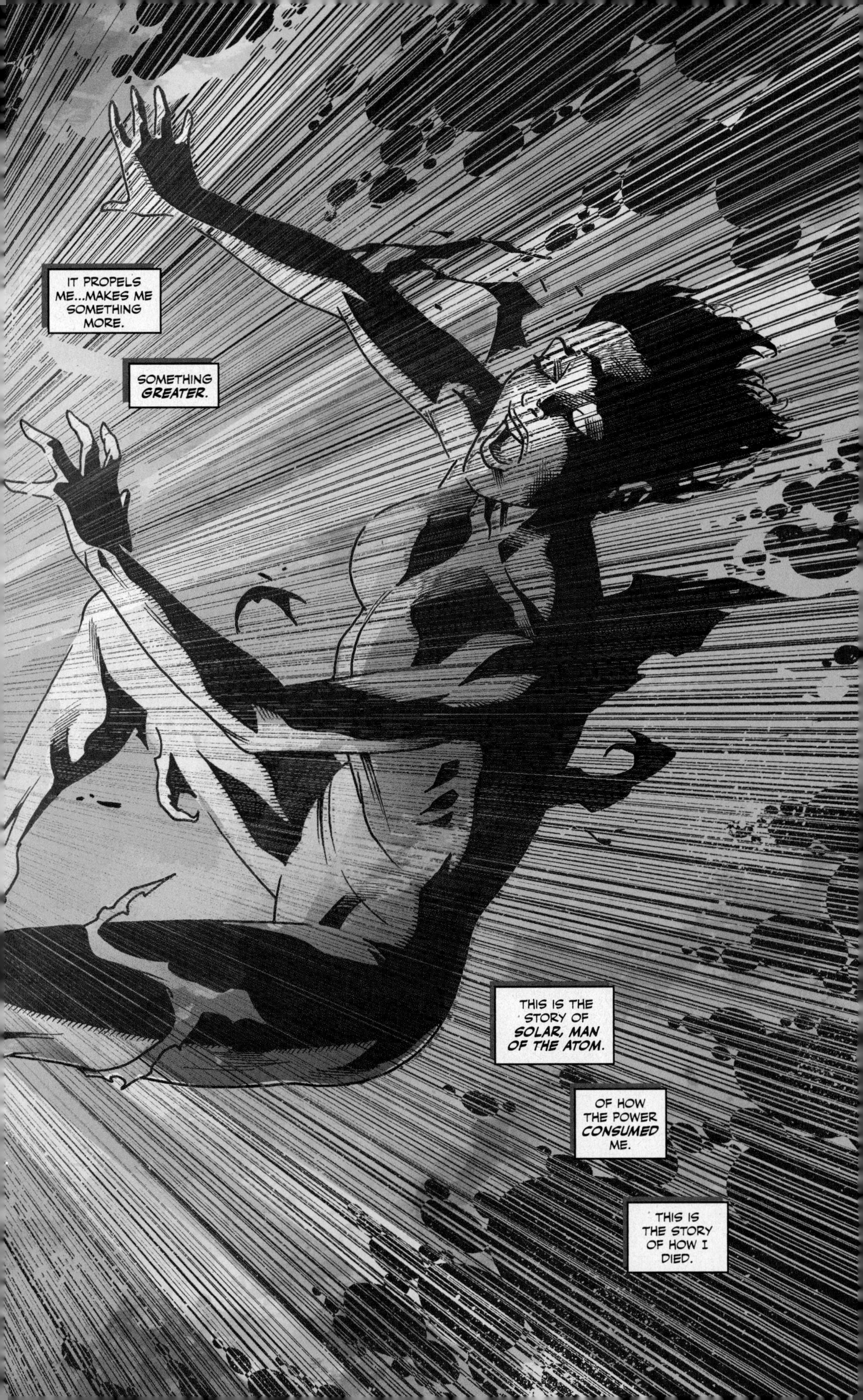
IT PROPELS ME...MAKES ME SOMETHING MORE.
SOMETHING *GREATER*.
THIS IS THE STORY OF *SOLAR, MAN OF THE ATOM*.
OF HOW THE POWER *CONSUMED* ME.
THIS IS THE STORY OF HOW I DIED.

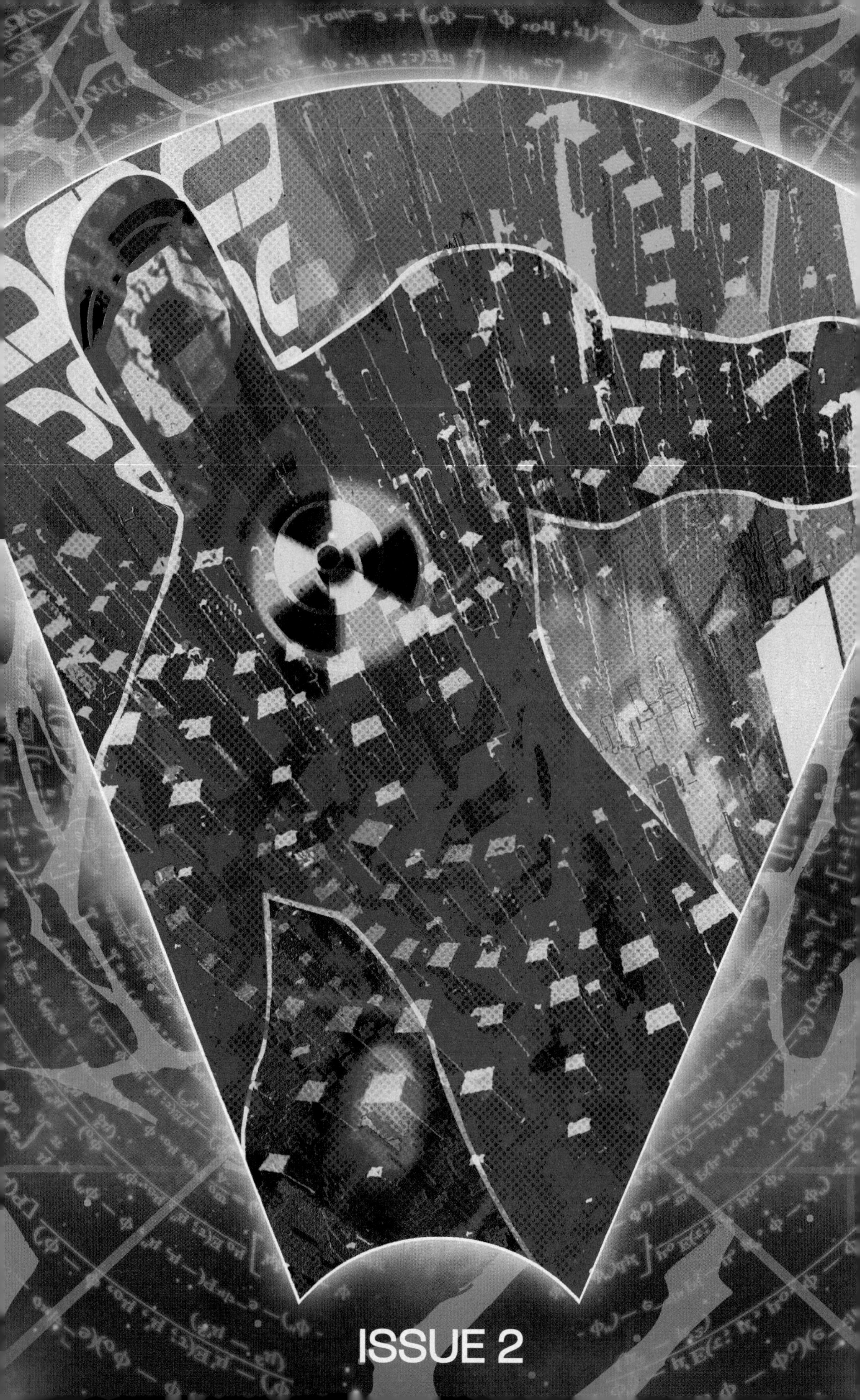
ISSUE 2

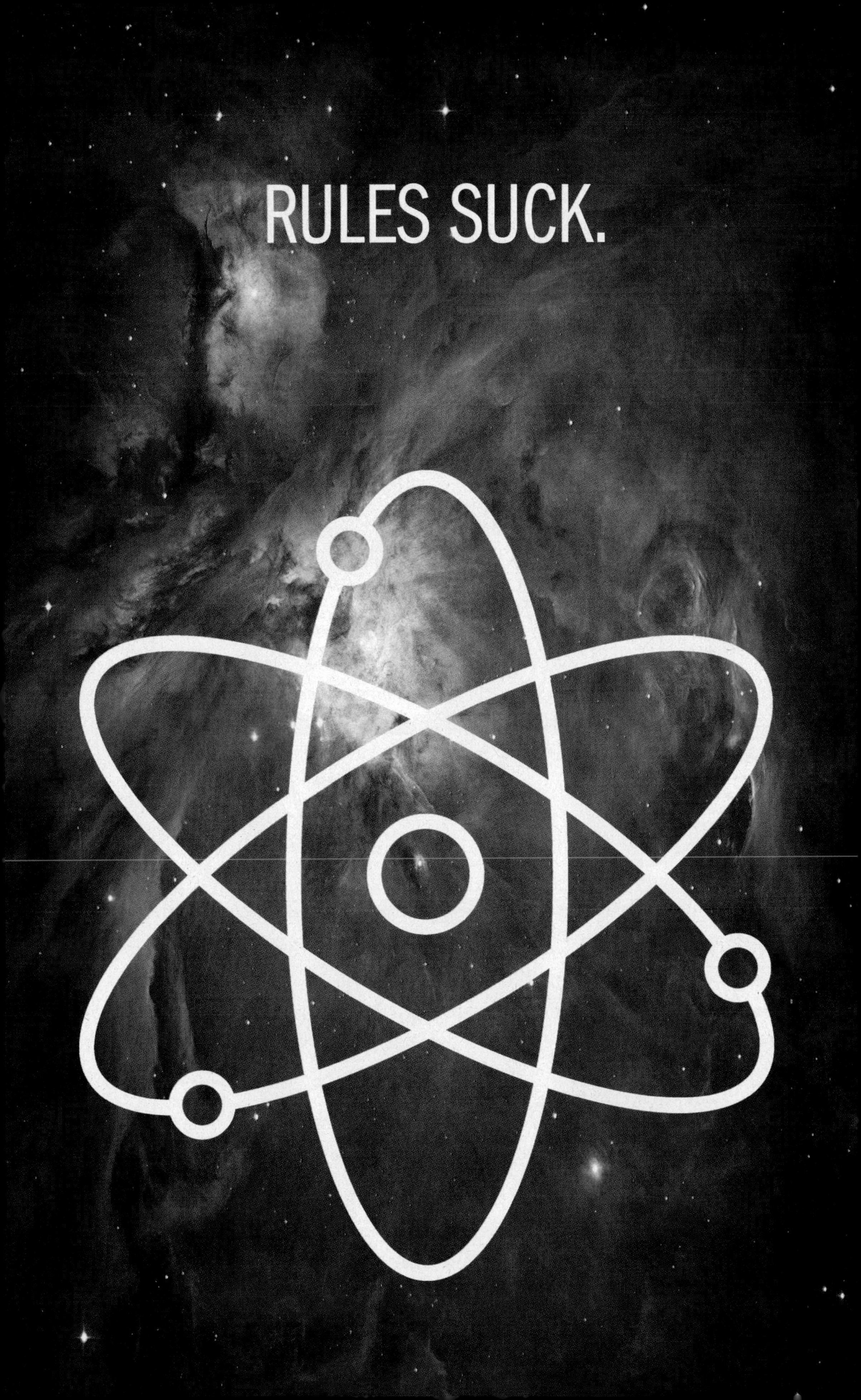
RULES SUCK.

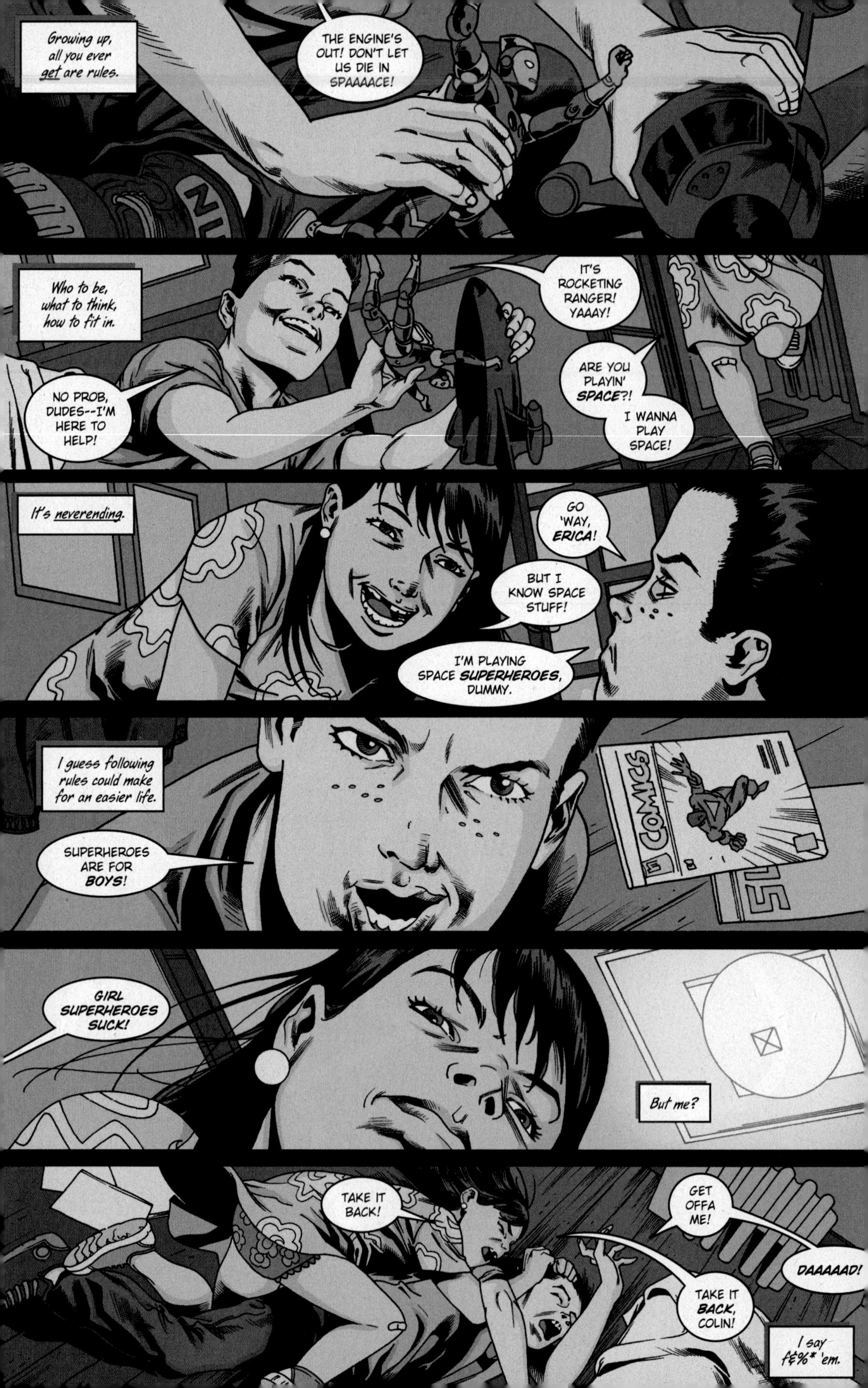
Growing up, all you ever get are rules.
THE ENGINE'S OUT! DON'T LET US DIE IN SPAAAACE!
Who to be, what to think, how to fit in.
NO PROB, DUDES--I'M HERE TO HELP!
IT'S ROCKETING RANGER! YAAAY!
ARE YOU PLAYIN' SPACE?!
I WANNA PLAY SPACE!
It's neverending.
GO 'WAY, ERICA!
BUT I KNOW SPACE STUFF!
I'M PLAYING SPACE SUPERHEROES, DUMMY.
I guess following rules could make for an easier life.
SUPERHEROES ARE FOR BOYS!
COMICS
GIRL SUPERHEROES SUCK!
But me?
TAKE IT BACK!
GET OFFA ME!
DAAAAAD!
TAKE IT BACK, COLIN!
I say f&%* 'em.

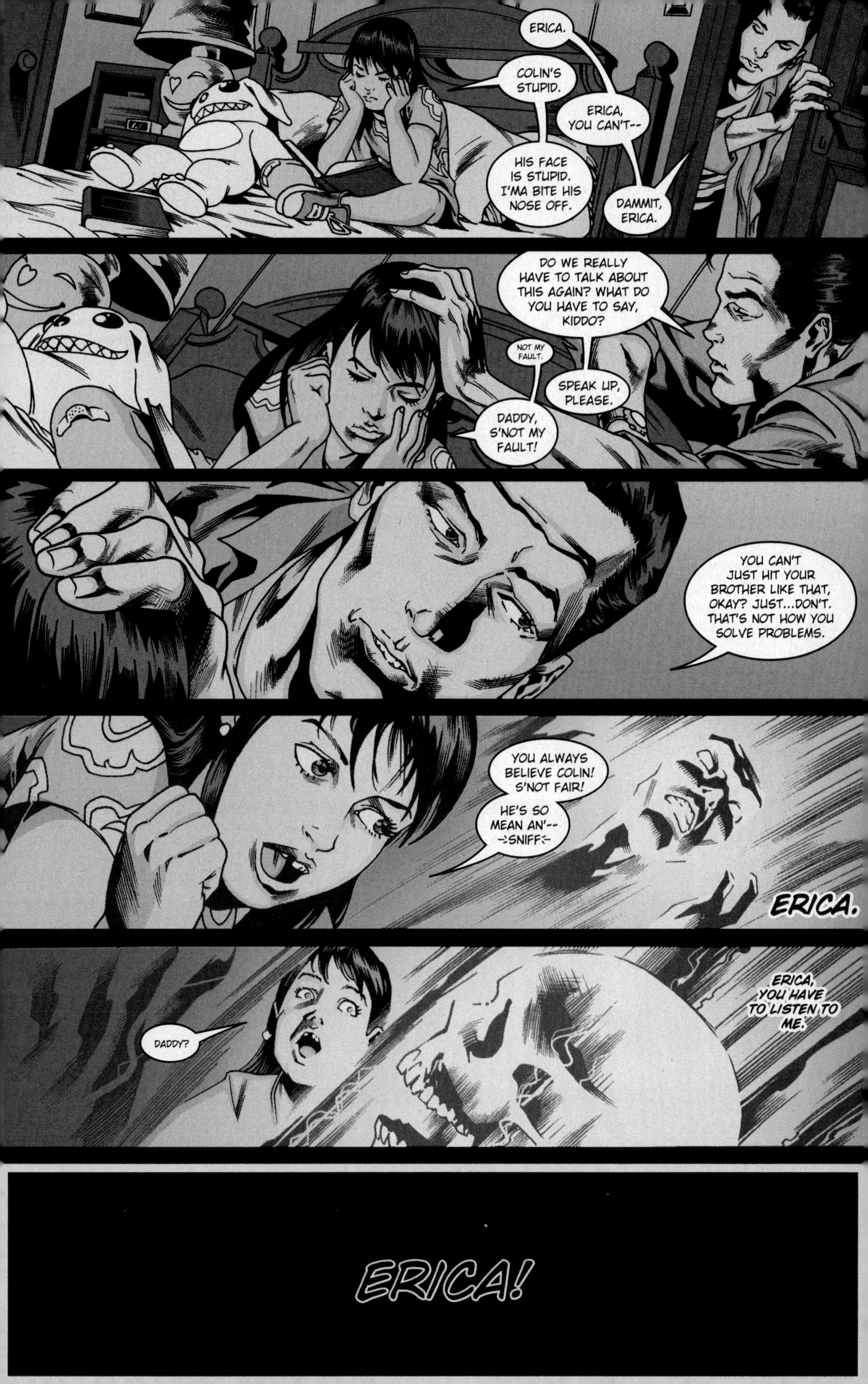
COLIN'S STUPID.
ERICA.
ERICA, YOU CAN'T--
HIS FACE IS STUPID. I'MA BITE HIS NOSE OFF.
DAMMIT, ERICA.
DO WE REALLY HAVE TO TALK ABOUT THIS AGAIN? WHAT DO YOU HAVE TO SAY, KIDDO?
NOT MY FAULT.
SPEAK UP, PLEASE.
DADDY, S'NOT MY FAULT!
YOU CAN'T JUST HIT YOUR BROTHER LIKE THAT, OKAY? JUST...DON'T. THAT'S NOT HOW YOU SOLVE PROBLEMS.
YOU ALWAYS BELIEVE COLIN! S'NOT FAIR!
HE'S SO MEAN AN'-- SNIFF
ERICA.
DADDY?
ERICA, YOU HAVE TO LISTEN TO ME.
ERICA!

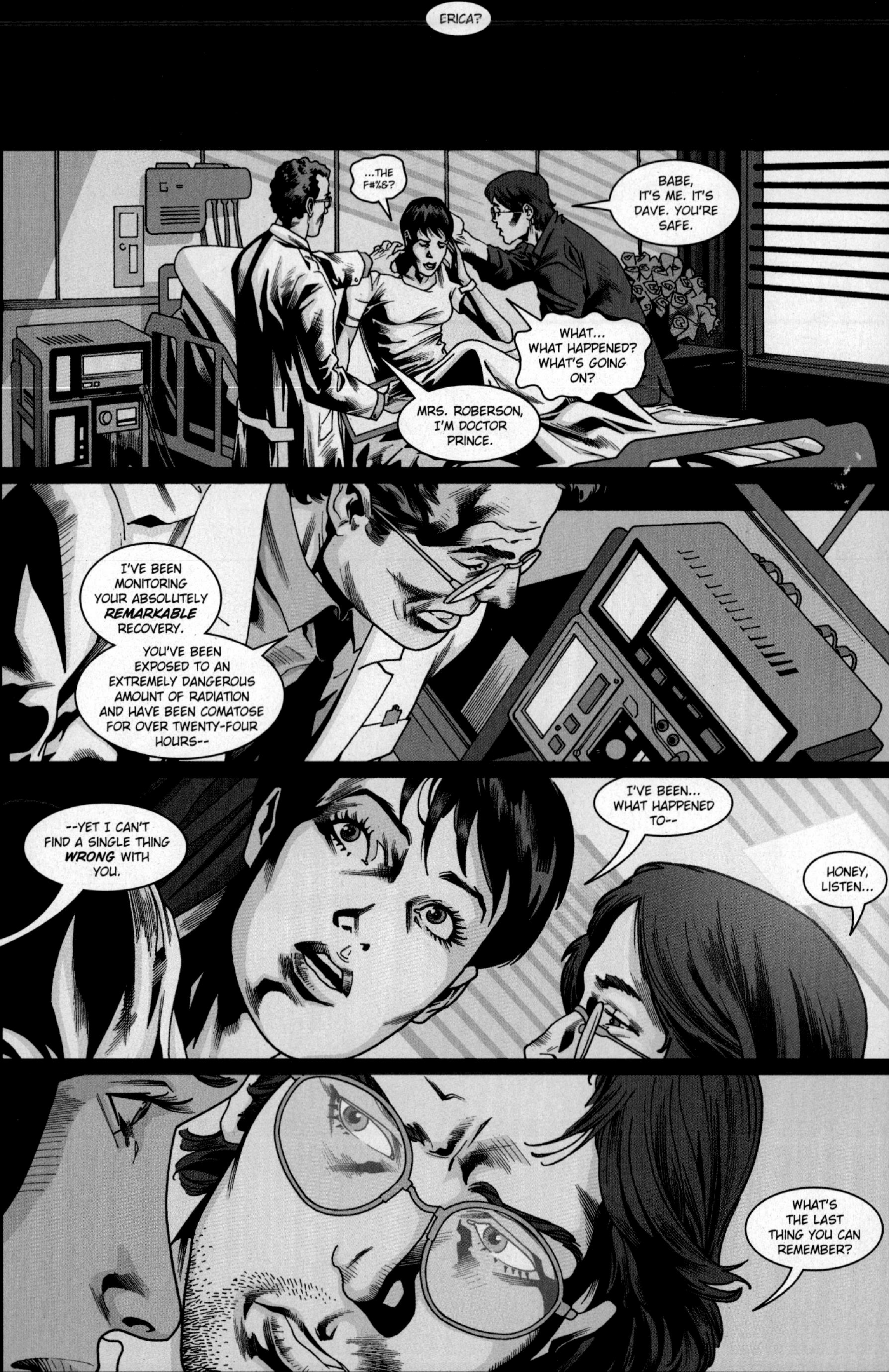
ERICA?
...THE F#%&?
BABE, IT'S ME. IT'S DAVE. YOU'RE SAFE.
WHAT... WHAT HAPPENED? WHAT'S GOING ON?
MRS. ROBERSON, I'M DOCTOR PRINCE.
I'VE BEEN MONITORING YOUR ABSOLUTELY REMARKABLE RECOVERY.
YOU'VE BEEN EXPOSED TO AN EXTREMELY DANGEROUS AMOUNT OF RADIATION AND HAVE BEEN COMATOSE FOR OVER TWENTY-FOUR HOURS--
--YET I CAN'T FIND A SINGLE THING WRONG WITH YOU.
I'VE BEEN... WHAT HAPPENED TO--
HONEY, LISTEN...
WHAT'S THE LAST THING YOU CAN REMEMBER?

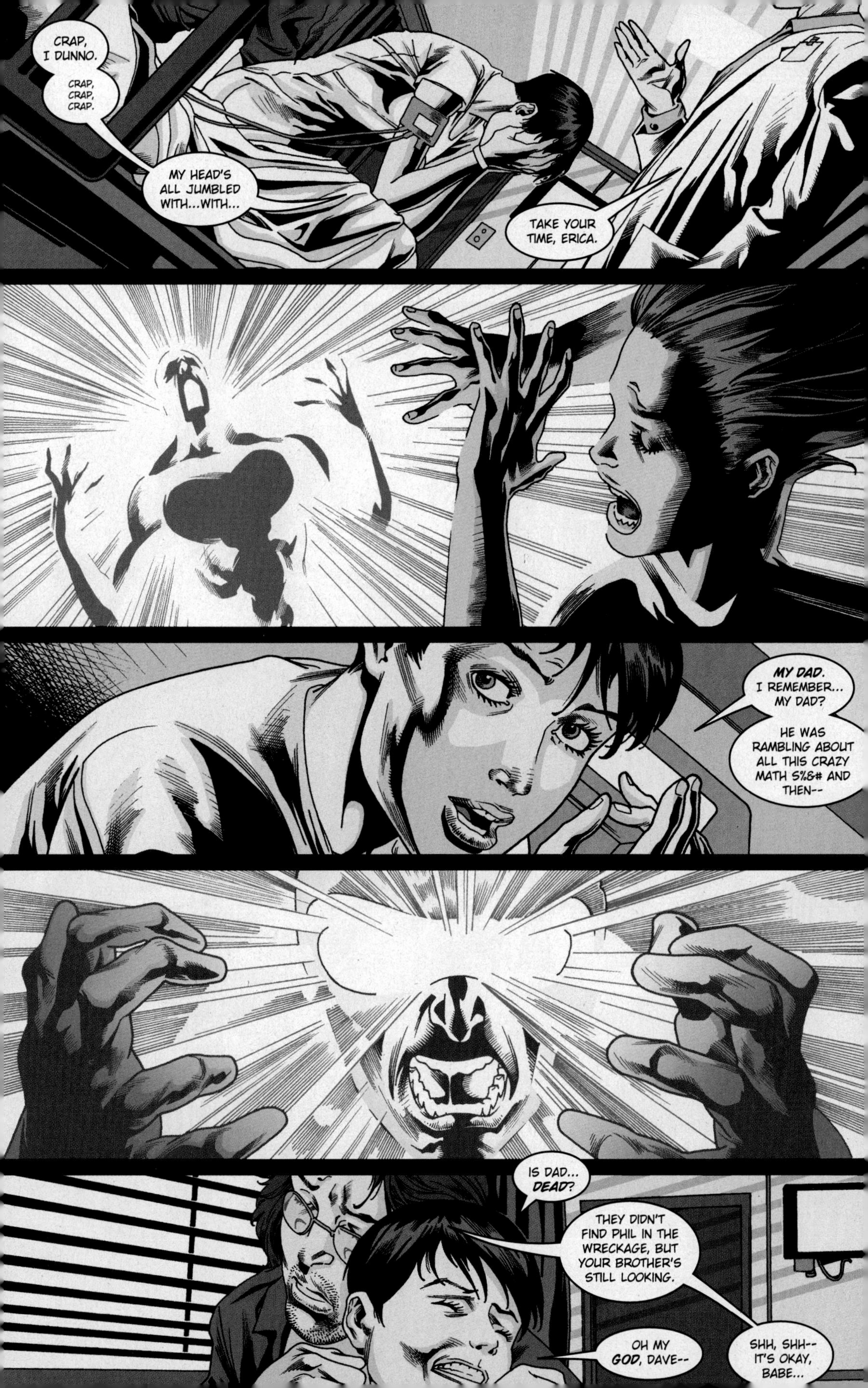
CRAP, I DUNNO.
CRAP, CRAP, CRAP.
MY HEAD'S ALL JUMBLED WITH...WITH...
TAKE YOUR TIME, ERICA.
MY DAD. I REMEMBER... MY DAD?
HE WAS RAMBLING ABOUT ALL THIS CRAZY MATH $%&# AND THEN--
IS DAD... DEAD?
THEY DIDN'T FIND PHIL IN THE WRECKAGE, BUT YOUR BROTHER'S STILL LOOKING.
OH MY GOD, DAVE--
SHH, SHH-- IT'S OKAY, BABE...

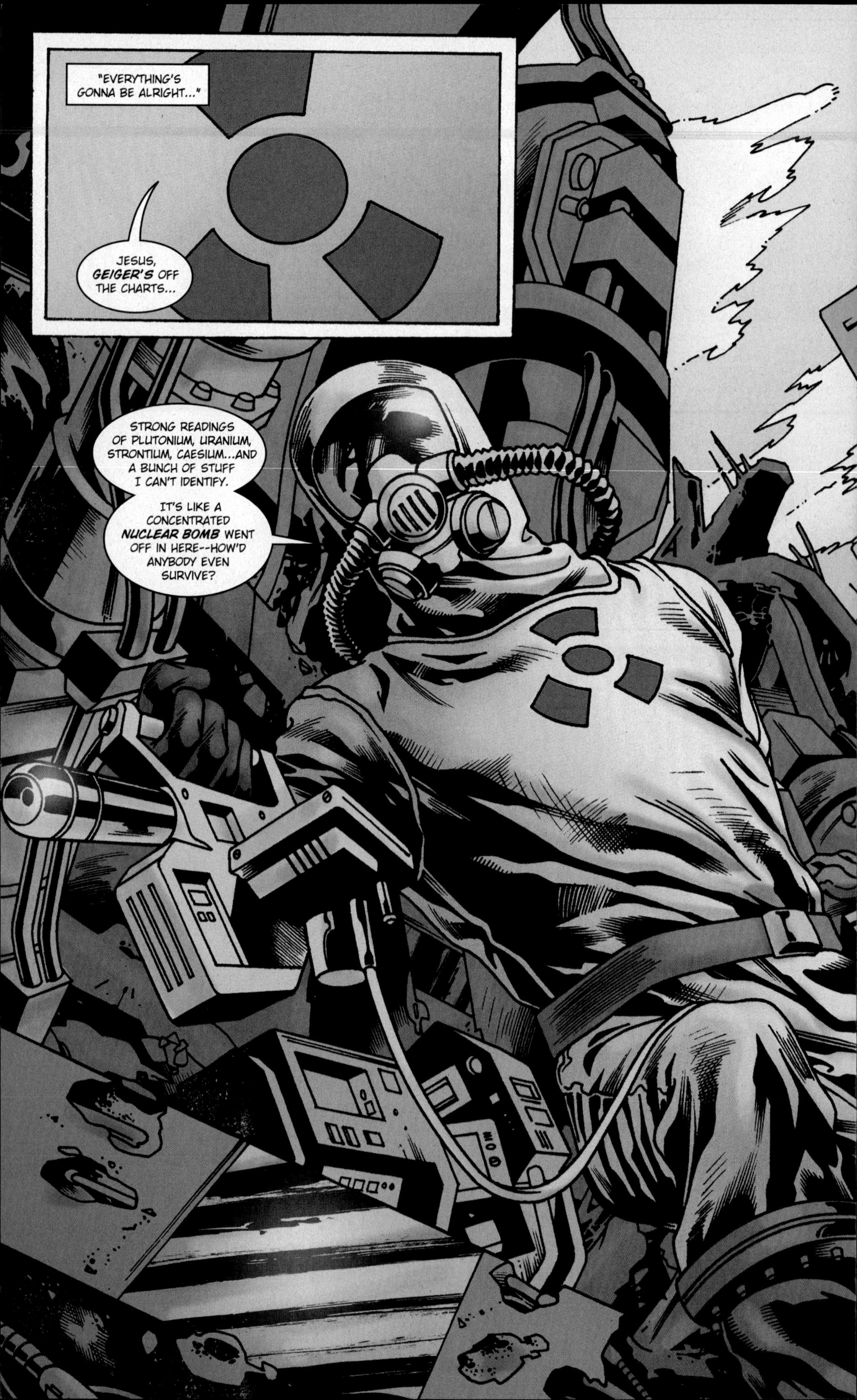
"EVERYTHING'S GONNA BE ALRIGHT..."
JESUS, **GEIGER'S** OFF THE CHARTS...
STRONG READINGS OF PLUTONIUM, URANIUM, STRONTIUM, CAESIUM...AND A BUNCH OF STUFF I CAN'T IDENTIFY.
IT'S LIKE A CONCENTRATED **NUCLEAR BOMB** WENT OFF IN HERE--HOW'D ANYBODY EVEN SURVIVE?

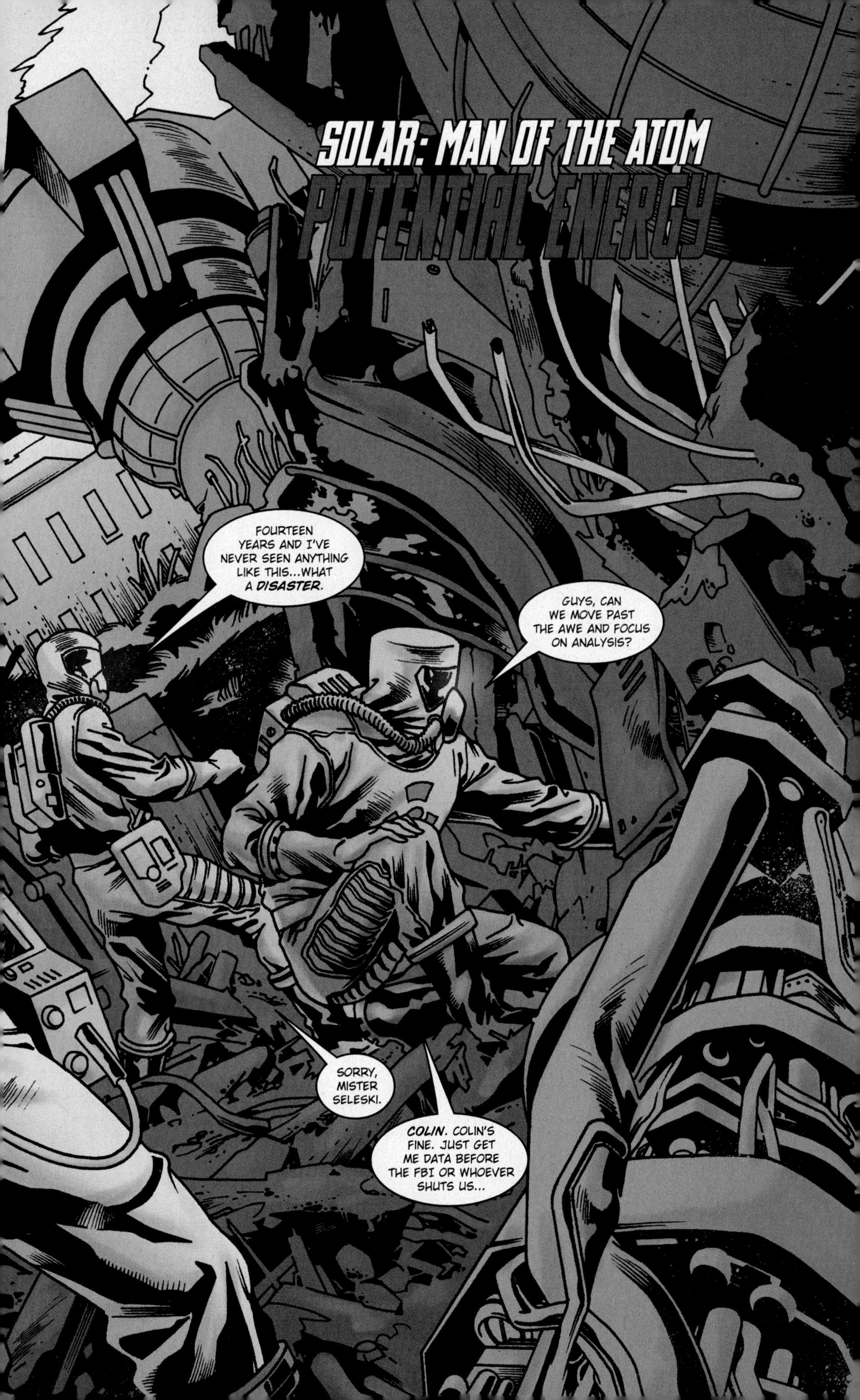
SOLAR: MAN OF THE ATOM
POTENTIAL ENERGY
FOURTEEN YEARS AND I'VE NEVER SEEN ANYTHING LIKE THIS...WHAT A DISASTER.
GUYS, CAN WE MOVE PAST THE AWE AND FOCUS ON ANALYSIS?
SORRY, MISTER SELESKI.
COLIN. COLIN'S FINE. JUST GET ME DATA BEFORE THE FBI OR WHOEVER SHUTS US...

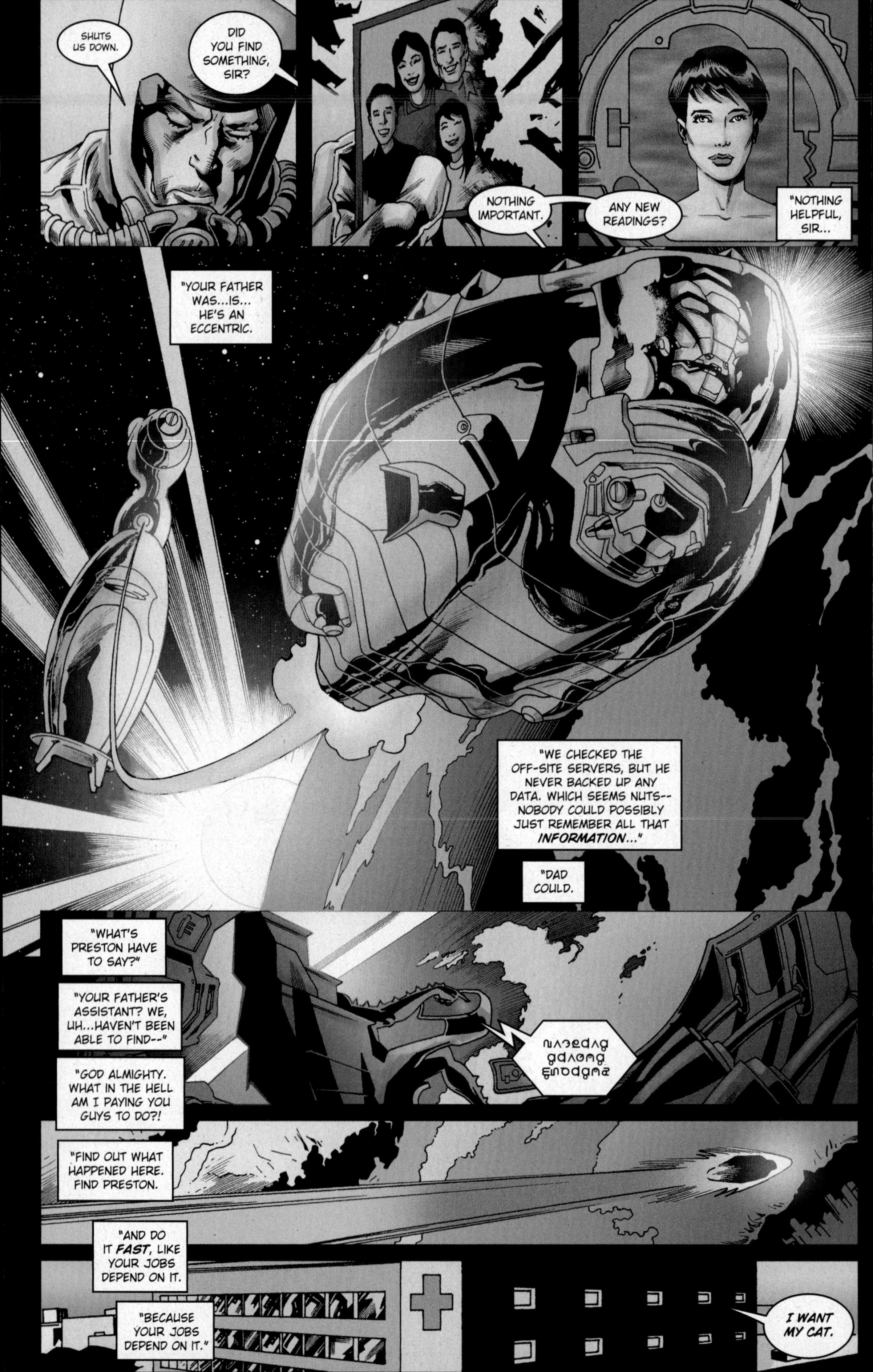
SHUTS US DOWN.
DID YOU FIND SOMETHING, SIR?
NOTHING IMPORTANT.
ANY NEW READINGS?
"NOTHING HELPFUL, SIR...
"YOUR FATHER WAS...IS... HE'S AN ECCENTRIC.
"WE CHECKED THE OFF-SITE SERVERS, BUT HE NEVER BACKED UP ANY DATA. WHICH SEEMS NUTS-- NOBODY COULD POSSIBLY JUST REMEMBER ALL THAT INFORMATION..."
"DAD COULD.
"WHAT'S PRESTON HAVE TO SAY?"
"YOUR FATHER'S ASSISTANT? WE, UH...HAVEN'T BEEN ABLE TO FIND--"
"GOD ALMIGHTY. WHAT IN THE HELL AM I PAYING YOU GUYS TO DO?!
"FIND OUT WHAT HAPPENED HERE. FIND PRESTON.
"AND DO IT FAST, LIKE YOUR JOBS DEPEND ON IT.
"BECAUSE YOUR JOBS DEPEND ON IT."
I WANT MY CAT.

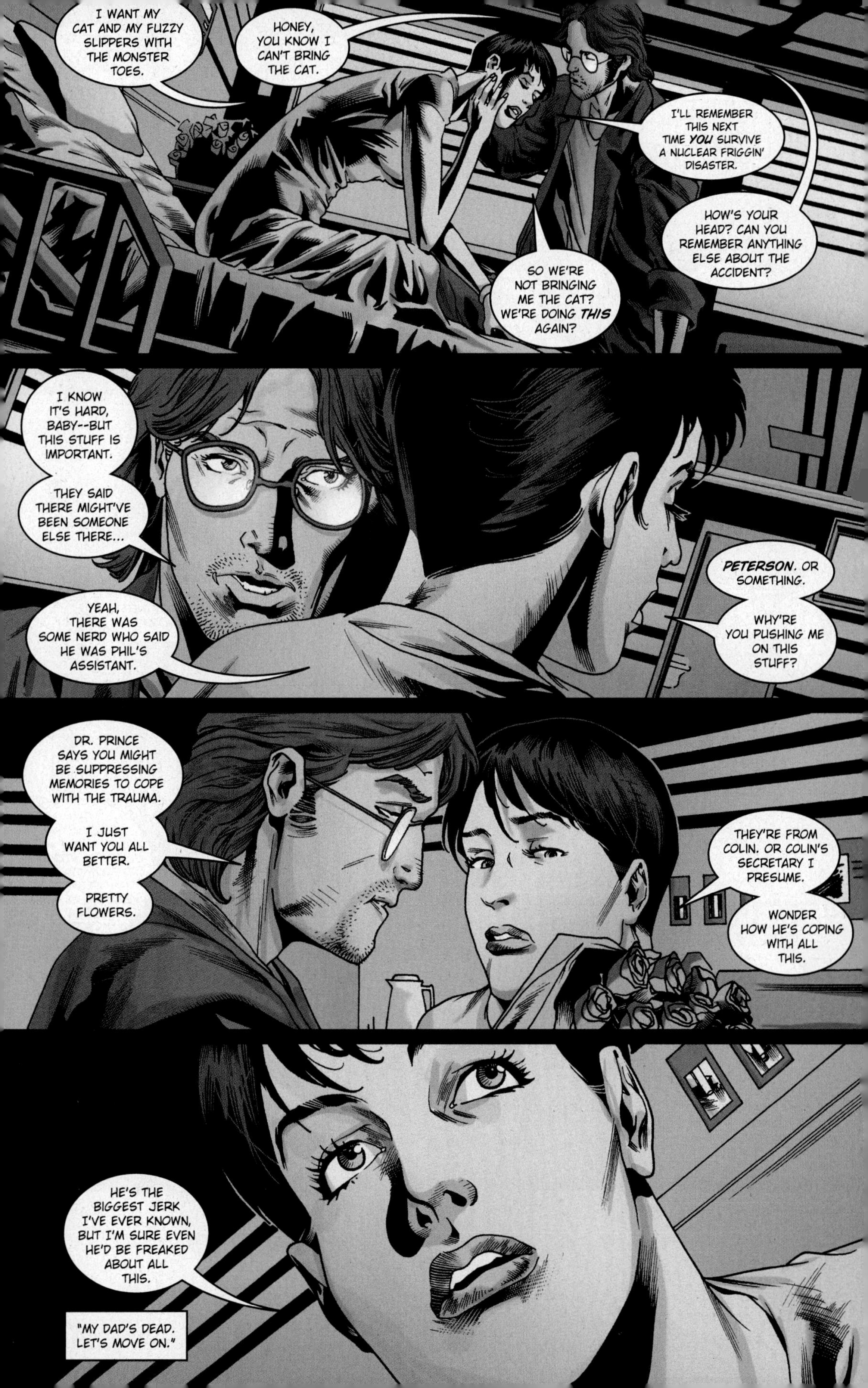
I WANT MY CAT AND MY FUZZY SLIPPERS WITH THE MONSTER TOES.
HONEY, YOU KNOW I CAN'T BRING THE CAT.
I'LL REMEMBER THIS NEXT TIME YOU SURVIVE A NUCLEAR FRIGGIN' DISASTER.
HOW'S YOUR HEAD? CAN YOU REMEMBER ANYTHING ELSE ABOUT THE ACCIDENT?
SO WE'RE NOT BRINGING ME THE CAT? WE'RE DOING THIS AGAIN?
I KNOW IT'S HARD, BABY--BUT THIS STUFF IS IMPORTANT.
THEY SAID THERE MIGHT'VE BEEN SOMEONE ELSE THERE...
YEAH, THERE WAS SOME NERD WHO SAID HE WAS PHIL'S ASSISTANT.
PETERSON. OR SOMETHING.
WHY'RE YOU PUSHING ME ON THIS STUFF?
DR. PRINCE SAYS YOU MIGHT BE SUPPRESSING MEMORIES TO COPE WITH THE TRAUMA.
I JUST WANT YOU ALL BETTER.
PRETTY FLOWERS.
THEY'RE FROM COLIN. OR COLIN'S SECRETARY I PRESUME.
WONDER HOW HE'S COPING WITH ALL THIS.
HE'S THE BIGGEST JERK I'VE EVER KNOWN, BUT I'M SURE EVEN HE'D BE FREAKED ABOUT ALL THIS.
"MY DAD'S DEAD. LET'S MOVE ON."

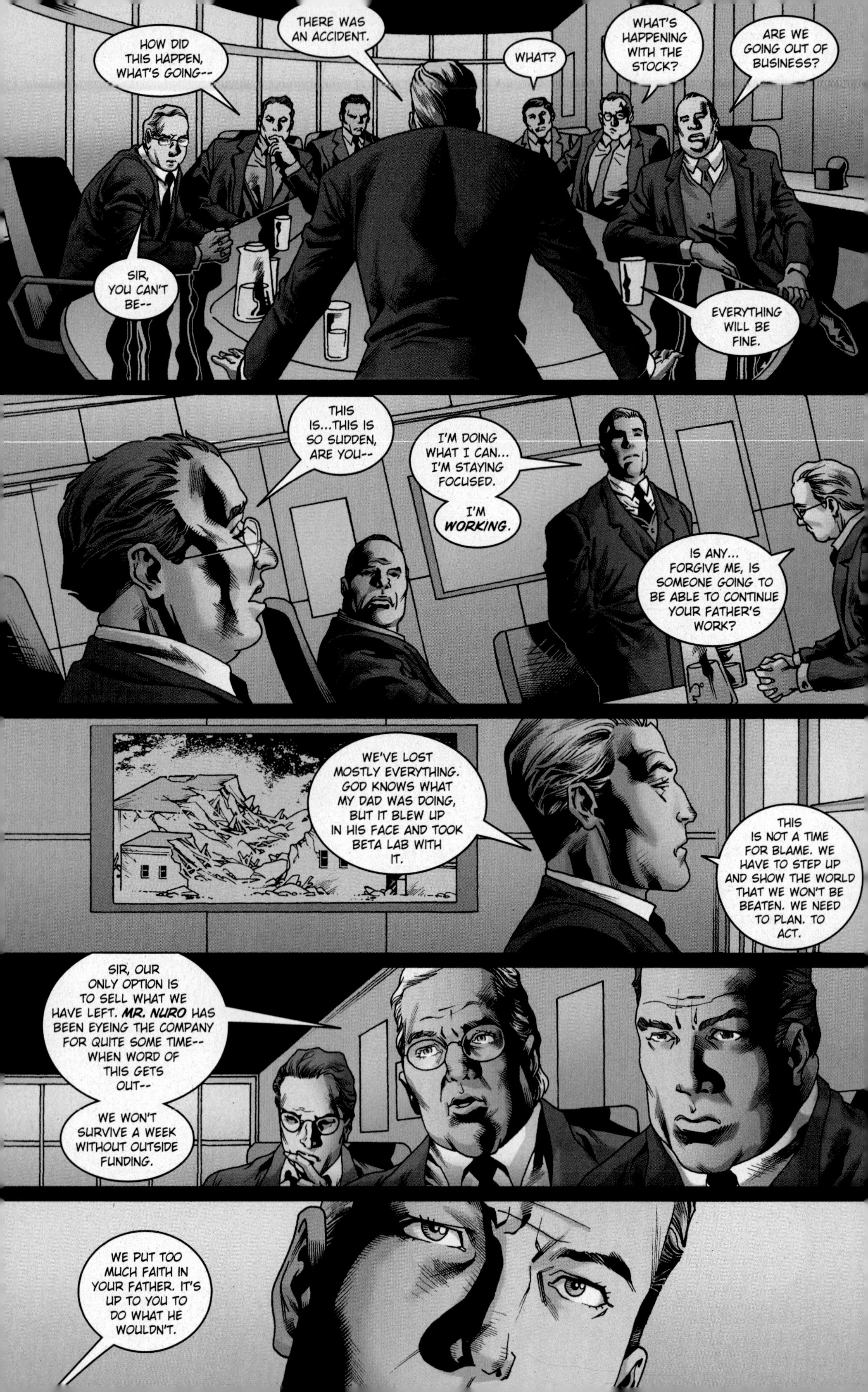
HOW DID THIS HAPPEN, WHAT'S GOING--
THERE WAS AN ACCIDENT.
WHAT?
WHAT'S HAPPENING WITH THE STOCK?
ARE WE GOING OUT OF BUSINESS?
SIR, YOU CAN'T BE--
EVERYTHING WILL BE FINE.
THIS IS...THIS IS SO SUDDEN, ARE YOU--
I'M DOING WHAT I CAN... I'M STAYING FOCUSED.
I'M **WORKING**.
IS ANY... FORGIVE ME, IS SOMEONE GOING TO BE ABLE TO CONTINUE YOUR FATHER'S WORK?
WE'VE LOST MOSTLY EVERYTHING. GOD KNOWS WHAT MY DAD WAS DOING, BUT IT BLEW UP IN HIS FACE AND TOOK BETA LAB WITH IT.
THIS IS NOT A TIME FOR BLAME. WE HAVE TO STEP UP AND SHOW THE WORLD THAT WE WON'T BE BEATEN. WE NEED TO PLAN. TO ACT.
SIR, OUR ONLY OPTION IS TO SELL WHAT WE HAVE LEFT. **MR. NURO** HAS BEEN EYEING THE COMPANY FOR QUITE SOME TIME-- WHEN WORD OF THIS GETS OUT--
WE WON'T SURVIVE A WEEK WITHOUT OUTSIDE FUNDING.
WE PUT TOO MUCH FAITH IN YOUR FATHER. IT'S UP TO YOU TO DO WHAT HE WOULDN'T.

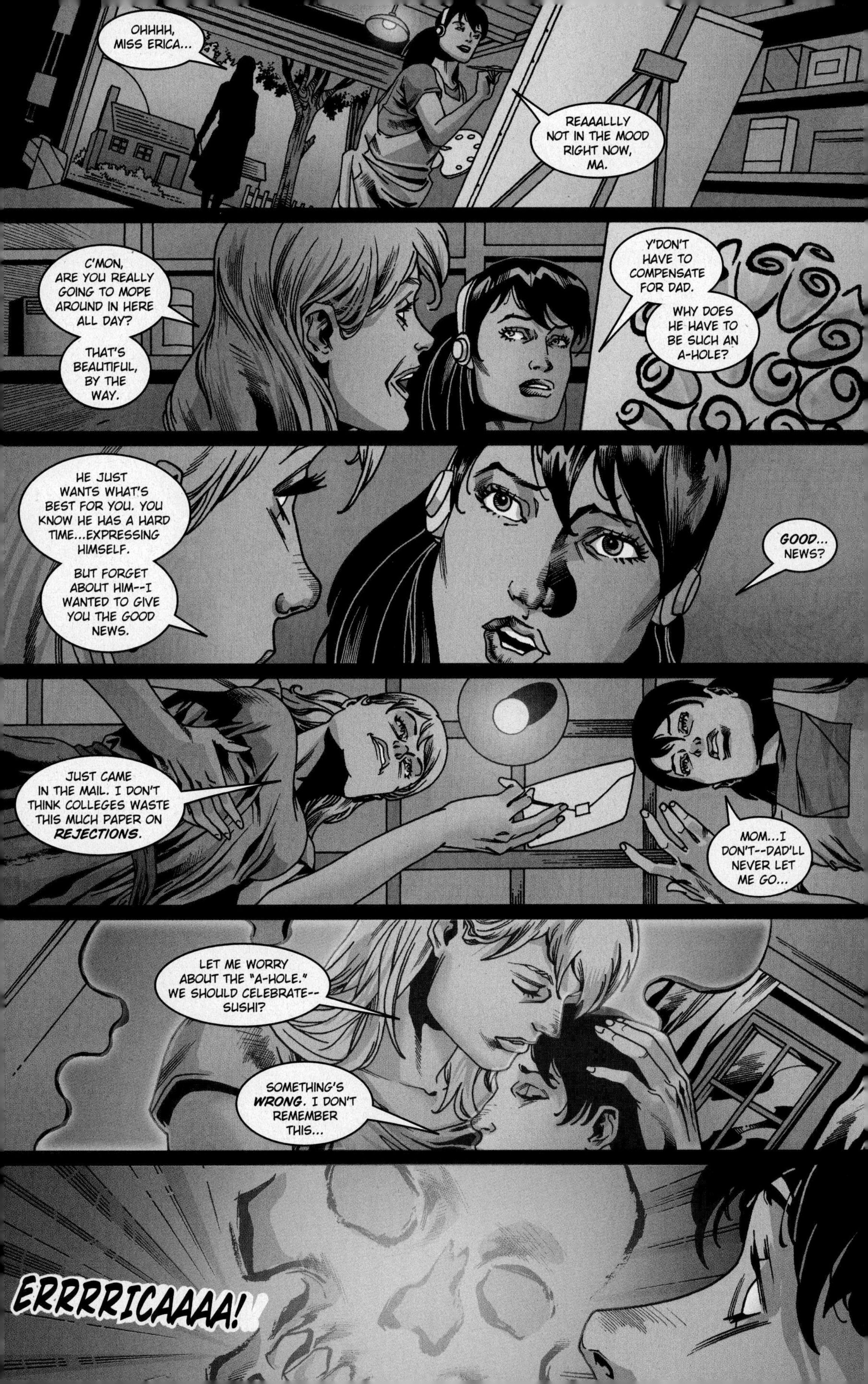
OHHHH, MISS ERICA...
REAAALLLY NOT IN THE MOOD RIGHT NOW, MA.
C'MON, ARE YOU REALLY GOING TO MOPE AROUND IN HERE ALL DAY?
THAT'S BEAUTIFUL, BY THE WAY.
Y'DON'T HAVE TO COMPENSATE FOR DAD.
WHY DOES HE HAVE TO BE SUCH AN A-HOLE?
HE JUST WANTS WHAT'S BEST FOR YOU. YOU KNOW HE HAS A HARD TIME...EXPRESSING HIMSELF.
BUT FORGET ABOUT HIM--I WANTED TO GIVE YOU THE GOOD NEWS.
GOOD... NEWS?
JUST CAME IN THE MAIL. I DON'T THINK COLLEGES WASTE THIS MUCH PAPER ON REJECTIONS.
MOM...I DON'T--DAD'LL NEVER LET ME GO...
LET ME WORRY ABOUT THE "A-HOLE." WE SHOULD CELEBRATE--SUSHI?
SOMETHING'S WRONG. I DON'T REMEMBER THIS...
ERRRRICAAAA!

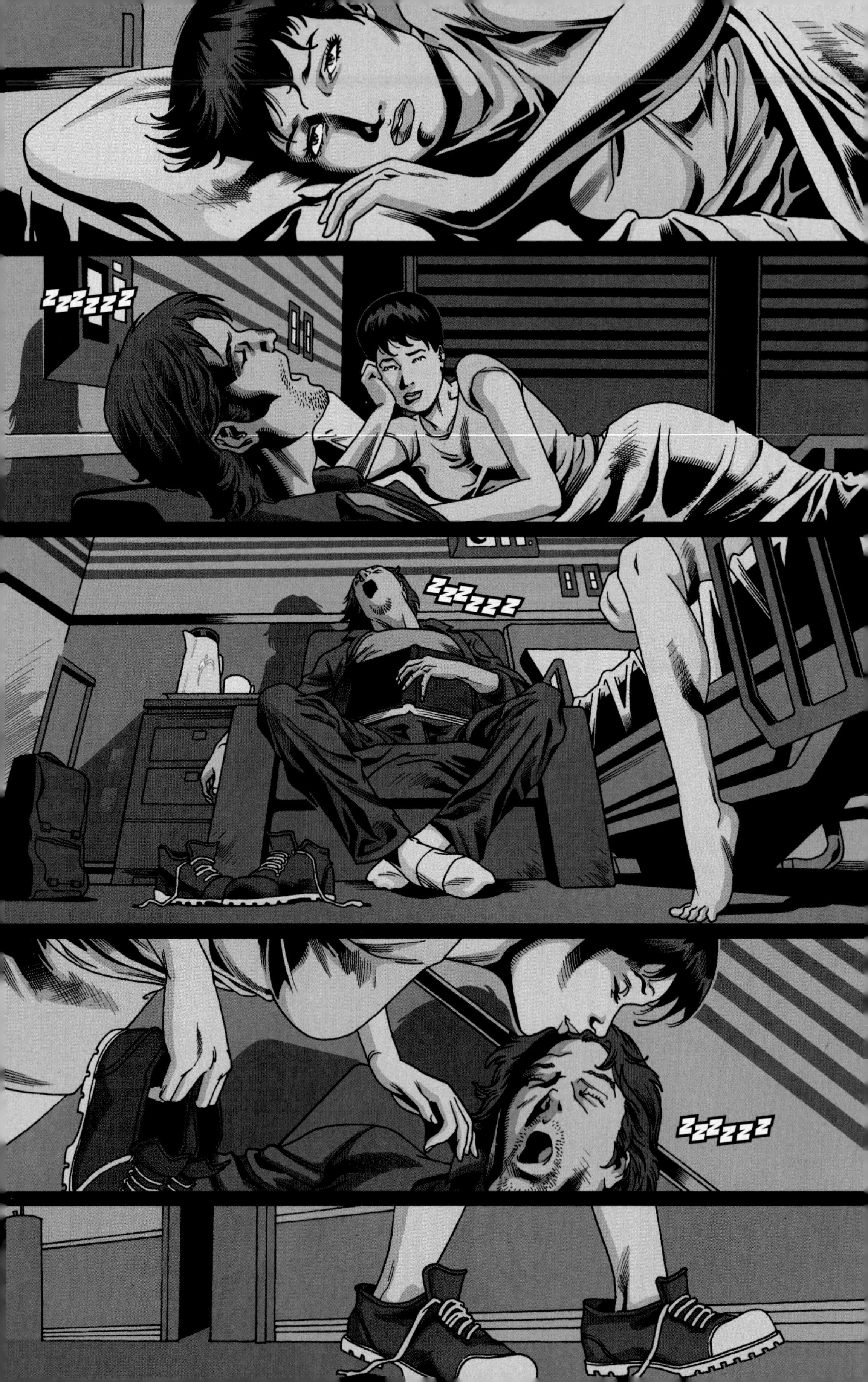
ZZZZZZ
ZZZZZZ
ZZZZZZ

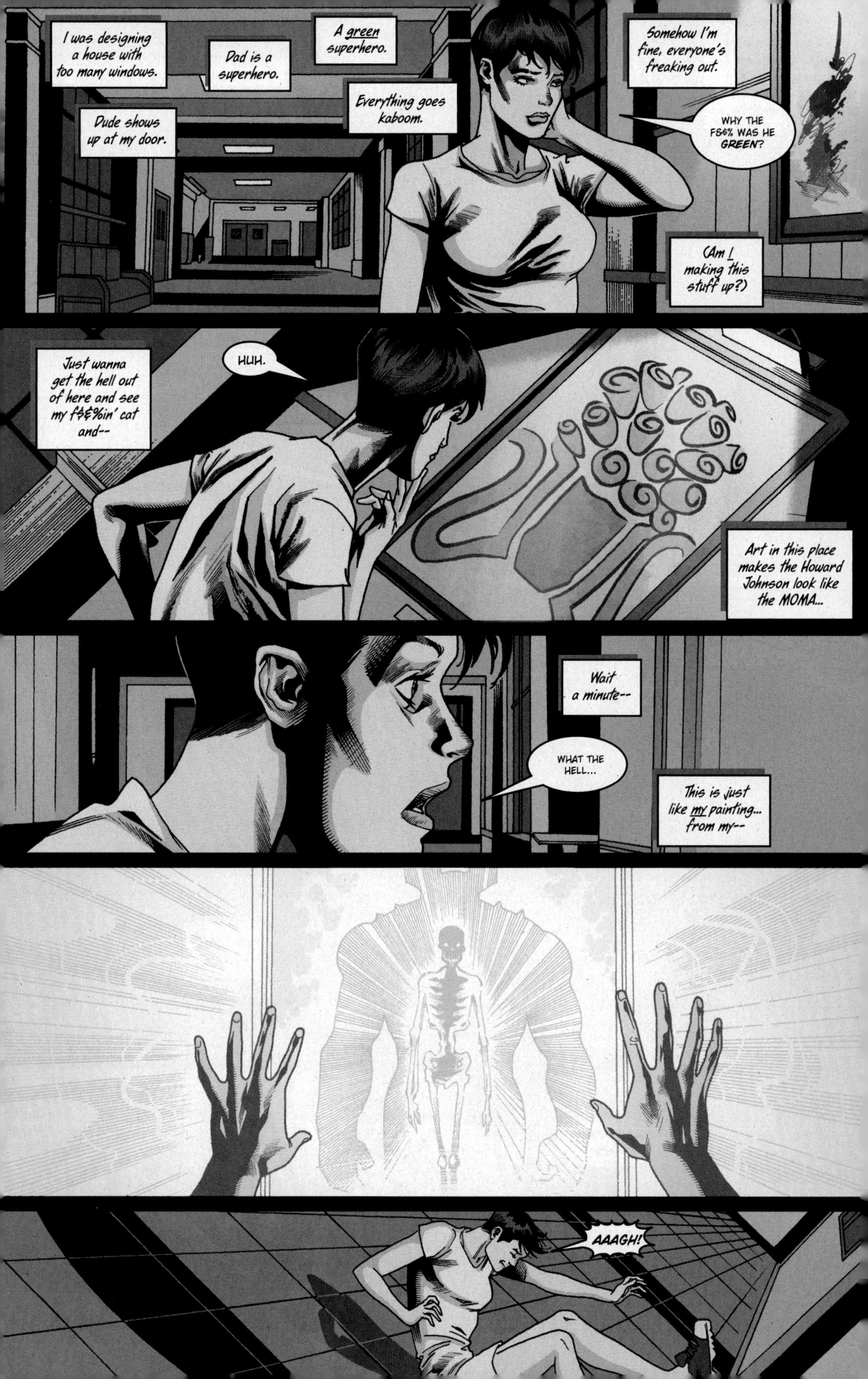
I was designing a house with too many windows.
Dude shows up at my door.
Dad is a superhero.
A green superhero.
Everything goes kaboom.
Somehow I'm fine, everyone's freaking out.
WHY THE F&$% WAS HE GREEN?
(Am I making this stuff up?)
Just wanna get the hell out of here and see my f$&%in' cat and--
HUH.
Art in this place makes the Howard Johnson look like the MOMA...
Wait a minute--
WHAT THE HELL...
This is just like my painting... from my--
AAAGH!

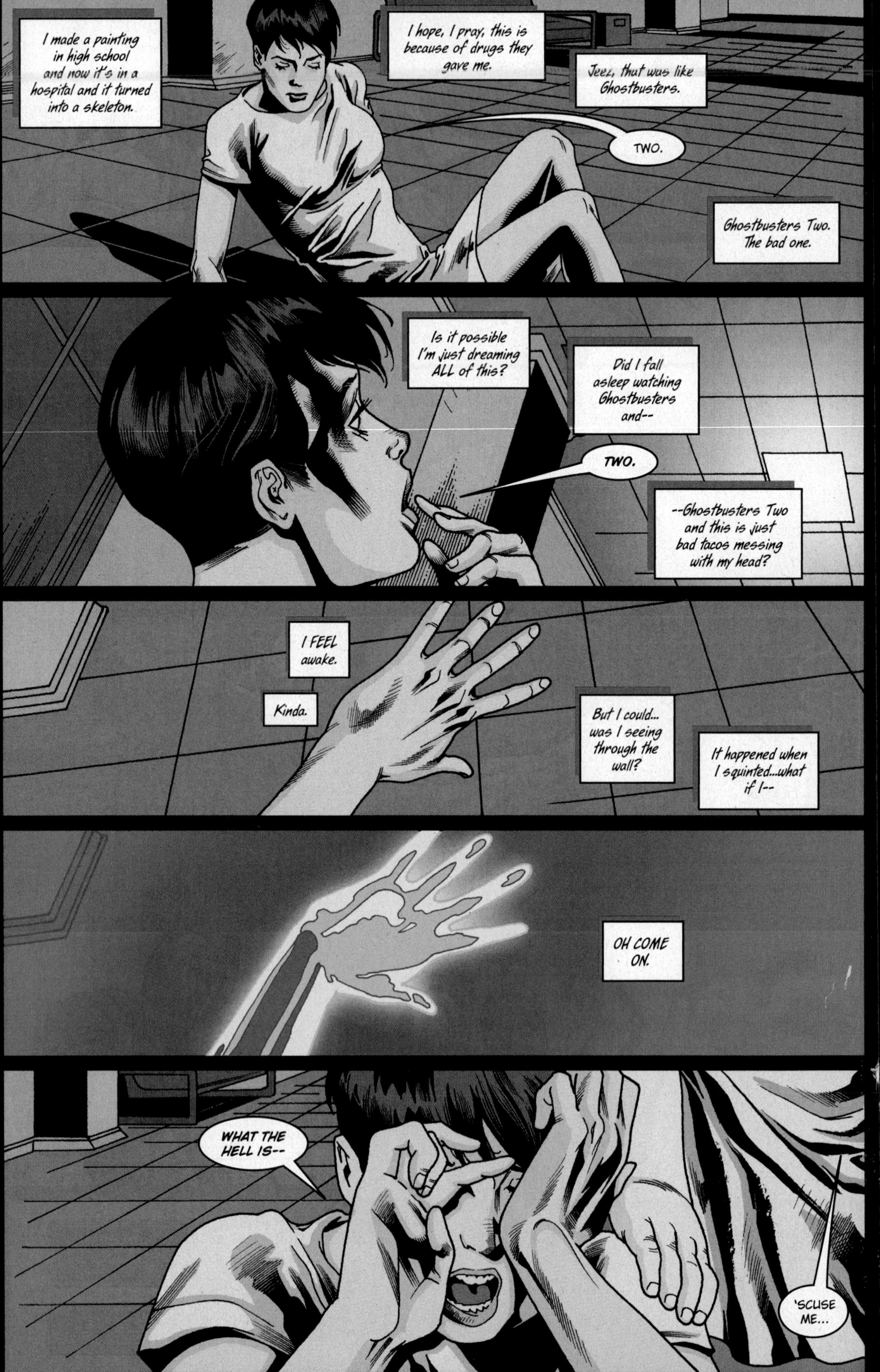

I made a painting in high school and now it's in a hospital and it turned into a skeleton.
I hope, I pray, this is because of drugs they gave me.
Jeez, that was like Ghostbusters.
TWO.
Ghostbusters Two. The bad one.
Is it possible I'm just dreaming ALL of this?
Did I fall asleep watching Ghostbusters and--
TWO.
--Ghostbusters Two and this is just bad tacos messing with my head?
I FEEL awake.
Kinda.
But I could... was I seeing through the wall?
It happened when I squinted...what if I--
OH COME ON.
WHAT THE HELL IS--
'SCUSE ME...

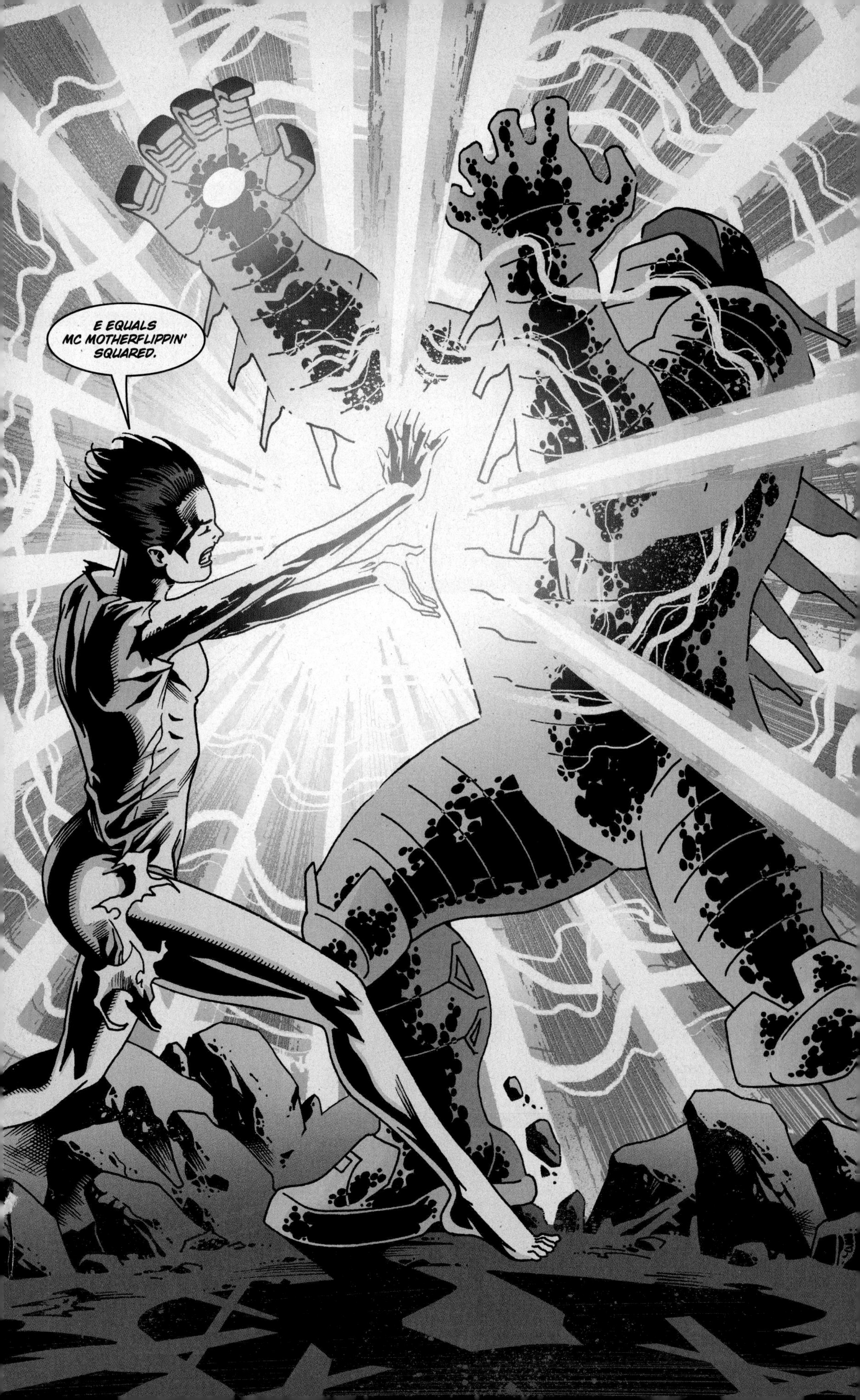
E EQUALS MC MOTHERFLIPPIN' SQUARED.

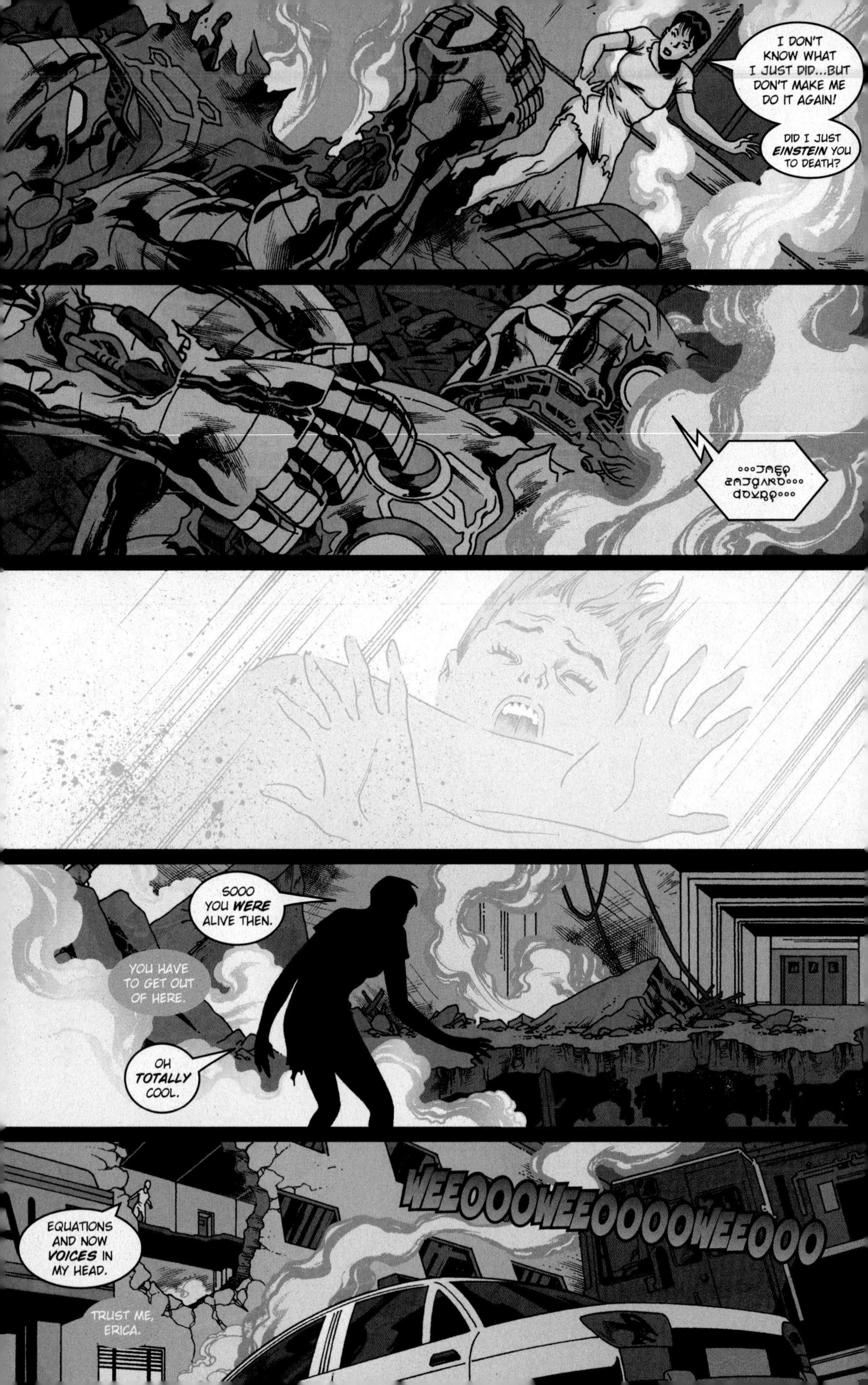
I DON'T KNOW WHAT I JUST DID...BUT DON'T MAKE ME DO IT AGAIN!
DID I JUST EINSTEIN YOU TO DEATH?
SOOO YOU WERE ALIVE THEN.
YOU HAVE TO GET OUT OF HERE.
OH TOTALLY COOL.
WEEOOOWEEOOOOWEEOOO
EQUATIONS AND NOW VOICES IN MY HEAD.
TRUST ME, ERICA.

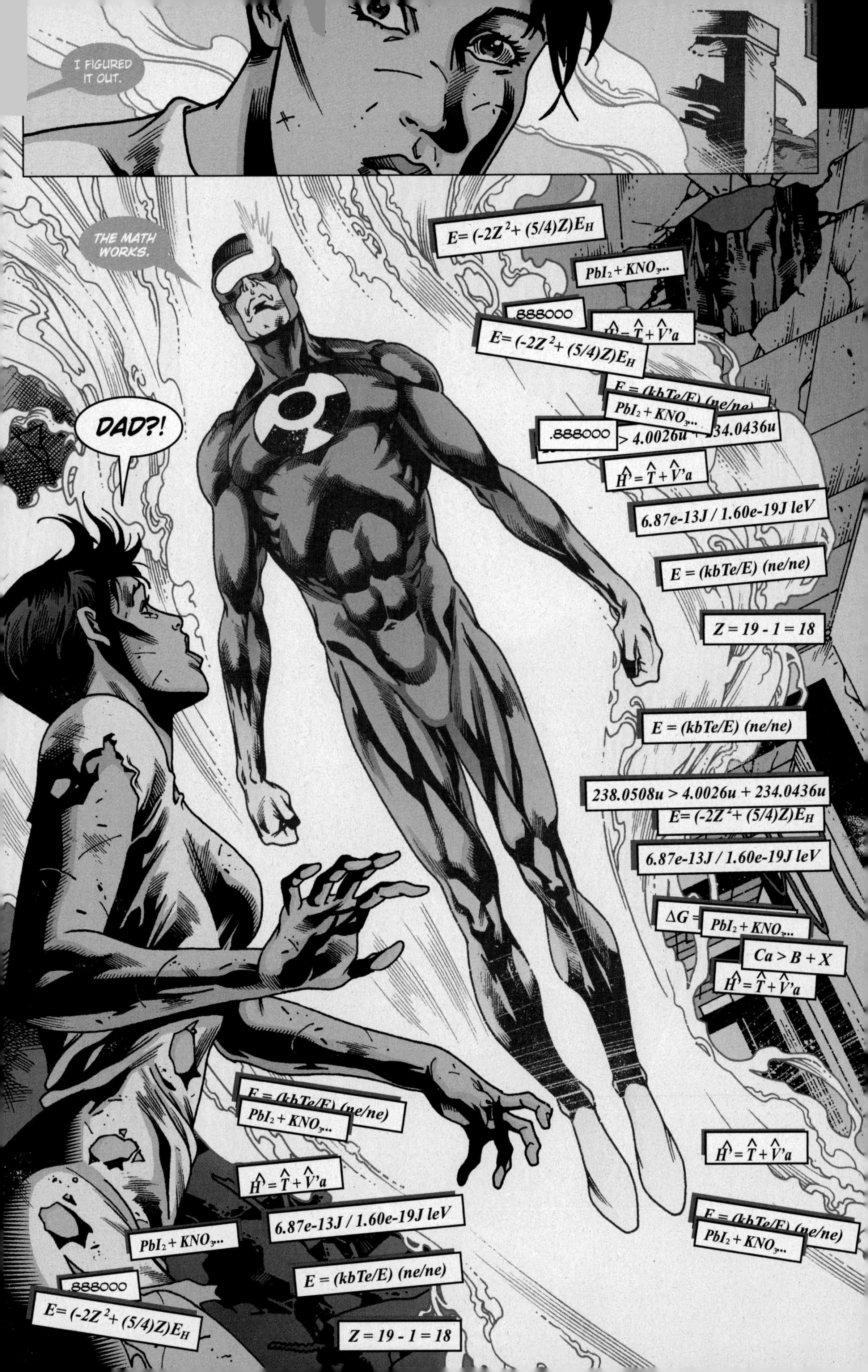
I FIGURED IT OUT.
THE MATH WORKS.
DAD?!
$E = (-2Z^2 + (5/4)Z)E_H$
$PbI_2 + KNO_3$...
.888000
$\hat{H} = \hat{T} + \hat{V}'a$
$E = (-2Z^2 + (5/4)Z)E_H$
$PbI_2 + KNO_3$...
.888000
$\hat{H} = \hat{T} + \hat{V}'a$
6.87e-13J / 1.60e-19J leV
E = (kbTe/E) (ne/ne)
Z = 19 - 1 = 18
E = (kbTe/E) (ne/ne)
238.0508u > 4.0026u + 234.0436u
$E = (-2Z^2 + (5/4)Z)E_H$
6.87e-13J / 1.60e-19J leV
$PbI_2 + KNO_3$...
Ca > B + X
$\hat{H} = \hat{T} + \hat{V}'a$
$PbI_2 + KNO_3$...
$\hat{H} = \hat{T} + \hat{V}'a$
$\hat{H} = \hat{T} + \hat{V}'a$
6.87e-13J / 1.60e-19J leV
$PbI_2 + KNO_3$...
$PbI_2 + KNO_3$...
E = (kbTe/E) (ne/ne)
.888000
$E = (-2Z^2 + (5/4)Z)E_H$
Z = 19 - 1 = 18

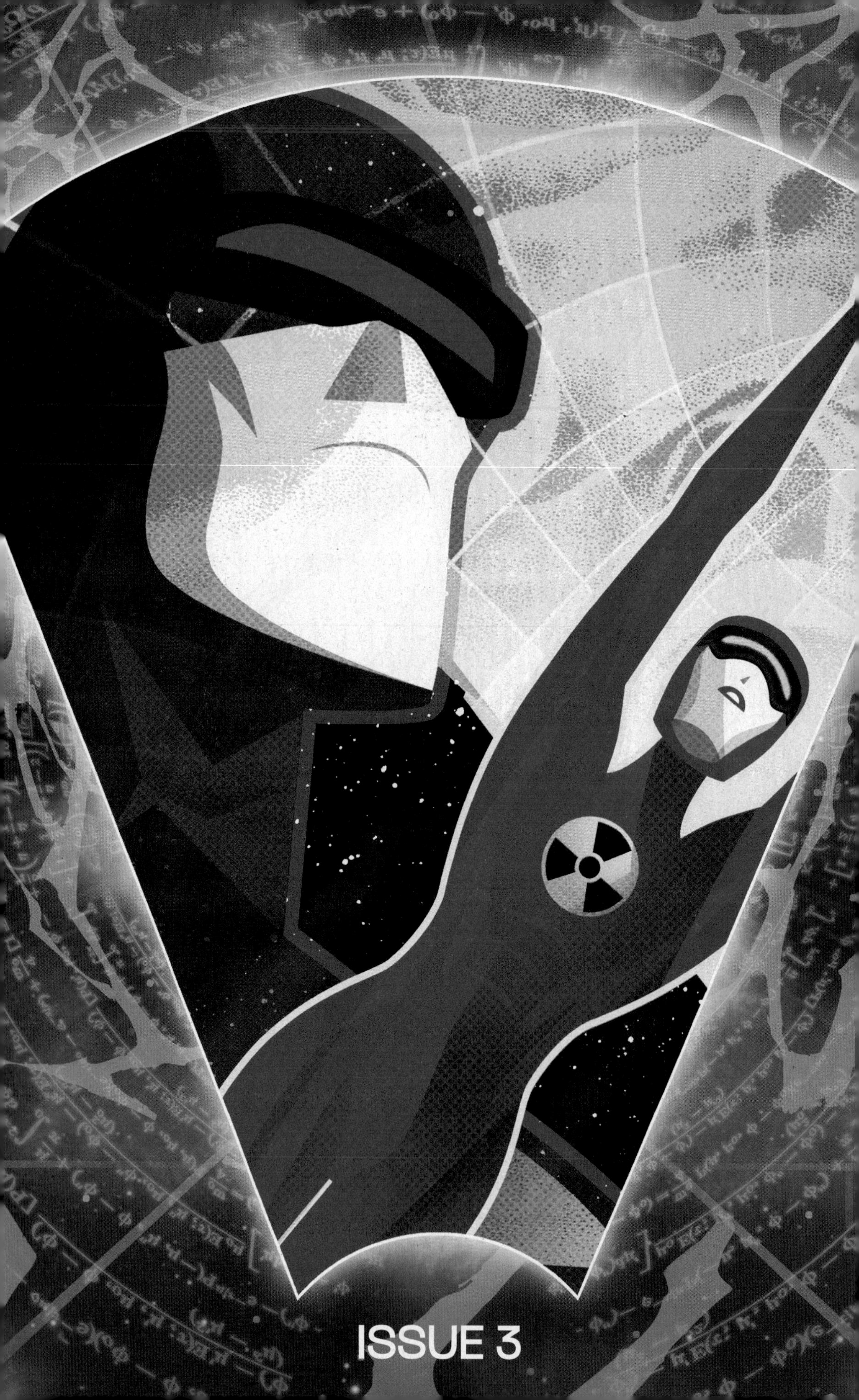
ISSUE 3

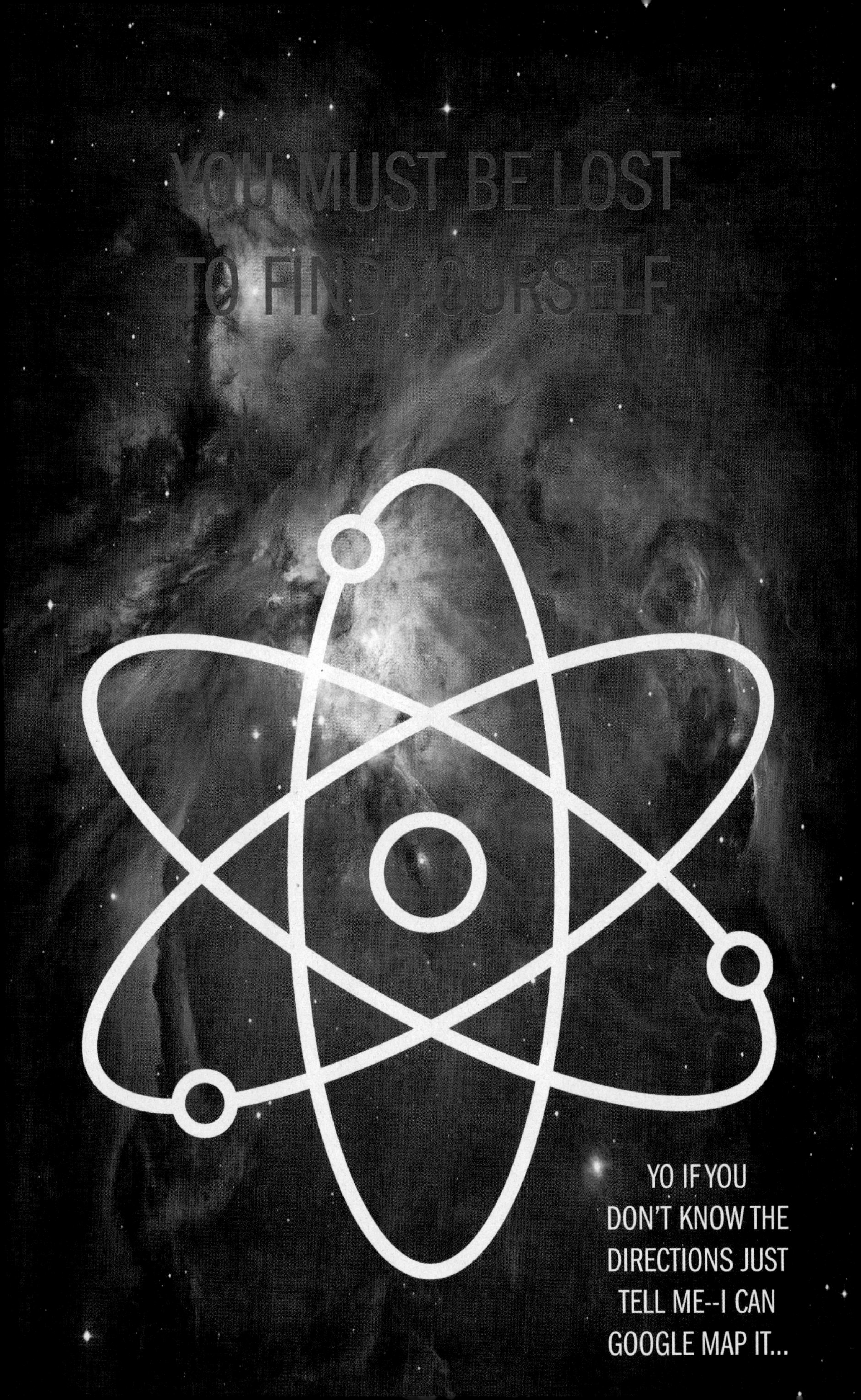
YOU MUST BE LOST
TO FIND YOURSELF.
YO IF YOU
DON'T KNOW THE
DIRECTIONS JUST
TELL ME--I CAN
GOOGLE MAP IT...

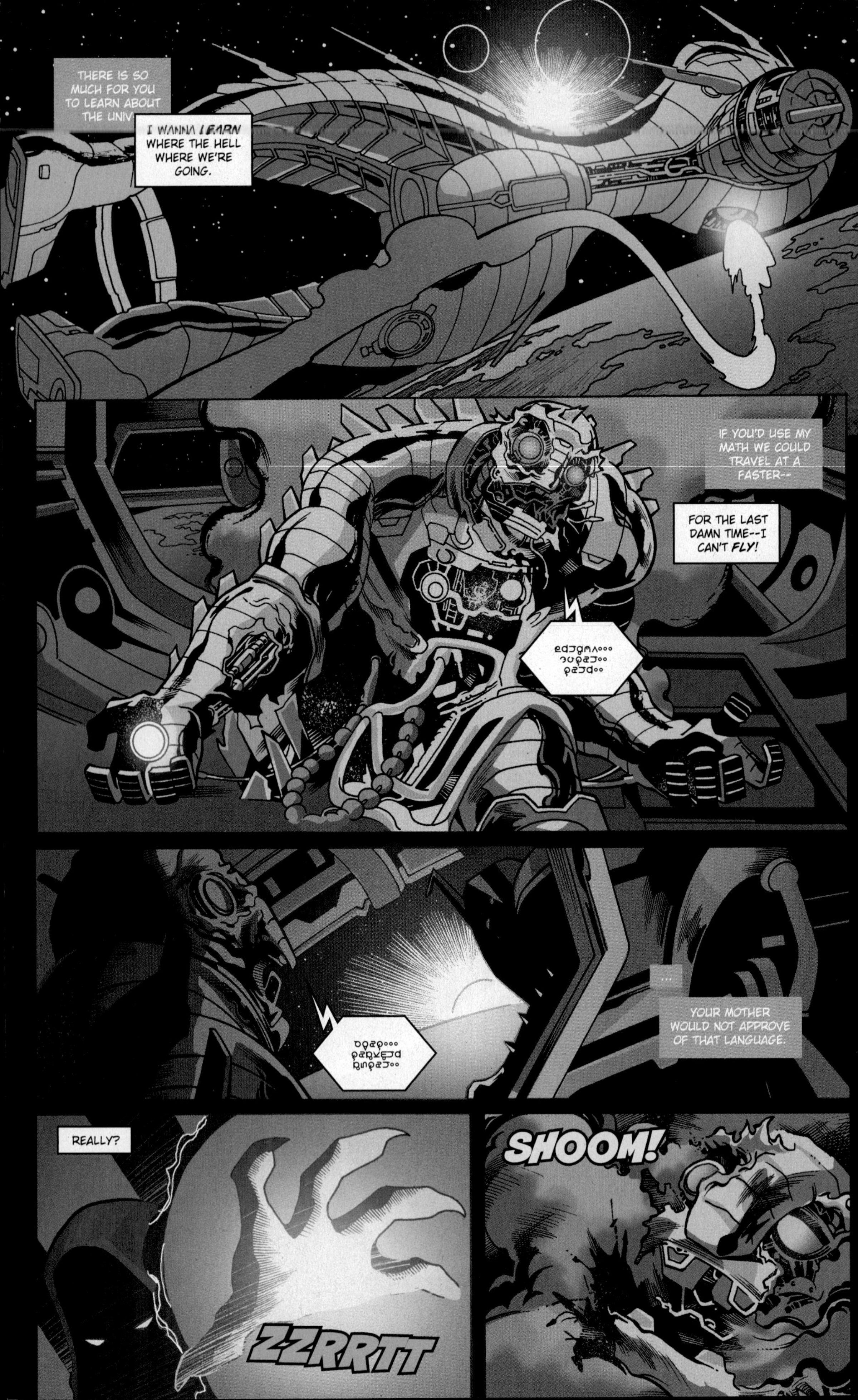
THERE IS SO MUCH FOR YOU TO LEARN ABOUT THE UNIV
I WANNA LEARN WHERE THE HELL WHERE WE'RE GOING.
IF YOU'D USE MY MATH WE COULD TRAVEL AT A FASTER--
FOR THE LAST DAMN TIME--I CAN'T FLY!
...
YOUR MOTHER WOULD NOT APPROVE OF THAT LANGUAGE.
REALLY?
ZZRRRTT
SHOOM!

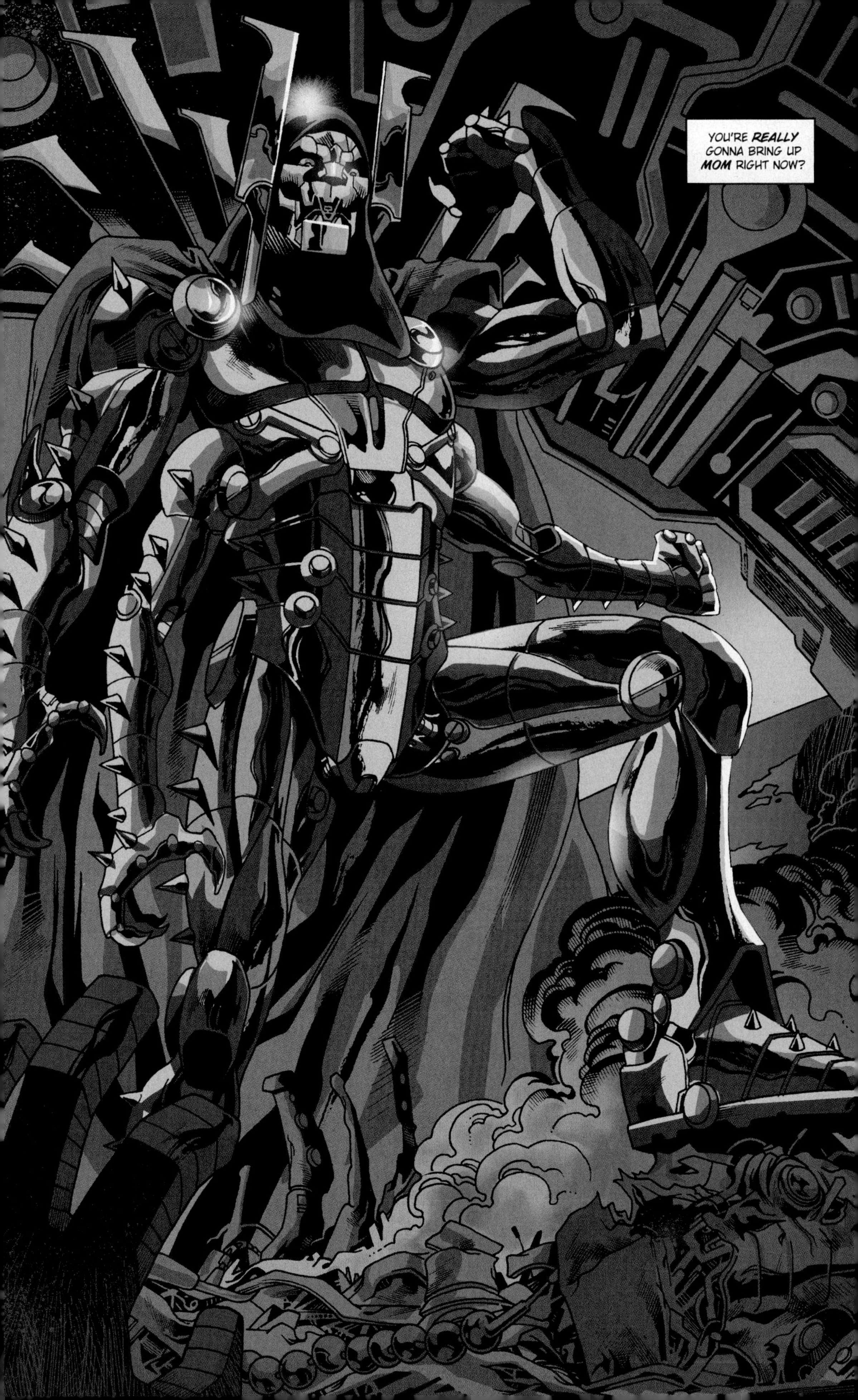
YOU'RE **REALLY** GONNA BRING UP **MOM** RIGHT NOW?

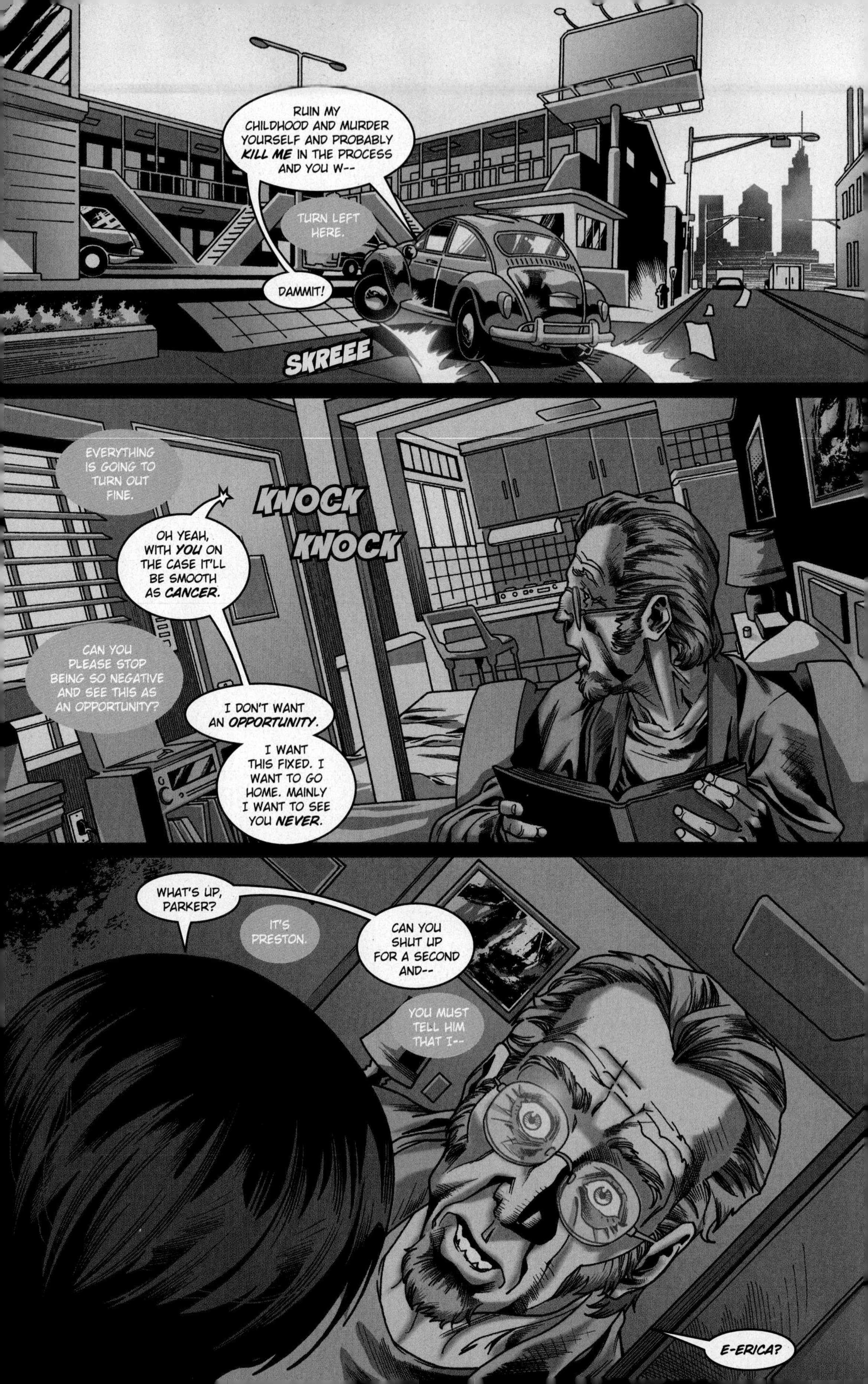
RUIN MY CHILDHOOD AND MURDER YOURSELF AND PROBABLY KILL ME IN THE PROCESS AND YOU W--
TURN LEFT HERE.
DAMMIT!
SKREEE
EVERYTHING IS GOING TO TURN OUT FINE.
KNOCK
KNOCK
OH YEAH, WITH YOU ON THE CASE IT'LL BE SMOOTH AS CANCER.
CAN YOU PLEASE STOP BEING SO NEGATIVE AND SEE THIS AS AN OPPORTUNITY?
I DON'T WANT AN OPPORTUNITY.
I WANT THIS FIXED. I WANT TO GO HOME. MAINLY I WANT TO SEE YOU NEVER.
WHAT'S UP, PARKER?
IT'S PRESTON.
CAN YOU SHUT UP FOR A SECOND AND--
YOU MUST TELL HIM THAT I--
E-ERICA?

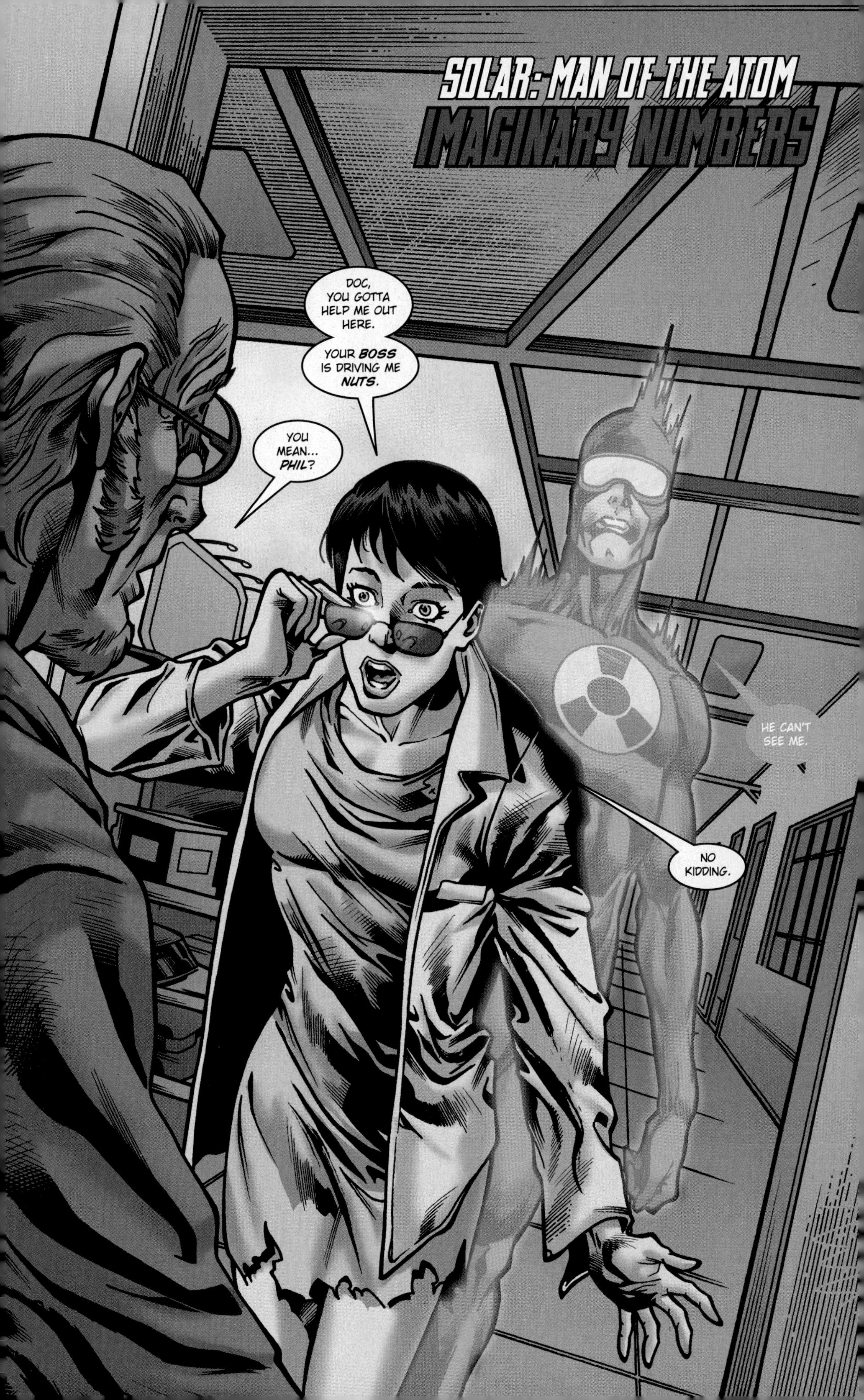
SOLAR: MAN OF THE ATOM
IMAGINARY NUMBERS
DOC, YOU GOTTA HELP ME OUT HERE.
YOUR BOSS IS DRIVING ME NUTS.
YOU MEAN... PHIL?
HE CAN'T SEE ME.
NO KIDDING.

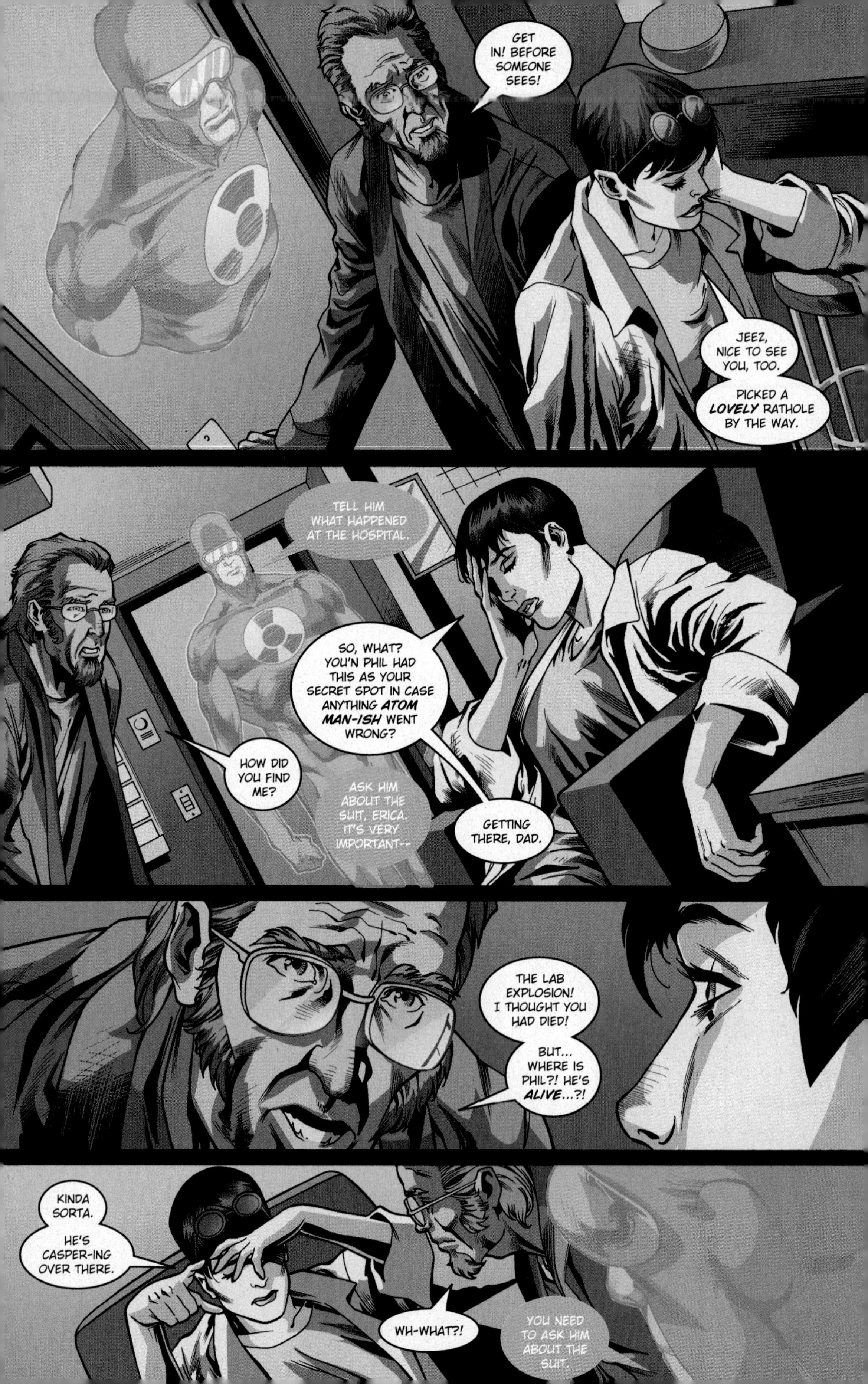
GET IN! BEFORE SOMEONE SEES!
JEEZ, NICE TO SEE YOU, TOO.
PICKED A **LOVELY** RATHOLE BY THE WAY.
TELL HIM WHAT HAPPENED AT THE HOSPITAL.
SO, WHAT? YOU'N PHIL HAD THIS AS YOUR SECRET SPOT IN CASE ANYTHING **ATOM MAN-ISH** WENT WRONG?
HOW DID YOU FIND ME?
ASK HIM ABOUT THE SUIT, ERICA. IT'S VERY IMPORTANT--
GETTING THERE, DAD.
THE LAB EXPLOSION! I THOUGHT YOU HAD DIED!
BUT... WHERE IS PHIL?! HE'S **ALIVE**...?!
KINDA SORTA.
HE'S CASPER-ING OVER THERE.
WH-WHAT?!
YOU NEED TO ASK HIM ABOUT THE SUIT.

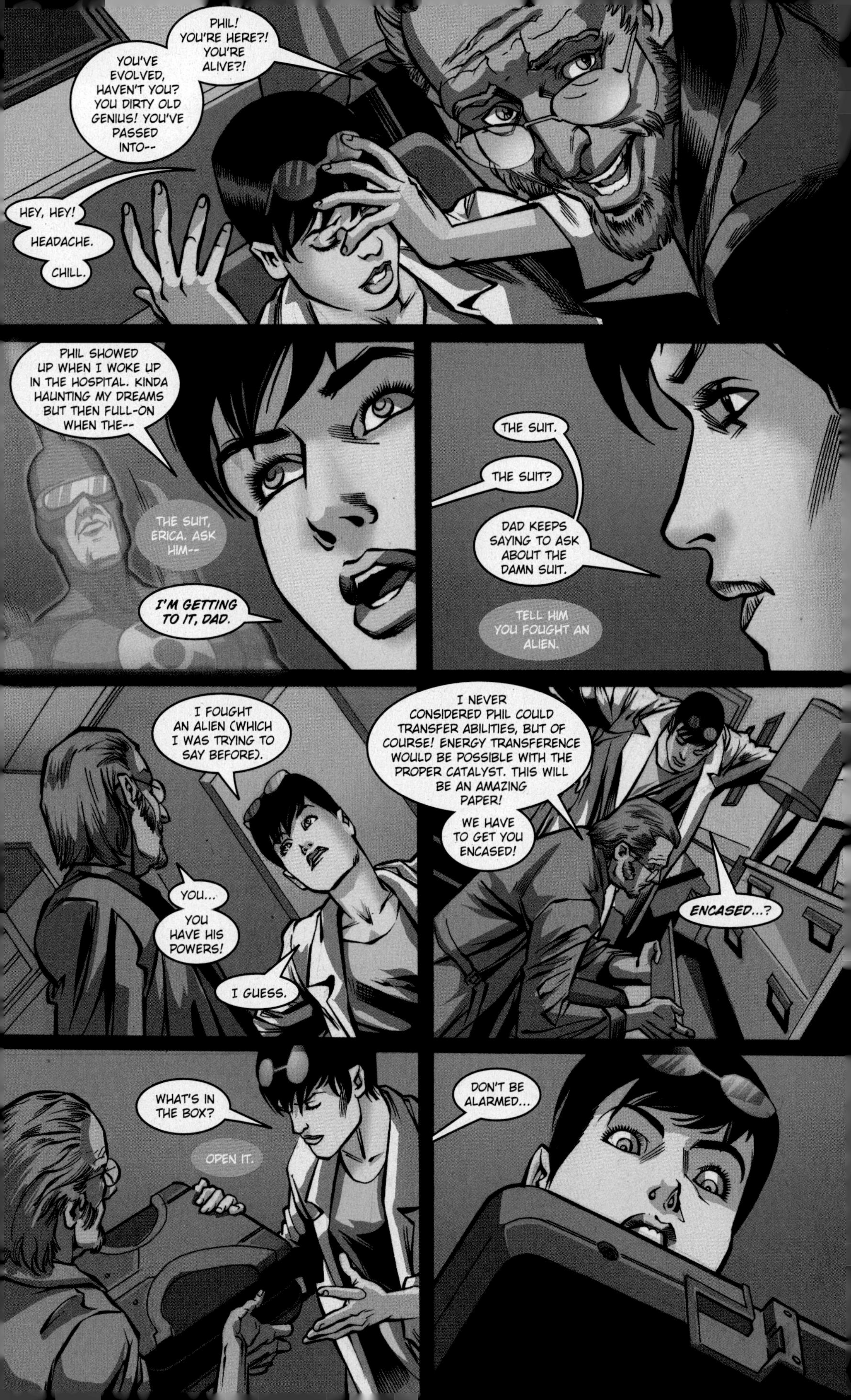
YOU'VE EVOLVED, HAVEN'T YOU? YOU DIRTY OLD GENIUS! YOU'VE PASSED INTO--
PHIL! YOU'RE HERE?! YOU'RE ALIVE?!
HEY, HEY!
HEADACHE.
CHILL.
PHIL SHOWED UP WHEN I WOKE UP IN THE HOSPITAL. KINDA HAUNTING MY DREAMS BUT THEN FULL-ON WHEN THE--
THE SUIT, ERICA. ASK HIM--
I'M GETTING TO IT, DAD.
THE SUIT.
THE SUIT?
DAD KEEPS SAYING TO ASK ABOUT THE DAMN SUIT.
TELL HIM YOU FOUGHT AN ALIEN.
I FOUGHT AN ALIEN (WHICH I WAS TRYING TO SAY BEFORE).
YOU...
YOU HAVE HIS POWERS!
I GUESS.
I NEVER CONSIDERED PHIL COULD TRANSFER ABILITIES, BUT OF COURSE! ENERGY TRANSFERENCE WOULD BE POSSIBLE WITH THE PROPER CATALYST. THIS WILL BE AN AMAZING PAPER!
WE HAVE TO GET YOU ENCASED!
ENCASED...?
WHAT'S IN THE BOX?
OPEN IT.
DON'T BE ALARMED...

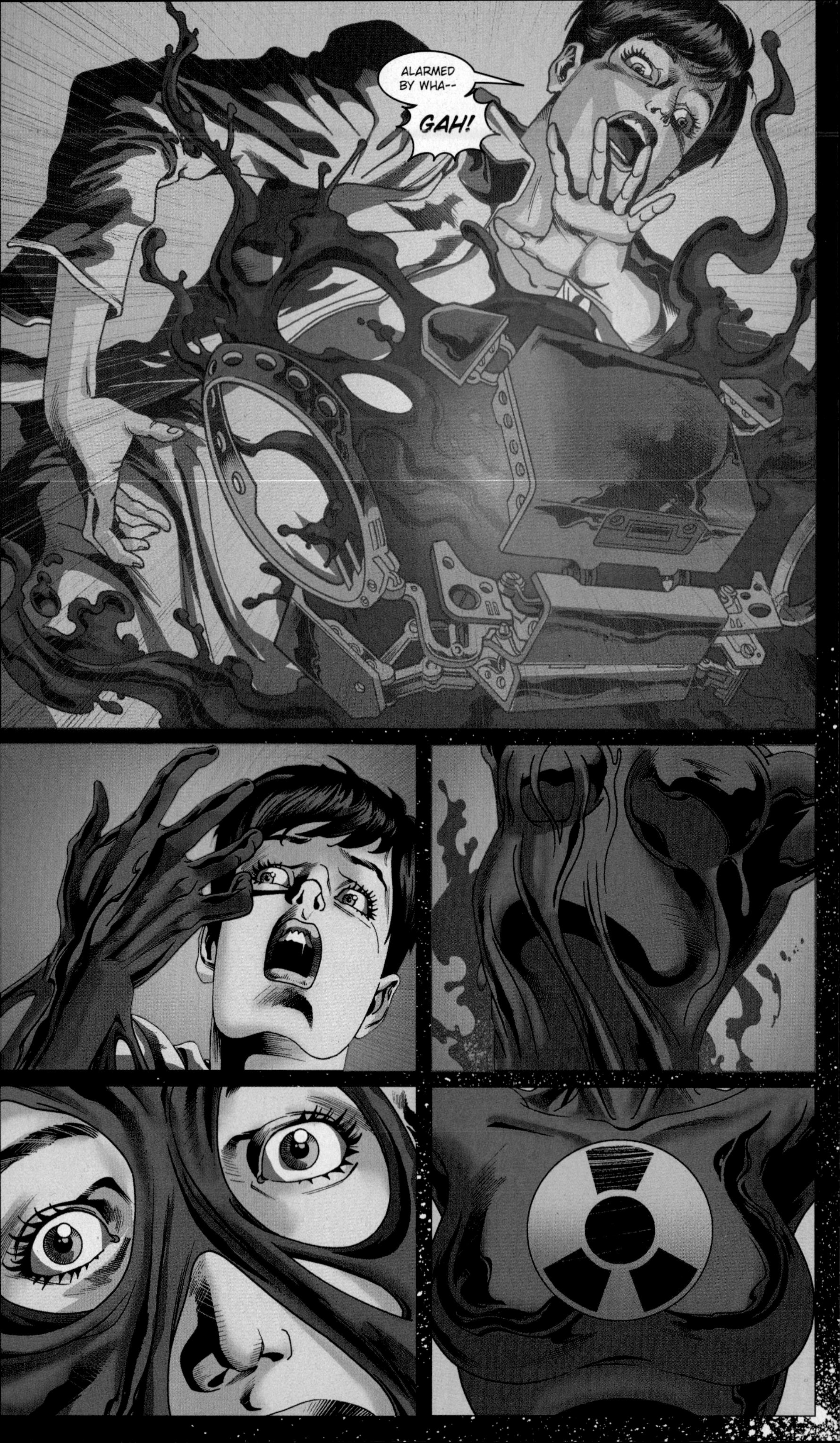
ALARMED
BY WHA--
GAH!

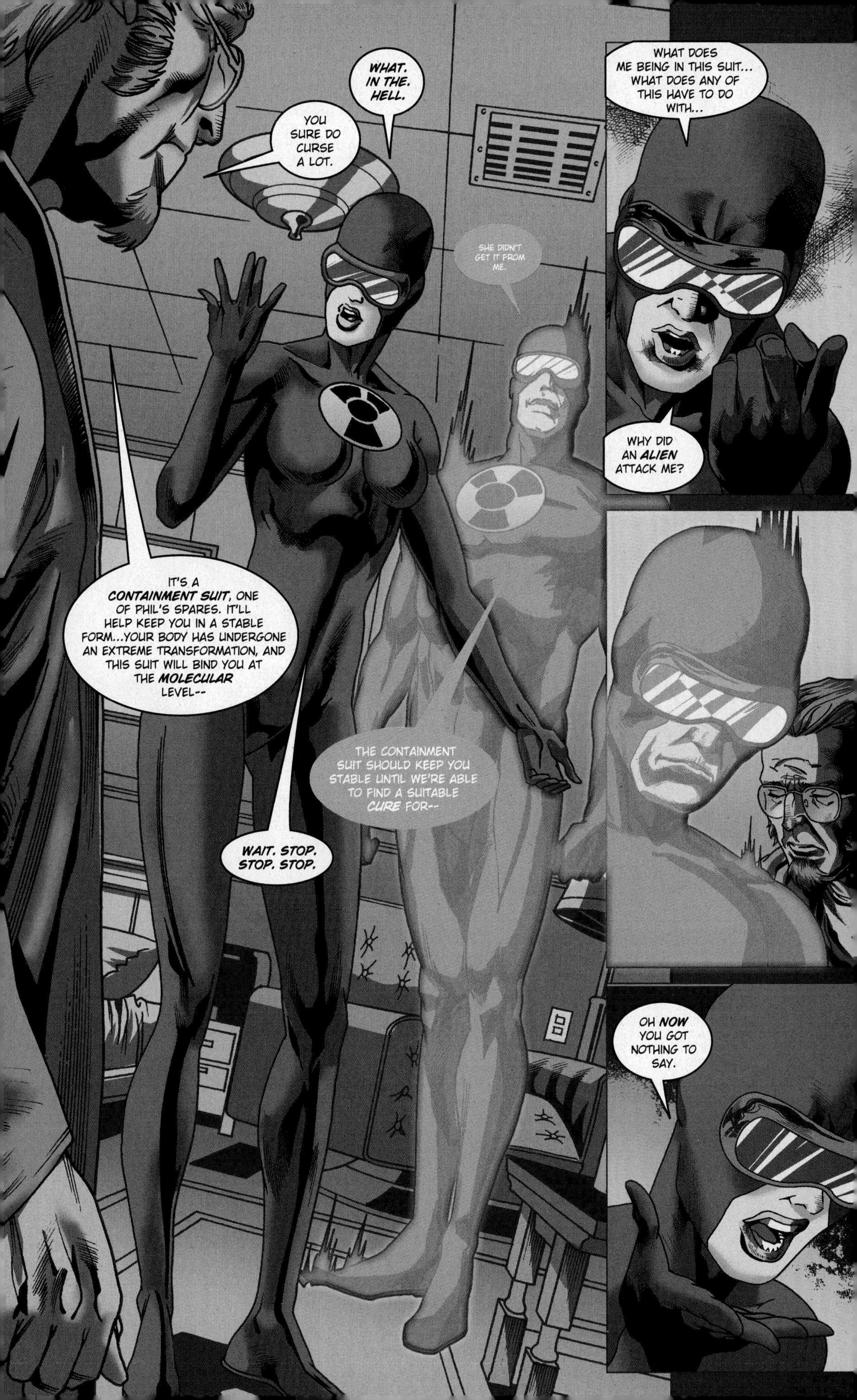

YOU SURE DO CURSE A LOT.
WHAT. IN THE. HELL.
SHE DIDN'T GET IT FROM ME.
IT'S A CONTAINMENT SUIT, ONE OF PHIL'S SPARES. IT'LL HELP KEEP YOU IN A STABLE FORM...YOUR BODY HAS UNDERGONE AN EXTREME TRANSFORMATION, AND THIS SUIT WILL BIND YOU AT THE MOLECULAR LEVEL--
THE CONTAINMENT SUIT SHOULD KEEP YOU STABLE UNTIL WE'RE ABLE TO FIND A SUITABLE CURE FOR--
WAIT. STOP. STOP. STOP.
WHAT DOES ME BEING IN THIS SUIT... WHAT DOES ANY OF THIS HAVE TO DO WITH...
WHY DID AN ALIEN ATTACK ME?
OH NOW YOU GOT NOTHING TO SAY.

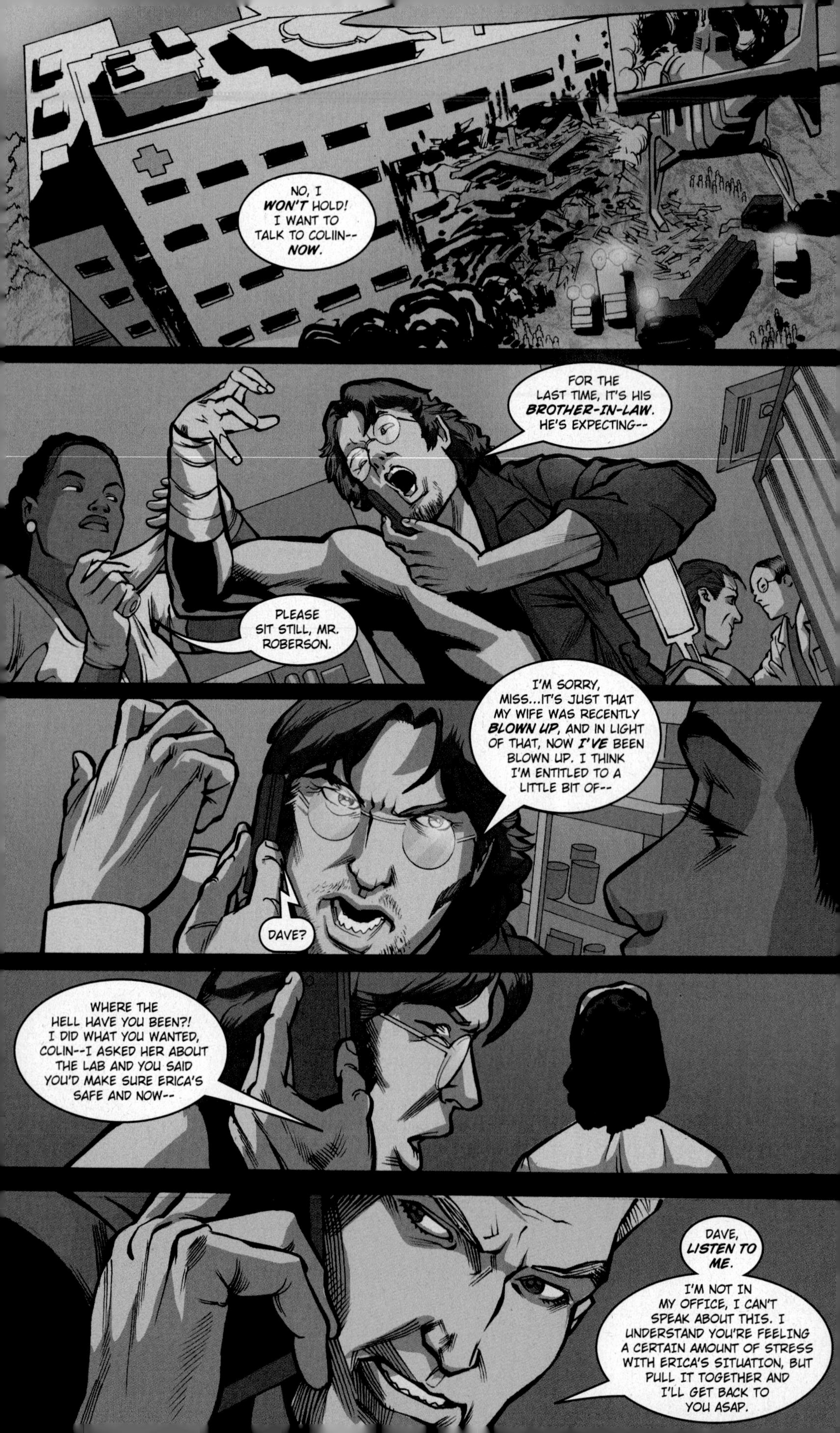
NO, I WON'T HOLD! I WANT TO TALK TO COLIIN-- NOW.
FOR THE LAST TIME, IT'S HIS BROTHER-IN-LAW. HE'S EXPECTING--
PLEASE SIT STILL, MR. ROBERSON.
I'M SORRY, MISS...IT'S JUST THAT MY WIFE WAS RECENTLY BLOWN UP, AND IN LIGHT OF THAT, NOW I'VE BEEN BLOWN UP. I THINK I'M ENTITLED TO A LITTLE BIT OF--
DAVE?
WHERE THE HELL HAVE YOU BEEN?! I DID WHAT YOU WANTED, COLIN--I ASKED HER ABOUT THE LAB AND YOU SAID YOU'D MAKE SURE ERICA'S SAFE AND NOW--
DAVE, LISTEN TO ME.
I'M NOT IN MY OFFICE, I CAN'T SPEAK ABOUT THIS. I UNDERSTAND YOU'RE FEELING A CERTAIN AMOUNT OF STRESS WITH ERICA'S SITUATION, BUT PULL IT TOGETHER AND I'LL GET BACK TO YOU ASAP.

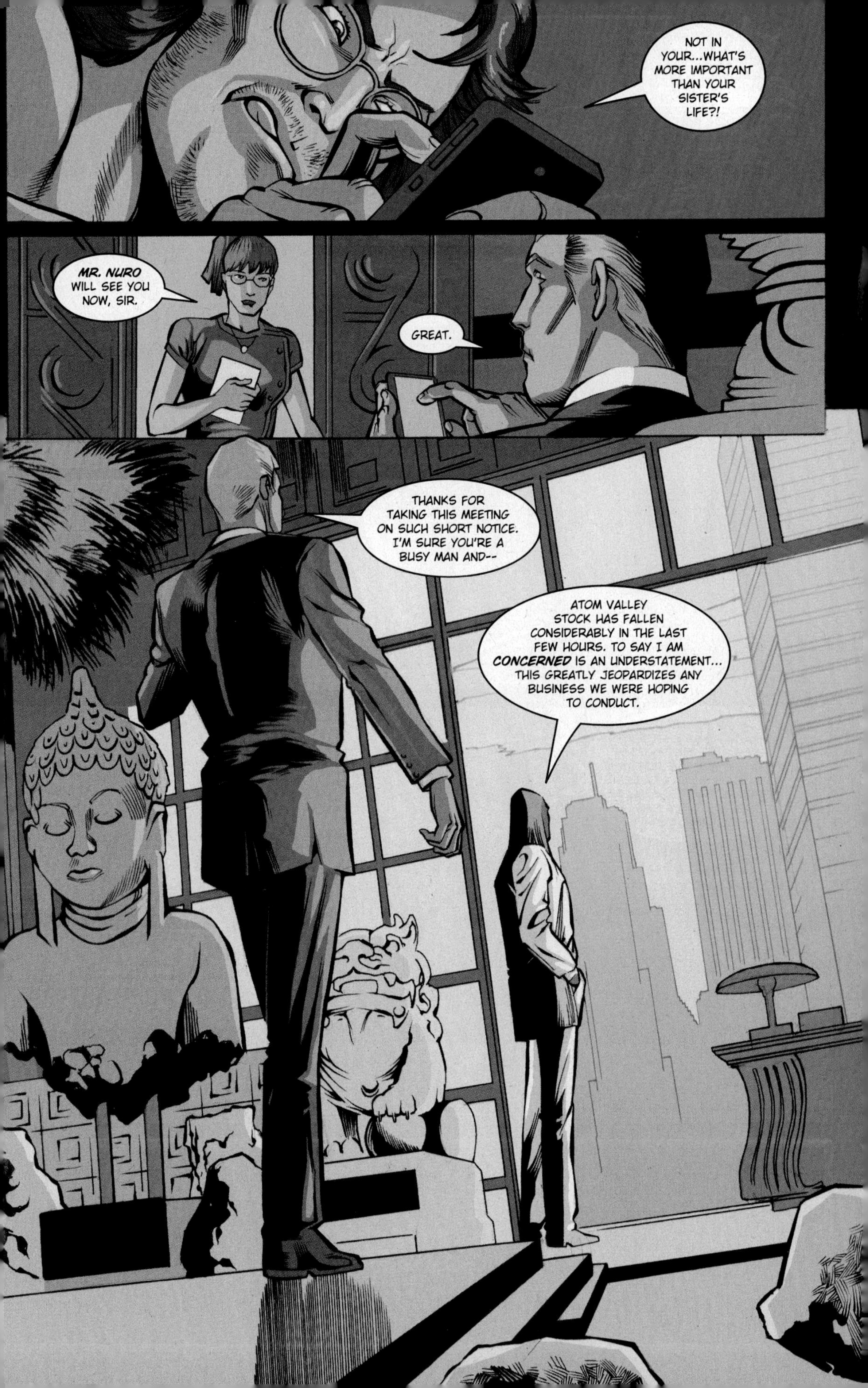
NOT IN YOUR...WHAT'S MORE IMPORTANT THAN YOUR SISTER'S LIFE?!
MR. NURO WILL SEE YOU NOW, SIR.
GREAT.
THANKS FOR TAKING THIS MEETING ON SUCH SHORT NOTICE. I'M SURE YOU'RE A BUSY MAN AND--
ATOM VALLEY STOCK HAS FALLEN CONSIDERABLY IN THE LAST FEW HOURS. TO SAY I AM CONCERNED IS AN UNDERSTATEMENT... THIS GREATLY JEOPARDIZES ANY BUSINESS WE WERE HOPING TO CONDUCT.

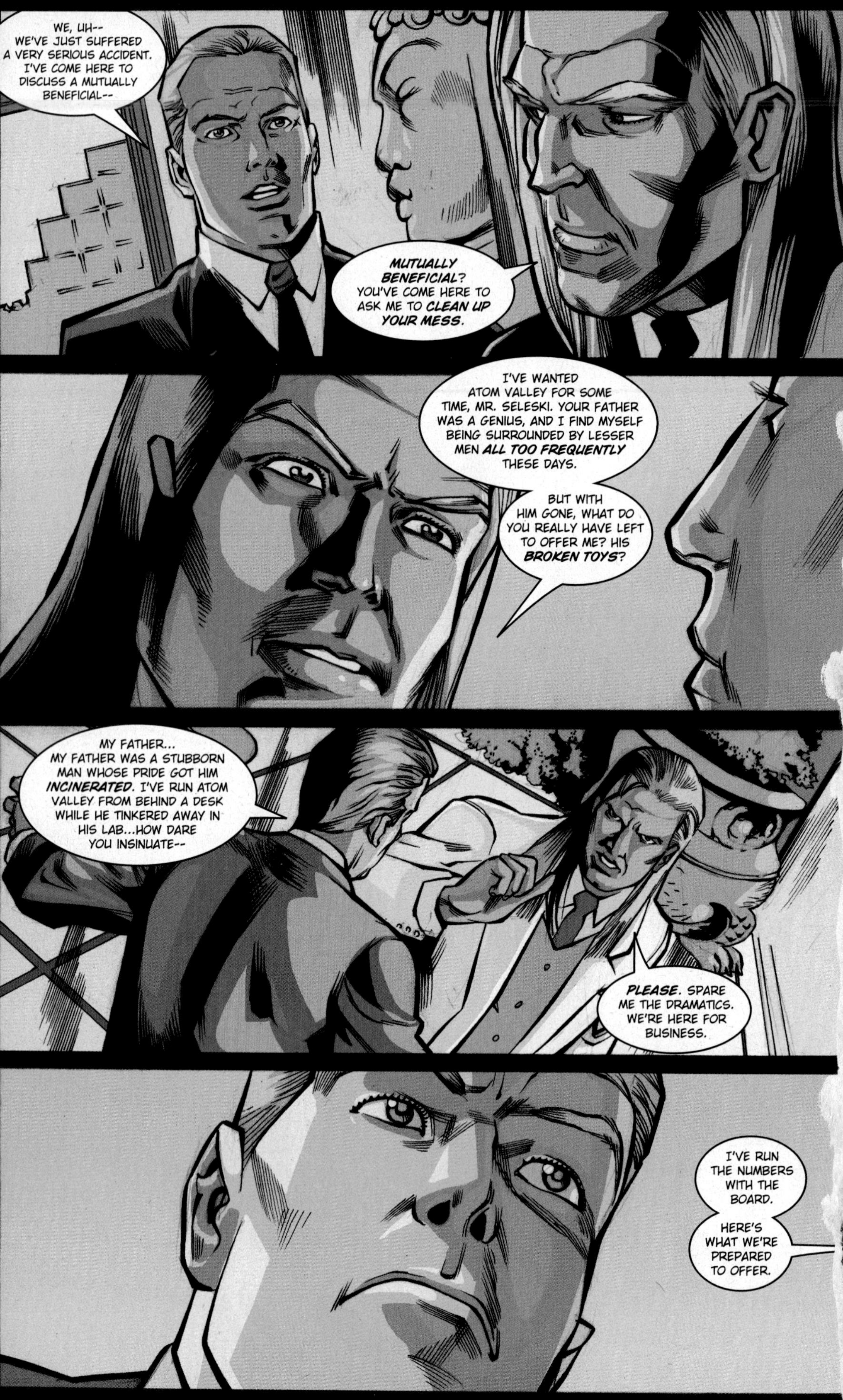
WE, UH-- WE'VE JUST SUFFERED A VERY SERIOUS ACCIDENT. I'VE COME HERE TO DISCUSS A MUTUALLY BENEFICIAL--
MUTUALLY BENEFICIAL? YOU'VE COME HERE TO ASK ME TO CLEAN UP YOUR MESS.
I'VE WANTED ATOM VALLEY FOR SOME TIME, MR. SELESKI. YOUR FATHER WAS A GENIUS, AND I FIND MYSELF BEING SURROUNDED BY LESSER MEN ALL TOO FREQUENTLY THESE DAYS.
BUT WITH HIM GONE, WHAT DO YOU REALLY HAVE LEFT TO OFFER ME? HIS BROKEN TOYS?
MY FATHER... MY FATHER WAS A STUBBORN MAN WHOSE PRIDE GOT HIM INCINERATED. I'VE RUN ATOM VALLEY FROM BEHIND A DESK WHILE HE TINKERED AWAY IN HIS LAB...HOW DARE YOU INSINUATE--
PLEASE. SPARE ME THE DRAMATICS. WE'RE HERE FOR BUSINESS.
I'VE RUN THE NUMBERS WITH THE BOARD.
HERE'S WHAT WE'RE PREPARED TO OFFER.

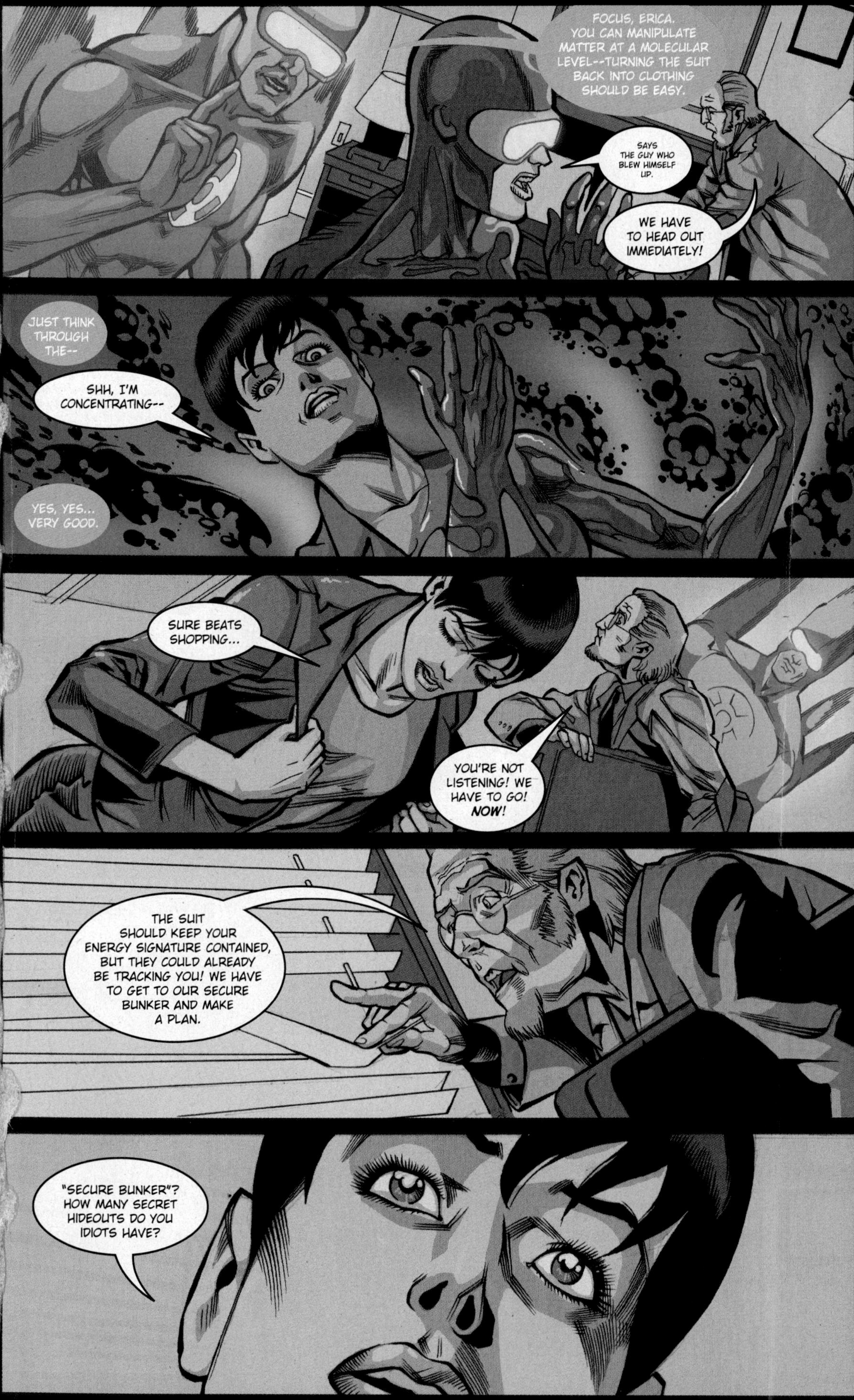
FOCUS, ERICA. YOU CAN MANIPULATE MATTER AT A MOLECULAR LEVEL--TURNING THE SUIT BACK INTO CLOTHING SHOULD BE EASY.
SAYS THE GUY WHO BLEW HIMSELF UP.
WE HAVE TO HEAD OUT IMMEDIATELY!
JUST THINK THROUGH THE--
SHH, I'M CONCENTRATING--
YES, YES... VERY GOOD.
SURE BEATS SHOPPING...
YOU'RE NOT LISTENING! WE HAVE TO GO! NOW!
THE SUIT SHOULD KEEP YOUR ENERGY SIGNATURE CONTAINED, BUT THEY COULD ALREADY BE TRACKING YOU! WE HAVE TO GET TO OUR SECURE BUNKER AND MAKE A PLAN.
"SECURE BUNKER"? HOW MANY SECRET HIDEOUTS DO YOU IDIOTS HAVE?

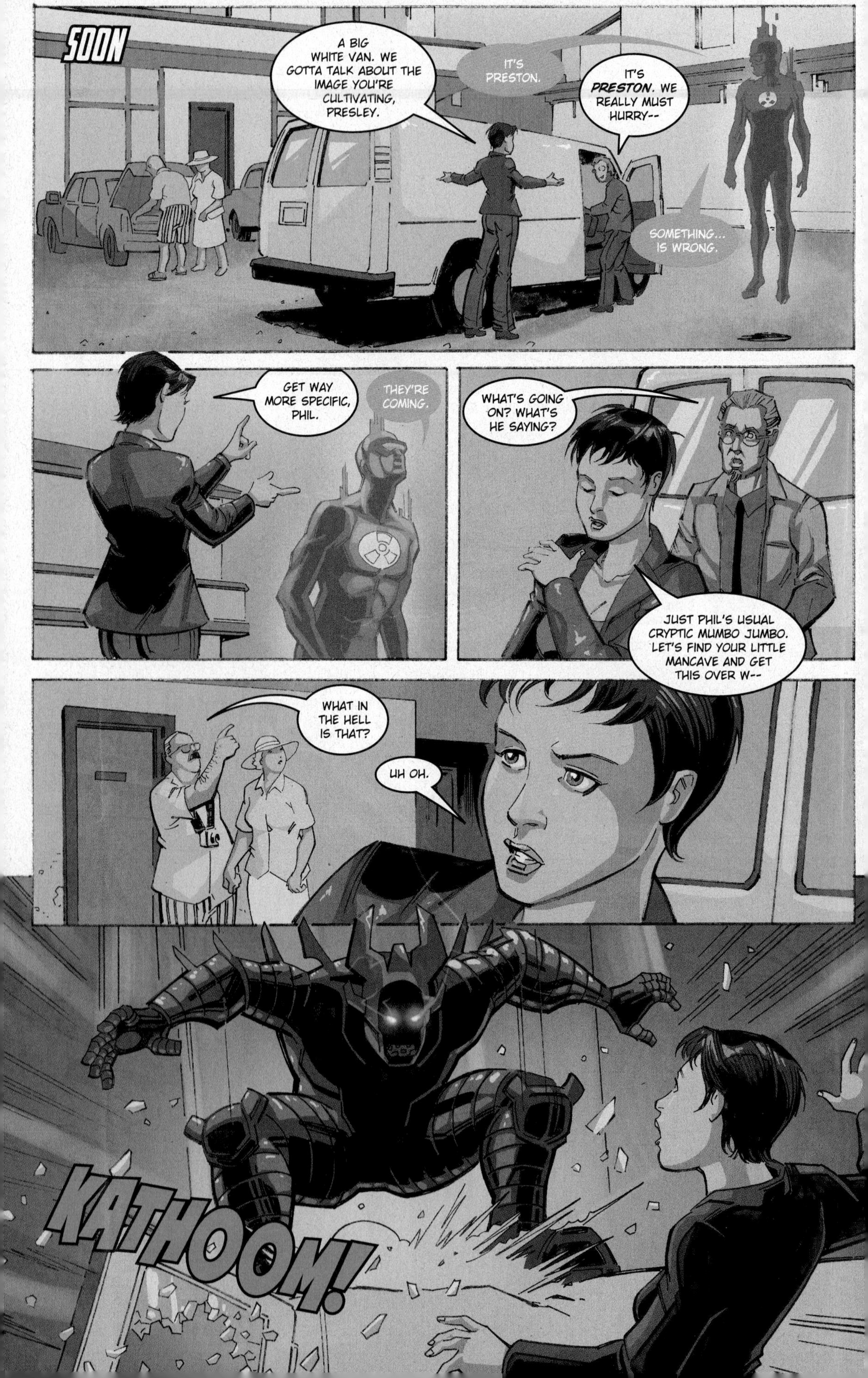
SOON
A BIG WHITE VAN. WE GOTTA TALK ABOUT THE IMAGE YOU'RE CULTIVATING, PRESLEY.
IT'S PRESTON.
IT'S PRESTON. WE REALLY MUST HURRY--
SOMETHING... IS WRONG.
GET WAY MORE SPECIFIC, PHIL.
THEY'RE COMING.
WHAT'S GOING ON? WHAT'S HE SAYING?
JUST PHIL'S USUAL CRYPTIC MUMBO JUMBO. LET'S FIND YOUR LITTLE MANCAVE AND GET THIS OVER W--
WHAT IN THE HELL IS THAT?
UH OH.
KATHOOM!

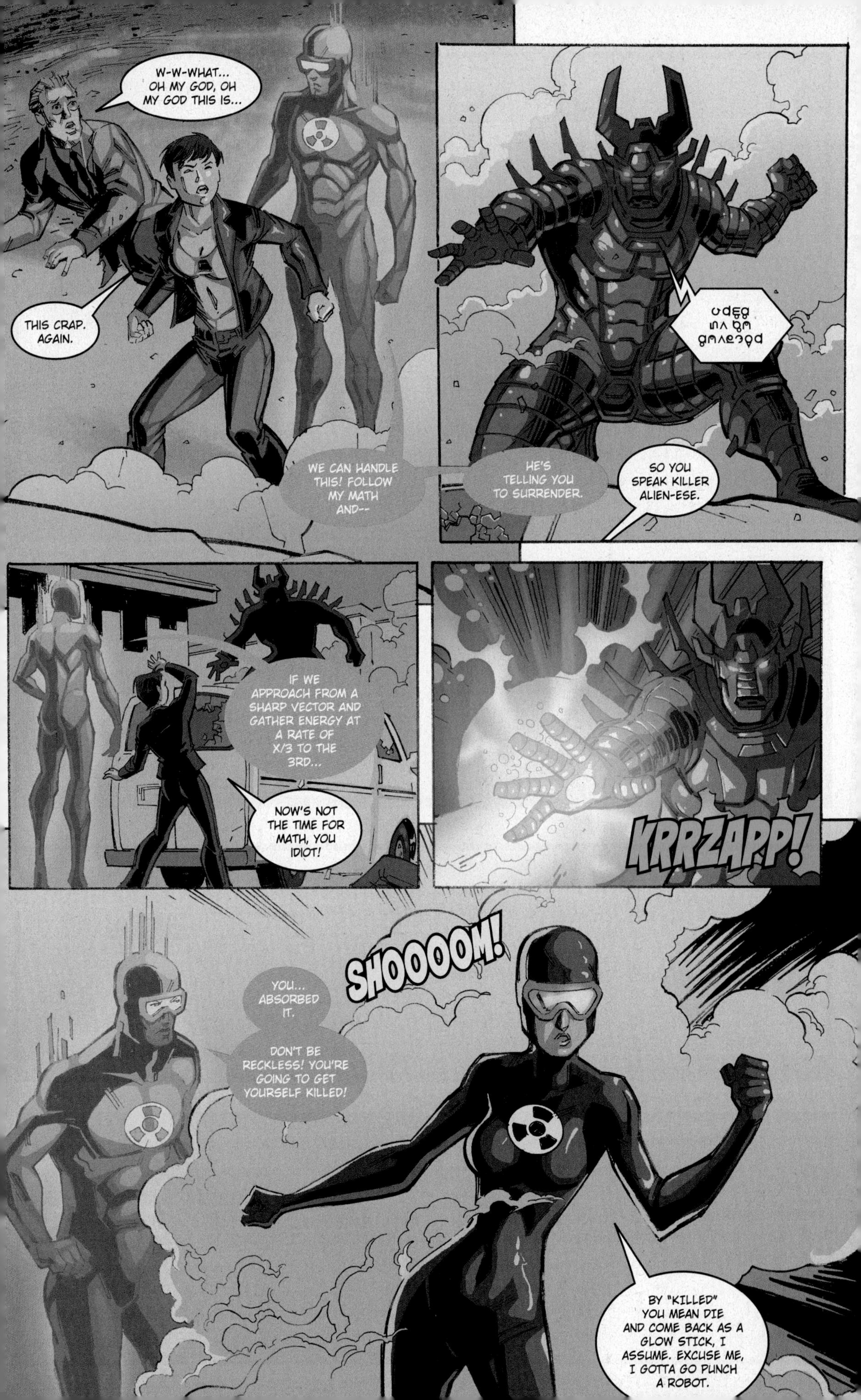
W-W-WHAT... OH MY GOD, OH MY GOD THIS IS...
THIS CRAP. AGAIN.
WE CAN HANDLE THIS! FOLLOW MY MATH AND--
HE'S TELLING YOU TO SURRENDER.
SO YOU SPEAK KILLER ALIEN-ESE.
IF WE APPROACH FROM A SHARP VECTOR AND GATHER ENERGY AT A RATE OF X/3 TO THE 3RD...
NOW'S NOT THE TIME FOR MATH, YOU IDIOT!
KRRZAPP!
SHOOOOM!
YOU... ABSORBED IT.
DON'T BE RECKLESS! YOU'RE GOING TO GET YOURSELF KILLED!
BY "KILLED" YOU MEAN DIE AND COME BACK AS A GLOW STICK, I ASSUME. EXCUSE ME, I GOTTA GO PUNCH A ROBOT.

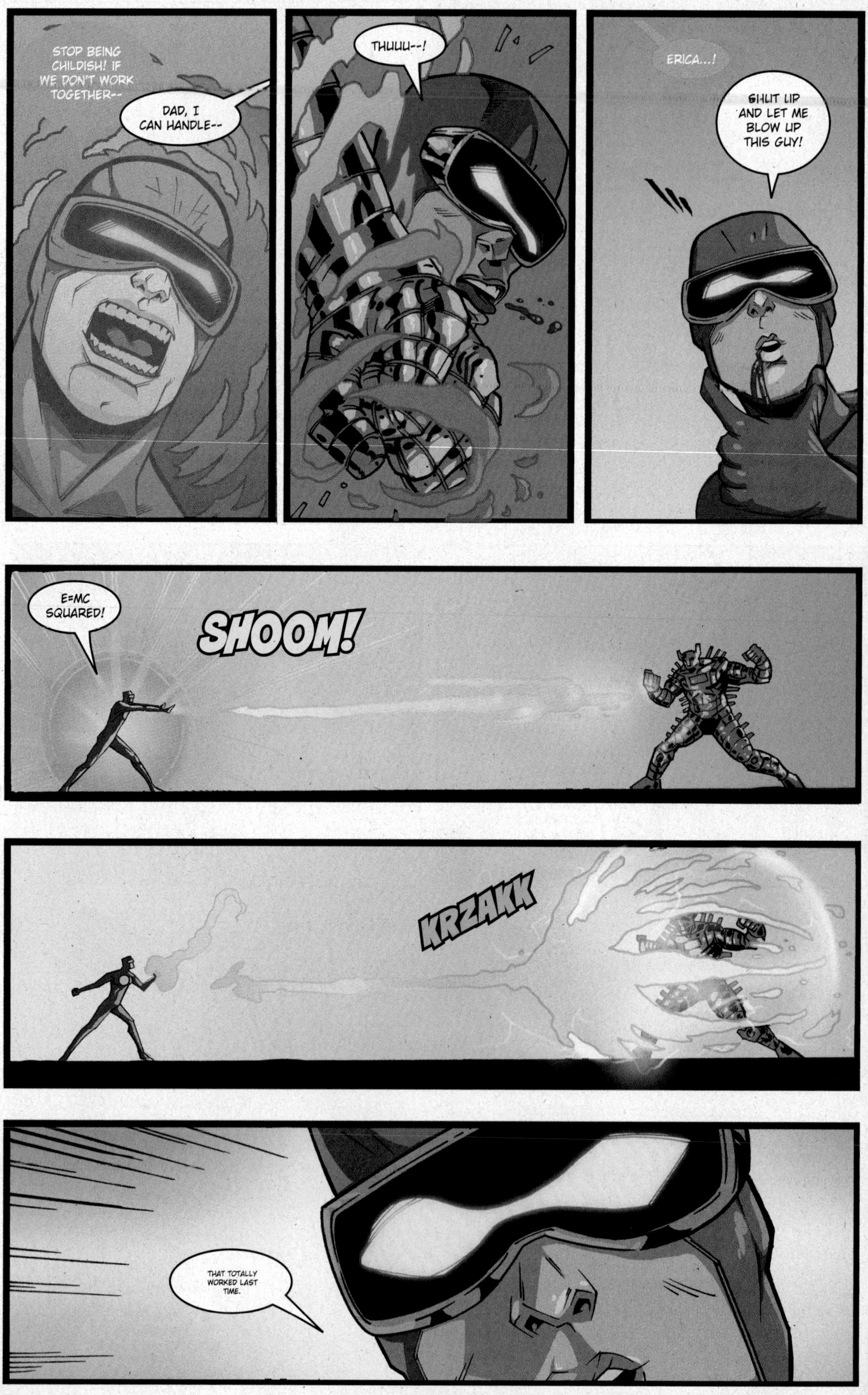
STOP BEING CHILDISH! IF WE DON'T WORK TOGETHER--
DAD, I CAN HANDLE--
THUUU--!
ERICA...!
SHUT UP AND LET ME BLOW UP THIS GUY!
E=MC SQUARED!
SHOOM!
KRZAKK
THAT TOTALLY WORKED LAST TIME.

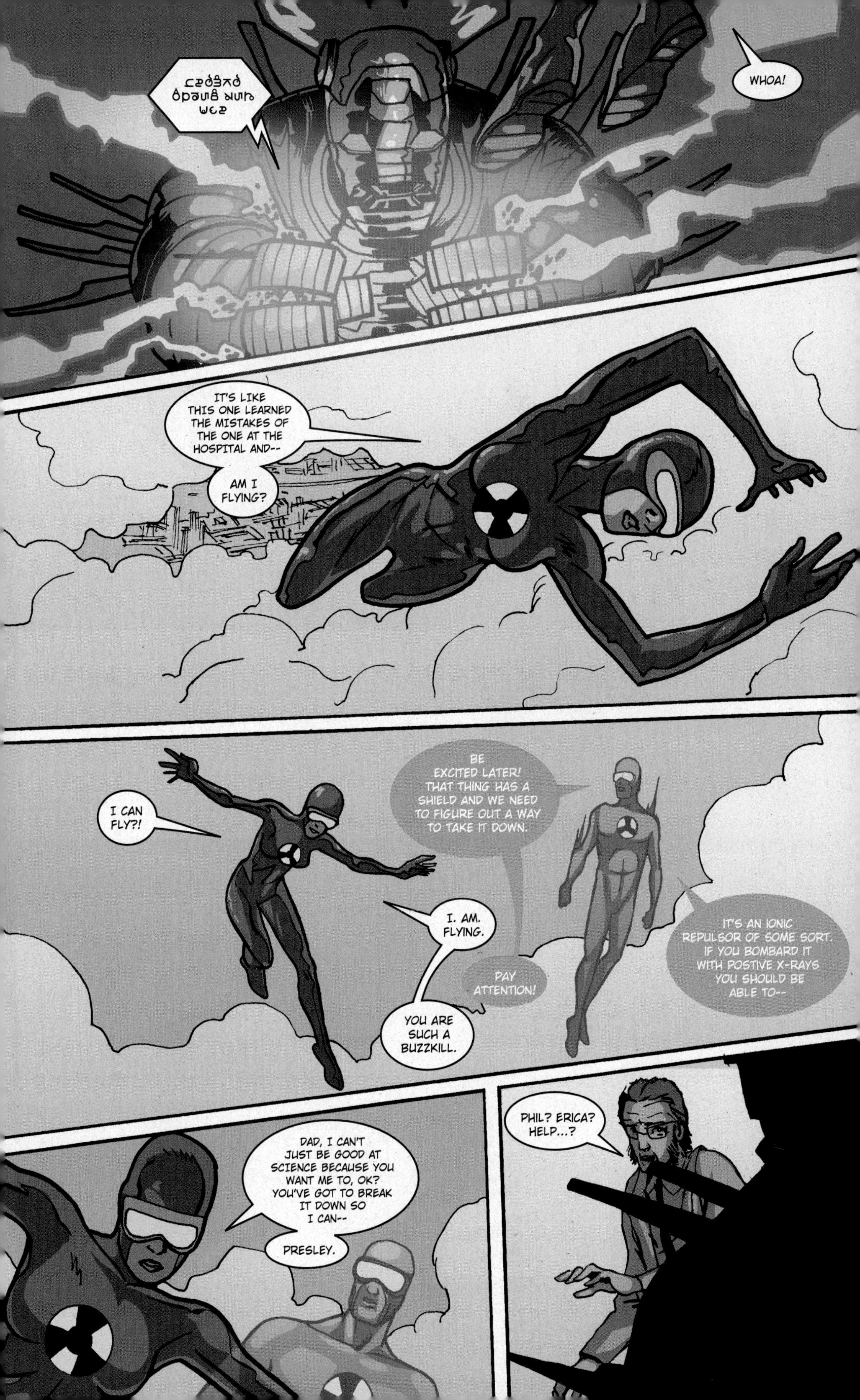
WHOA!
IT'S LIKE THIS ONE LEARNED THE MISTAKES OF THE ONE AT THE HOSPITAL AND--
AM I FLYING?
I CAN FLY?!
BE EXCITED LATER! THAT THING HAS A SHIELD AND WE NEED TO FIGURE OUT A WAY TO TAKE IT DOWN.
I. AM. FLYING.
PAY ATTENTION!
YOU ARE SUCH A BUZZKILL.
IT'S AN IONIC REPULSOR OF SOME SORT. IF YOU BOMBARD IT WITH POSTIVE X-RAYS YOU SHOULD BE ABLE TO--
DAD, I CAN'T JUST BE GOOD AT SCIENCE BECAUSE YOU WANT ME TO, OK? YOU'VE GOT TO BREAK IT DOWN SO I CAN--
PRESLEY.
PHIL? ERICA? HELP...?

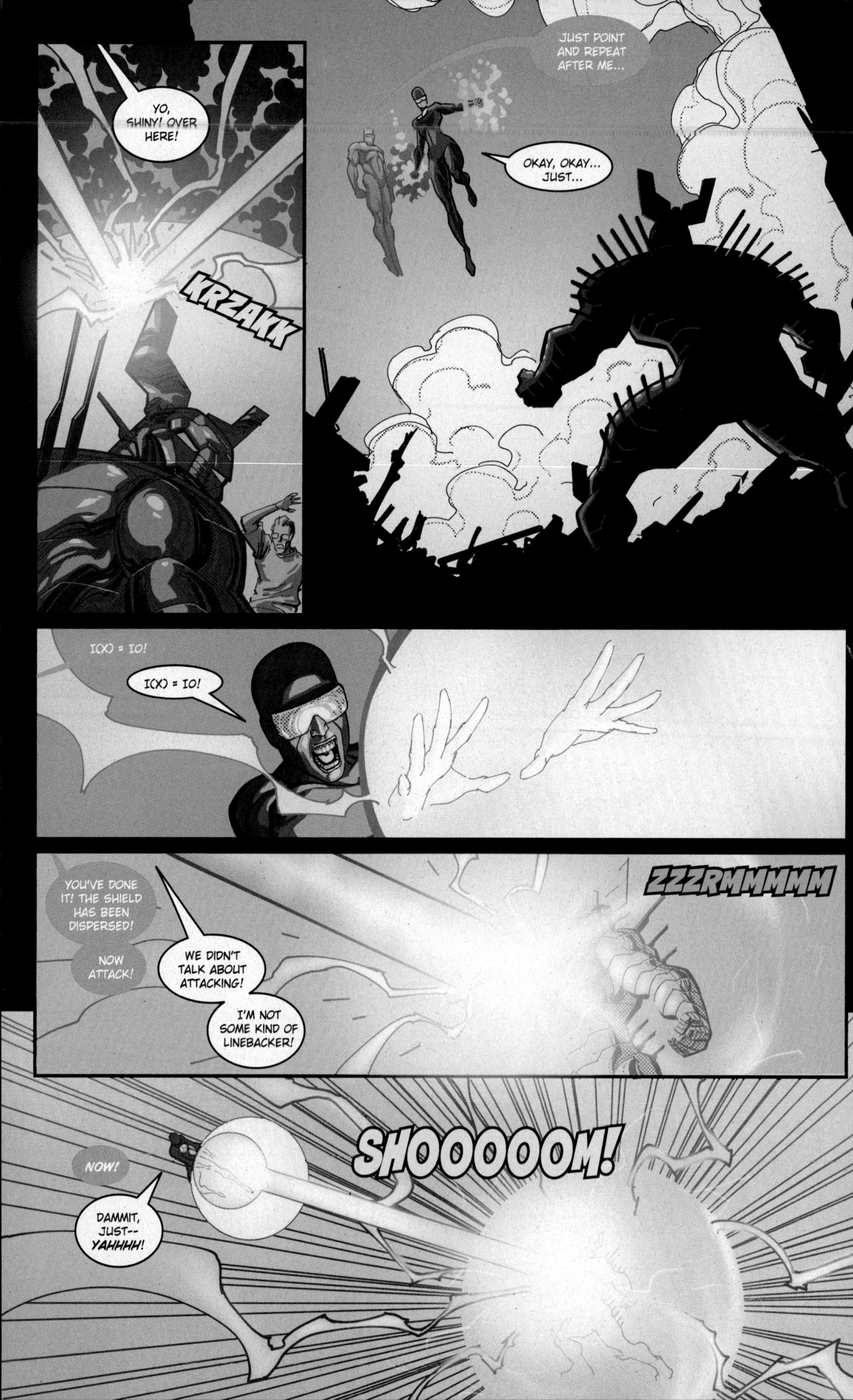

YO, SHINY! OVER HERE!
KRZAKK
JUST POINT AND REPEAT AFTER ME...
OKAY, OKAY... JUST...
I(X) = IO!
I(X) = IO!
ZZZRMMMMM
YOU'VE DONE IT! THE SHIELD HAS BEEN DISPERSED!
NOW ATTACK!
WE DIDN'T TALK ABOUT ATTACKING!
I'M NOT SOME KIND OF LINEBACKER!
SHOOOOOM!
NOW!
DAMMIT, JUST-- YAHHHH!

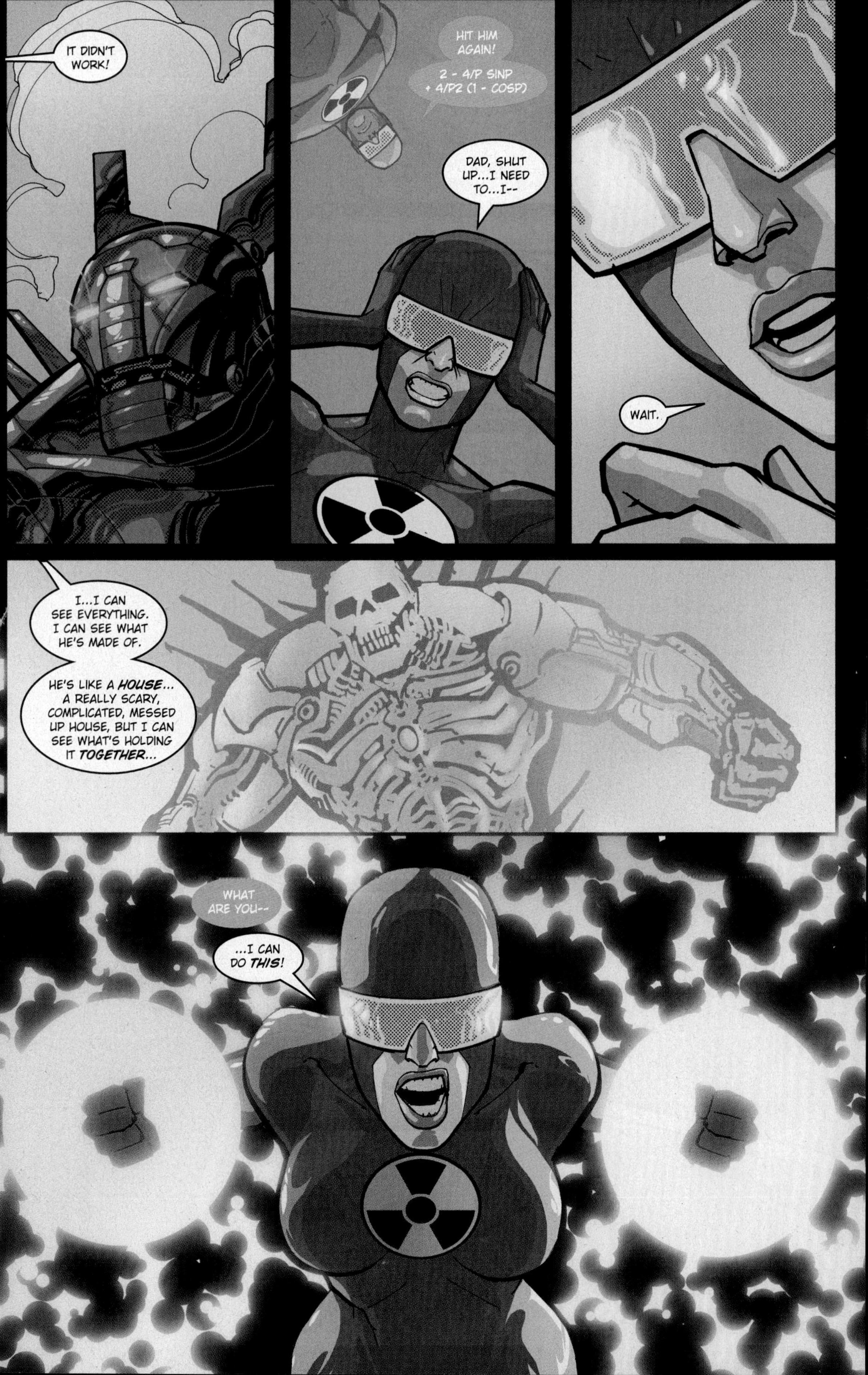
IT DIDN'T WORK!
HIT HIM AGAIN!
2 - 4/P SINP + 4/P2 (1 - COSP)
DAD, SHUT UP...I NEED TO...I--
WAIT.
I...I CAN SEE EVERYTHING. I CAN SEE WHAT HE'S MADE OF.
HE'S LIKE A HOUSE... A REALLY SCARY, COMPLICATED, MESSED UP HOUSE, BUT I CAN SEE WHAT'S HOLDING IT TOGETHER...
WHAT ARE YOU--
...I CAN DO THIS!

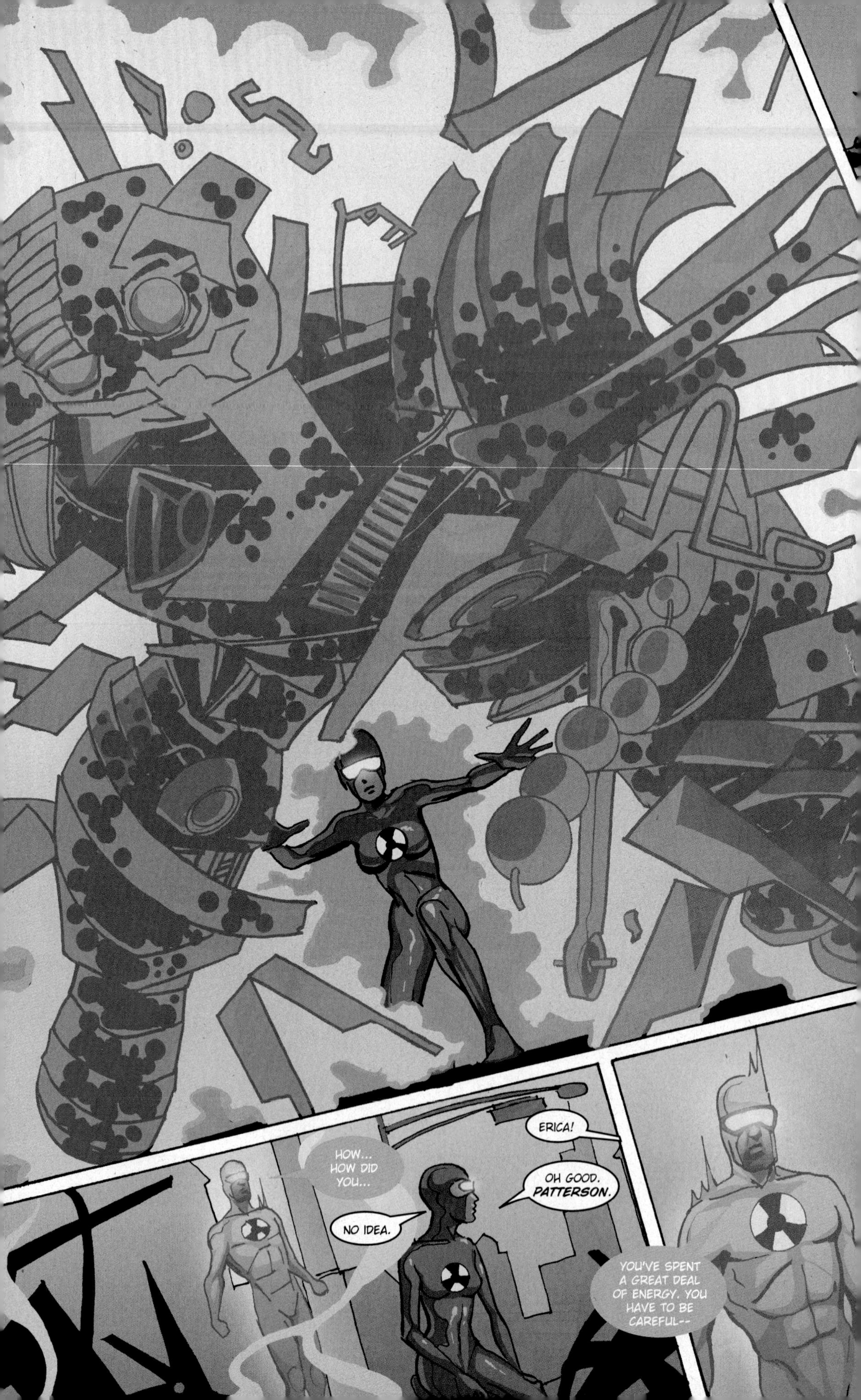
ERICA!
HOW... HOW DID YOU...
OH GOOD. PATTERSON.
NO IDEA.
YOU'VE SPENT A GREAT DEAL OF ENERGY. YOU HAVE TO BE CAREFUL--

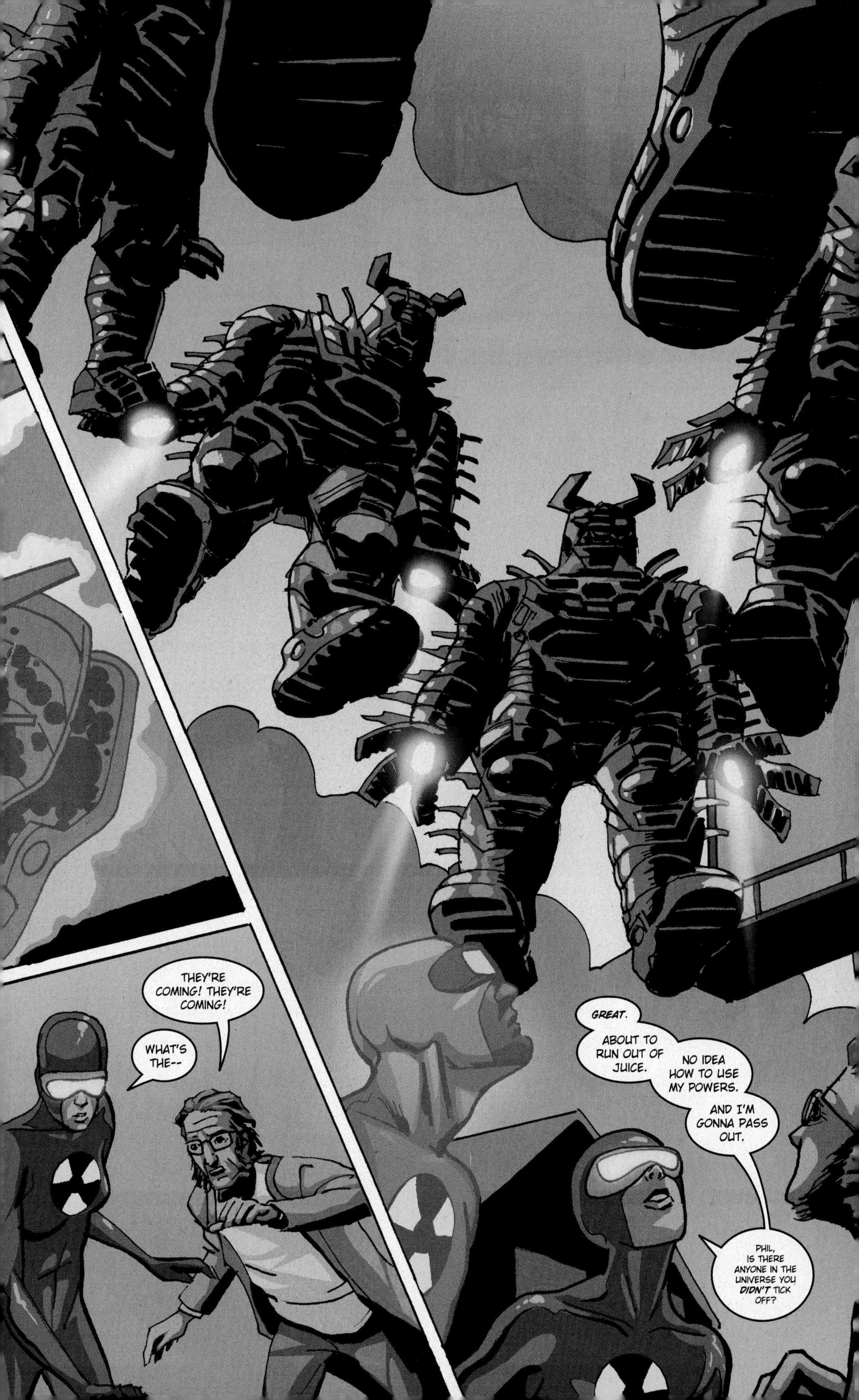
THEY'RE COMING! THEY'RE COMING!
WHAT'S THE--
GREAT.
ABOUT TO RUN OUT OF JUICE.
NO IDEA HOW TO USE MY POWERS.
AND I'M GONNA PASS OUT.
PHIL, IS THERE ANYONE IN THE UNIVERSE YOU DIDN'T TICK OFF?

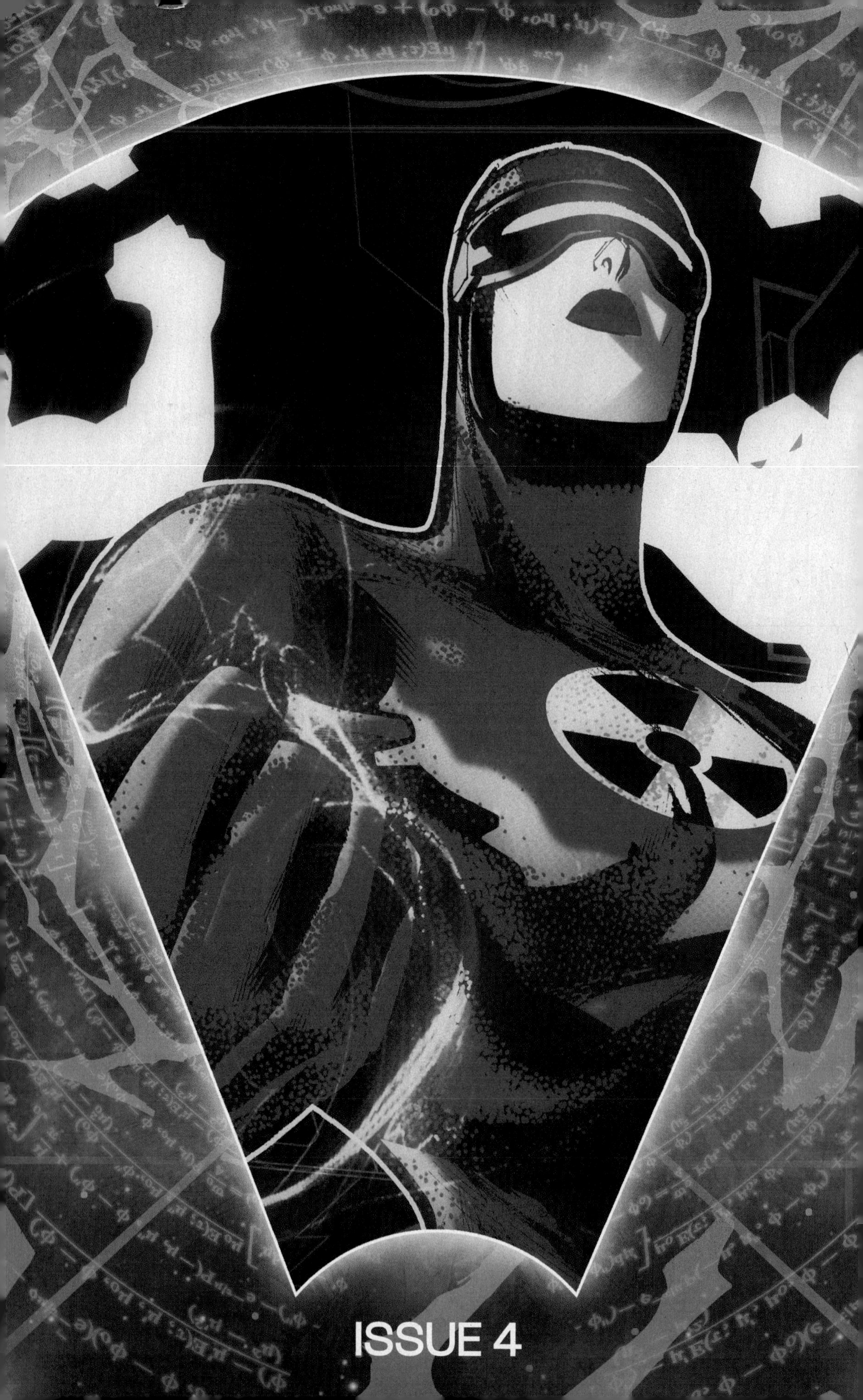
ISSUE 4

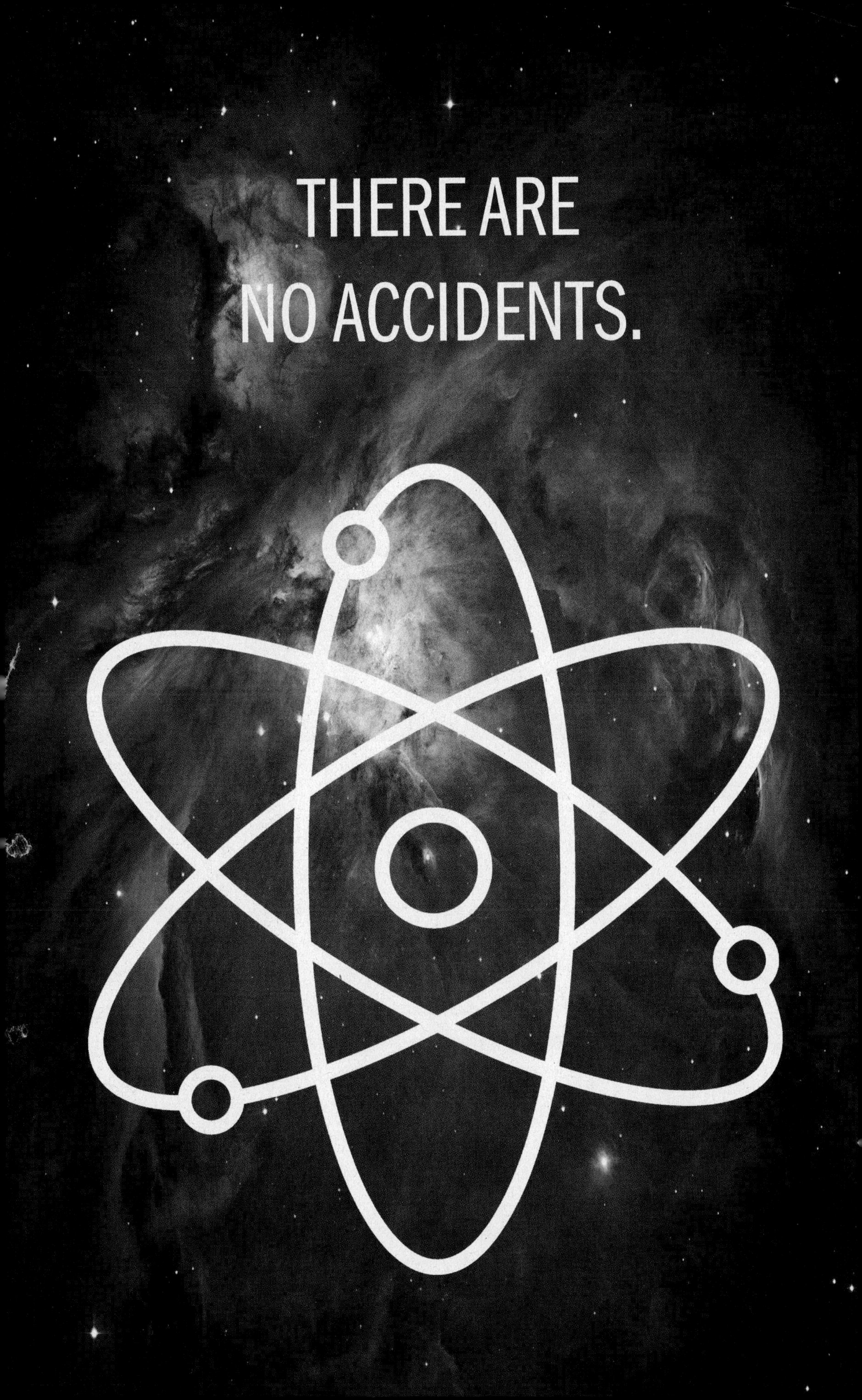
THERE ARE
NO ACCIDENTS.

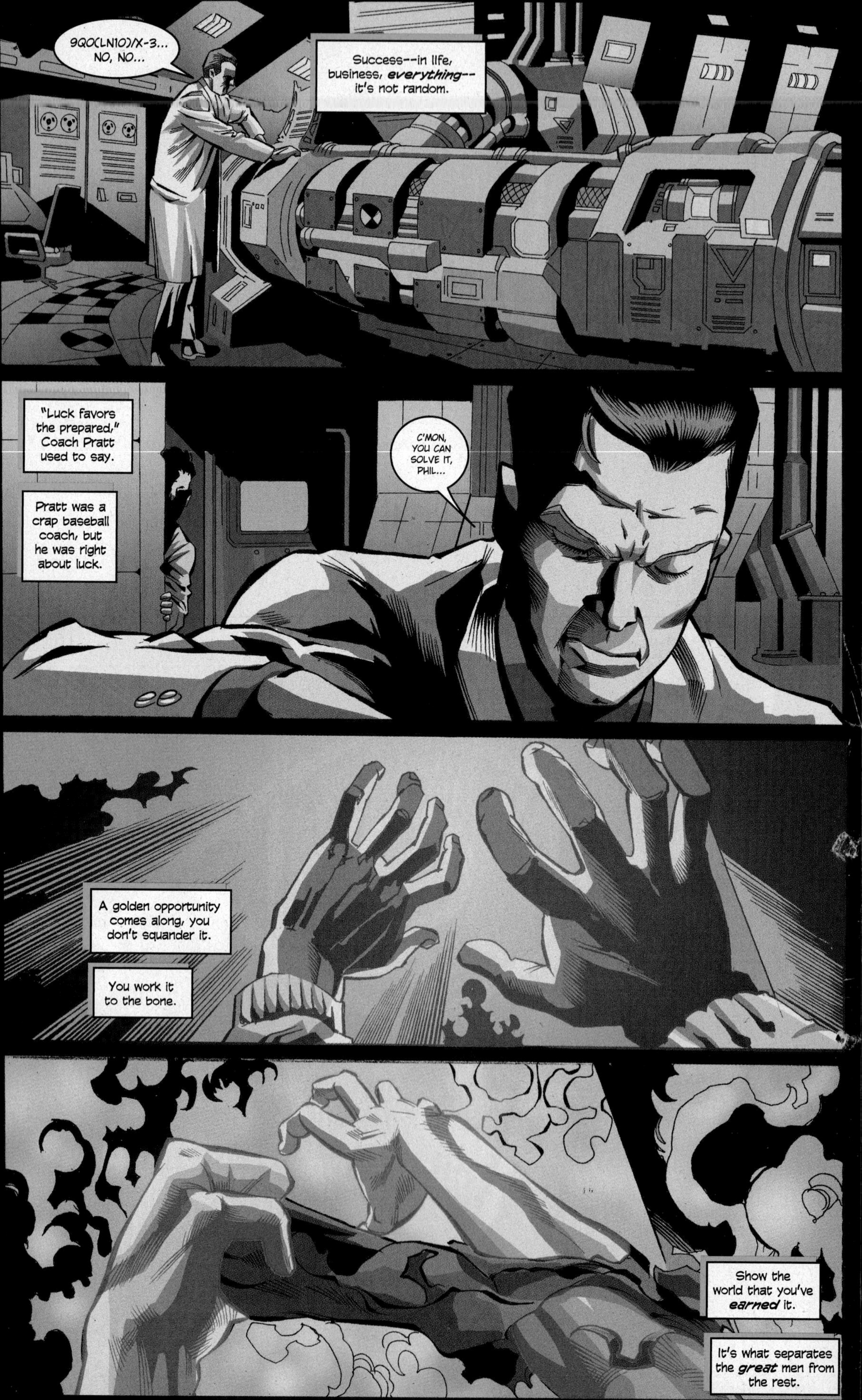
9QO(LN10)/X-3... NO, NO...
Success--in life, business, *everything*-- it's not random.
"Luck favors the prepared," Coach Pratt used to say.
C'MON, YOU CAN SOLVE IT, PHIL...
Pratt was a crap baseball coach, but he was right about luck.
A golden opportunity comes along, you don't squander it.
You work it to the bone.
Show the world that you've *earned* it.
It's what separates the *great* men from the rest.

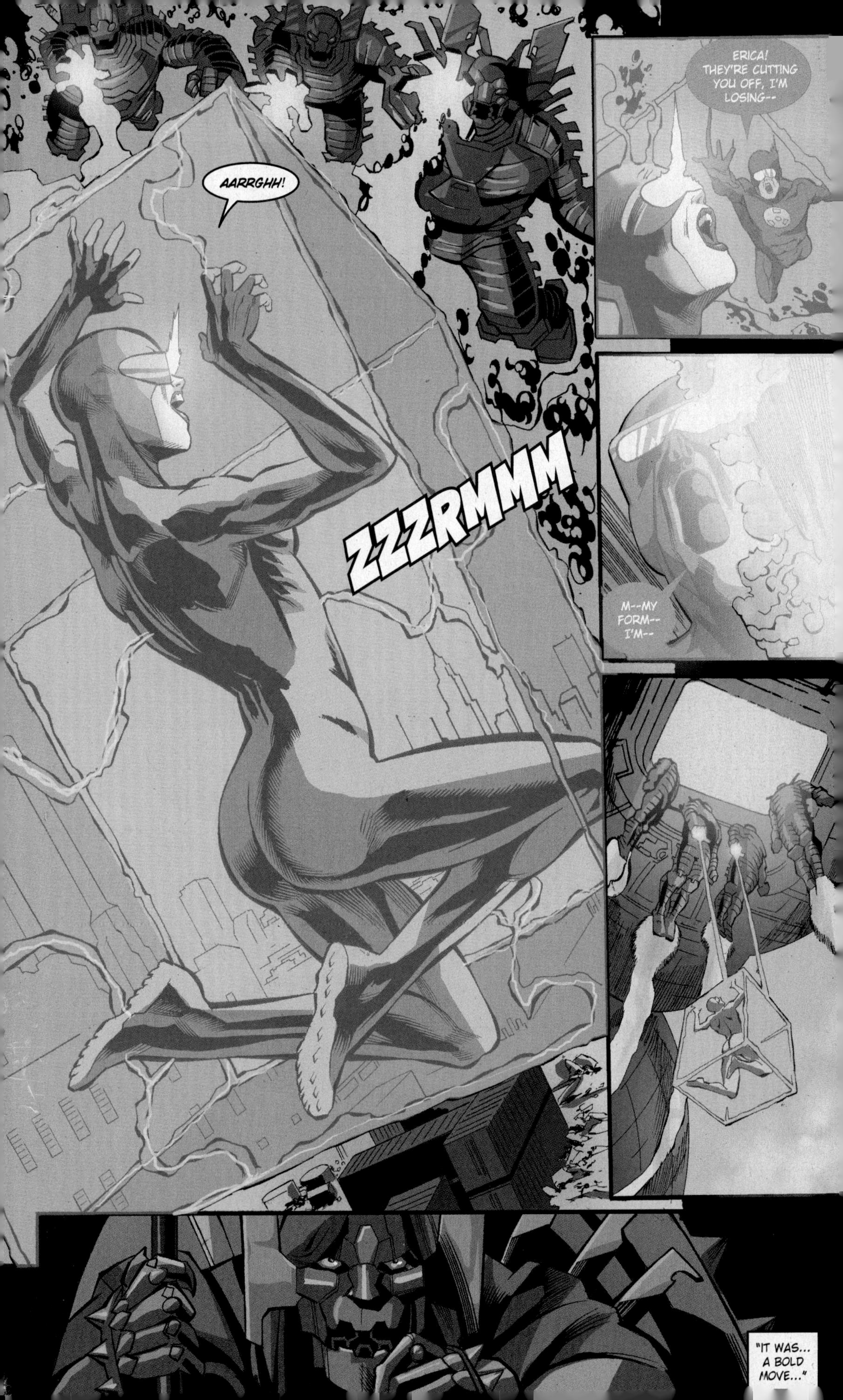

AARRGHH!
ERICA! THEY'RE CUTTING YOU OFF, I'M LOSING--
ZZZRMMM
M--MY FORM-- I'M--
"IT WAS... A BOLD MOVE..."

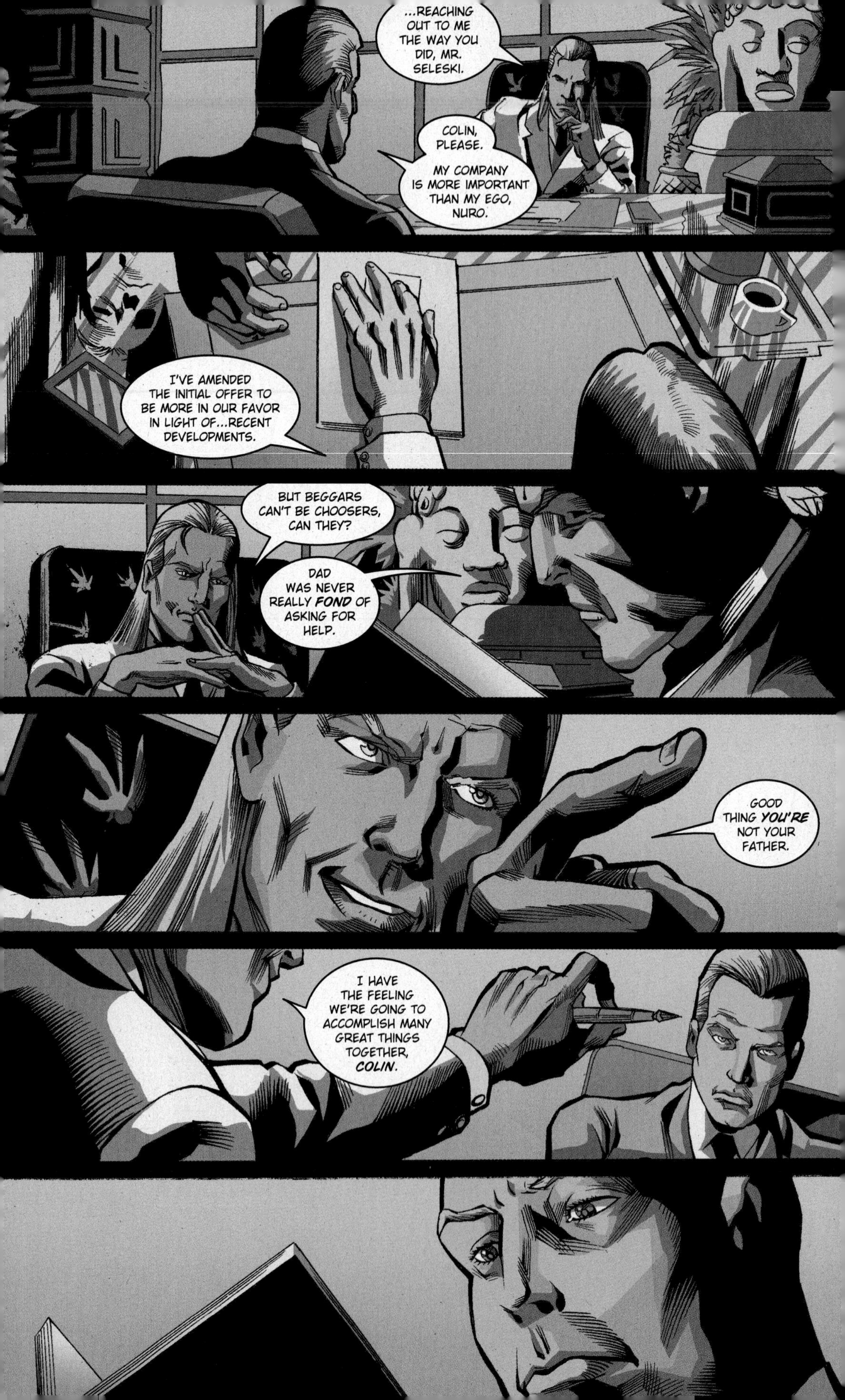
...REACHING OUT TO ME THE WAY YOU DID, MR. SELESKI.
COLIN, PLEASE.
MY COMPANY IS MORE IMPORTANT THAN MY EGO, NURO.
I'VE AMENDED THE INITIAL OFFER TO BE MORE IN OUR FAVOR IN LIGHT OF...RECENT DEVELOPMENTS.
BUT BEGGARS CAN'T BE CHOOSERS, CAN THEY?
DAD WAS NEVER REALLY *FOND* OF ASKING FOR HELP.
GOOD THING *YOU'RE* NOT YOUR FATHER.
I HAVE THE FEELING WE'RE GOING TO ACCOMPLISH MANY GREAT THINGS TOGETHER, *COLIN*.

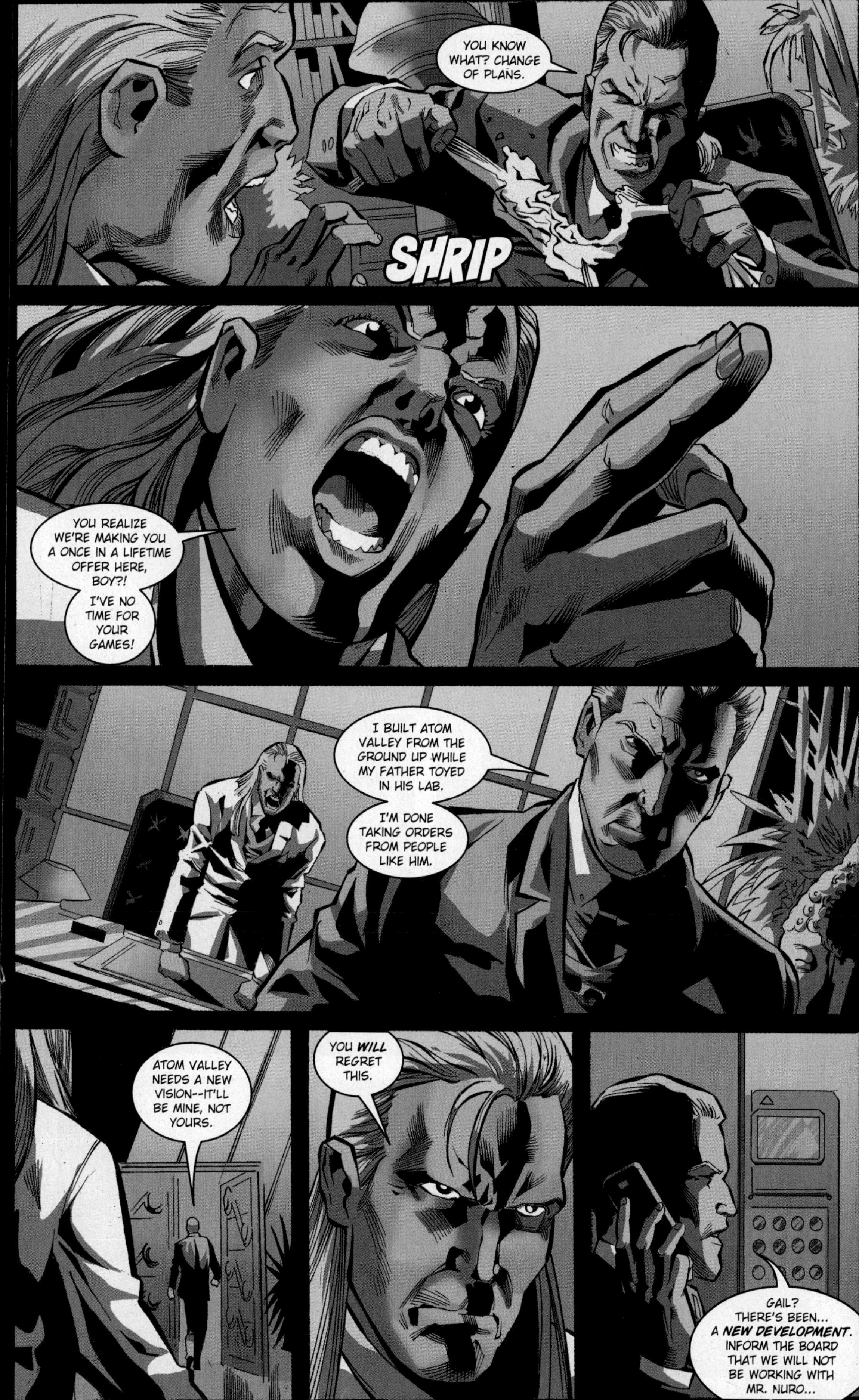
YOU KNOW WHAT? CHANGE OF PLANS.
SHRIP
YOU REALIZE WE'RE MAKING YOU A ONCE IN A LIFETIME OFFER HERE, BOY?!
I'VE NO TIME FOR YOUR GAMES!
I BUILT ATOM VALLEY FROM THE GROUND UP WHILE MY FATHER TOYED IN HIS LAB.
I'M DONE TAKING ORDERS FROM PEOPLE LIKE HIM.
ATOM VALLEY NEEDS A NEW VISION--IT'LL BE MINE, NOT YOURS.
YOU WILL REGRET THIS.
GAIL? THERE'S BEEN... A NEW DEVELOPMENT. INFORM THE BOARD THAT WE WILL NOT BE WORKING WITH MR. NURO...

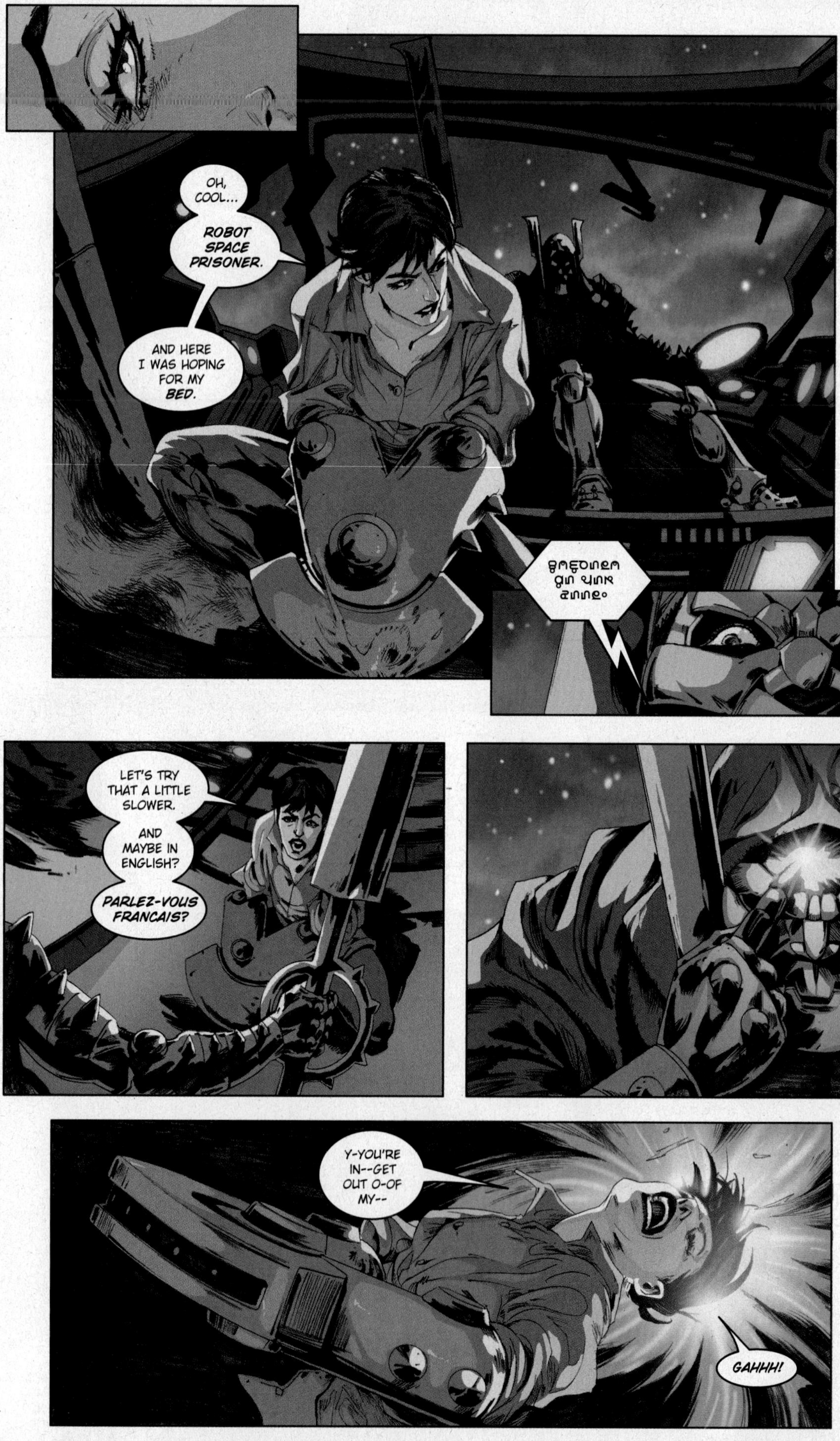
OH, COOL... ROBOT SPACE PRISONER.
AND HERE I WAS HOPING FOR MY BED.
LET'S TRY THAT A LITTLE SLOWER.
AND MAYBE IN ENGLISH?
PARLEZ-VOUS FRANCAIS?
Y-YOU'RE IN--GET OUT O-OF MY--
GAHHH!

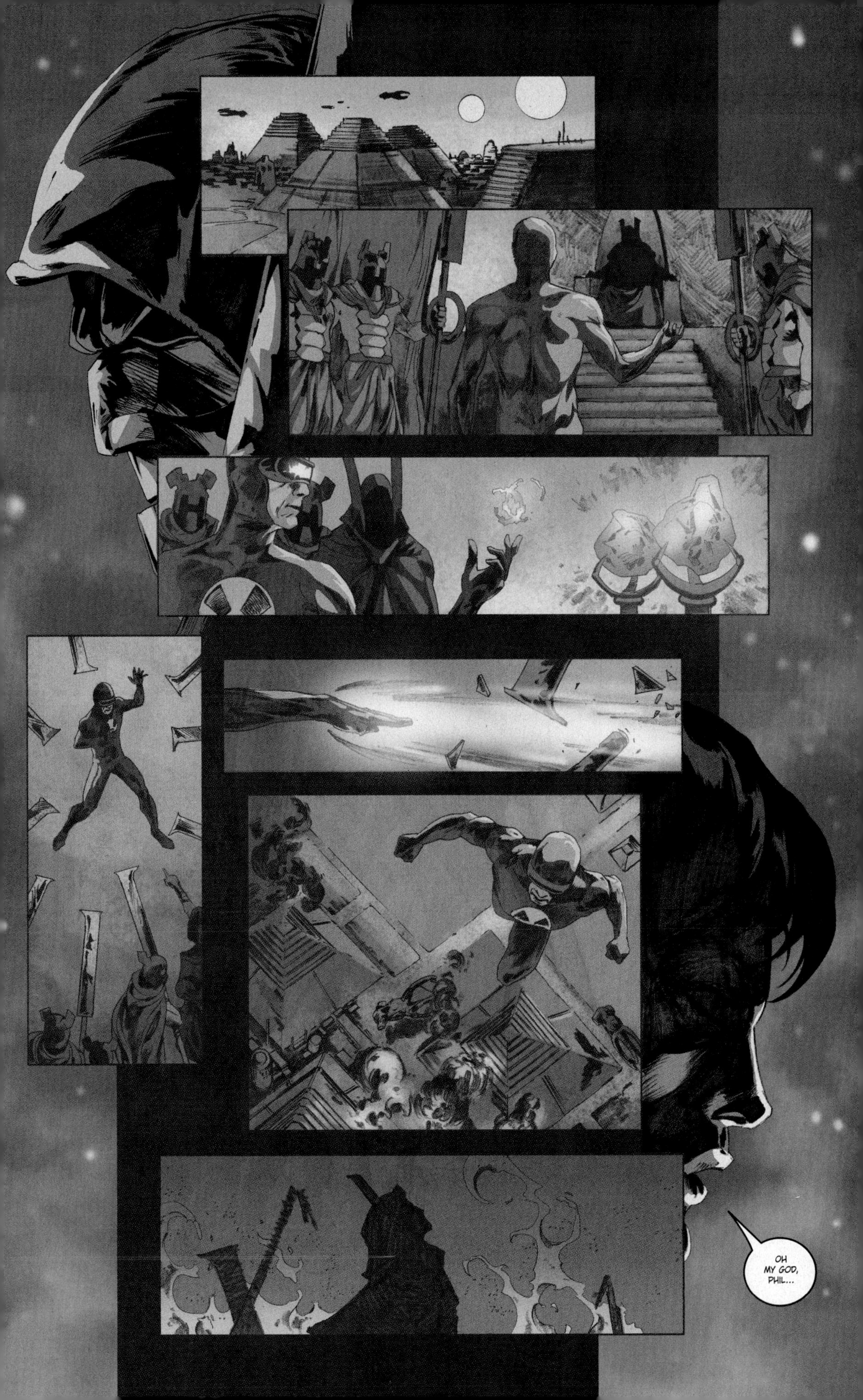
OH MY GOD, PHIL...

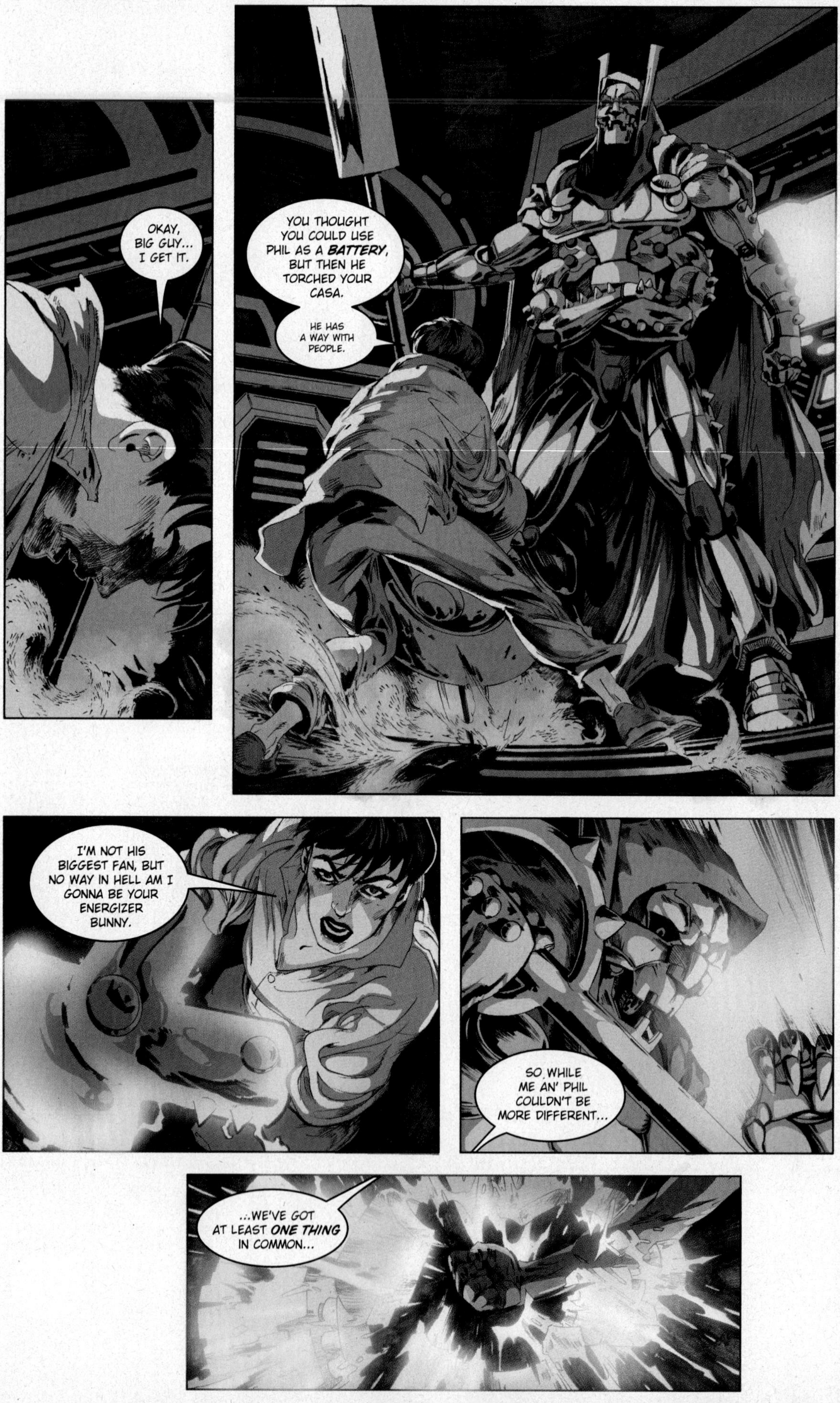
OKAY, BIG GUY... I GET IT.
YOU THOUGHT YOU COULD USE PHIL AS A **BATTERY**, BUT THEN HE TORCHED YOUR CASA.
HE HAS A WAY WITH PEOPLE.
I'M NOT HIS BIGGEST FAN, BUT NO WAY IN HELL AM I GONNA BE YOUR ENERGIZER BUNNY.
SO WHILE ME AN' PHIL COULDN'T BE MORE DIFFERENT...
...WE'VE GOT AT LEAST **ONE THING** IN COMMON...

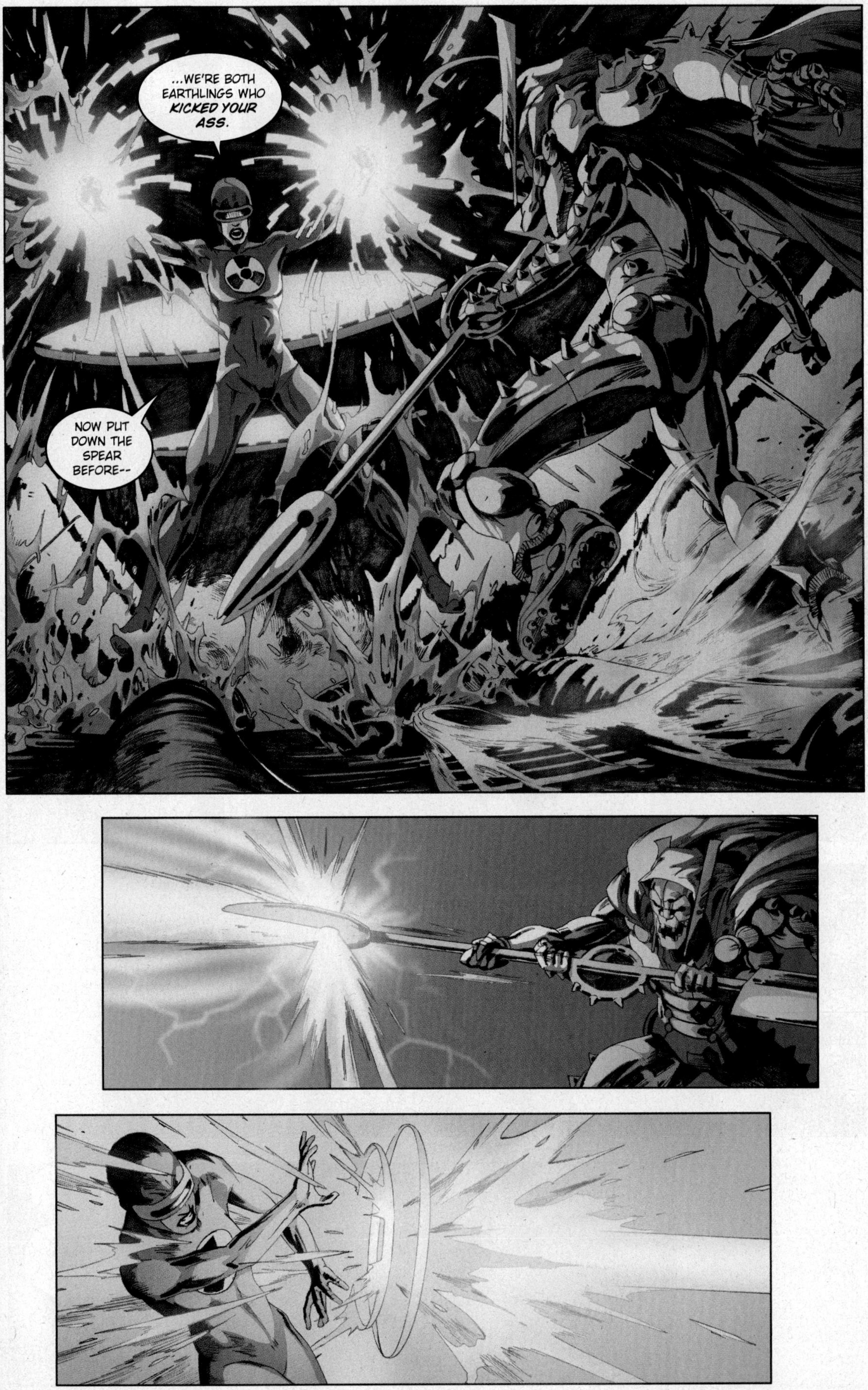
...WE'RE BOTH EARTHLINGS WHO KICKED YOUR ASS.
NOW PUT DOWN THE SPEAR BEFORE--

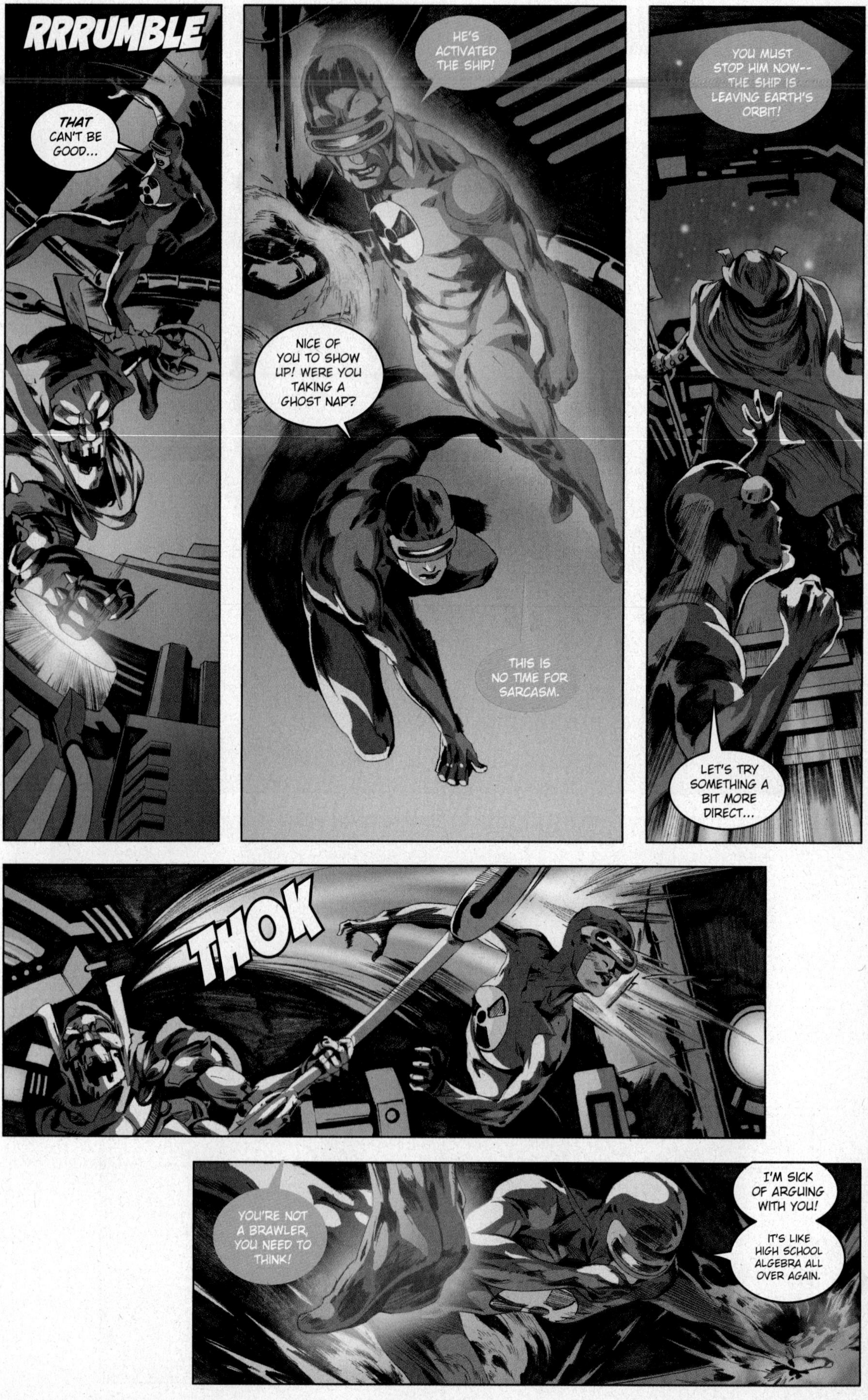
RRRUMBLE
THAT CAN'T BE GOOD...
HE'S ACTIVATED THE SHIP!
NICE OF YOU TO SHOW UP! WERE YOU TAKING A GHOST NAP?
THIS IS NO TIME FOR SARCASM.
YOU MUST STOP HIM NOW-- THE SHIP IS LEAVING EARTH'S ORBIT!
LET'S TRY SOMETHING A BIT MORE DIRECT...
THOK
YOU'RE NOT A BRAWLER, YOU NEED TO THINK!
I'M SICK OF ARGUING WITH YOU!
IT'S LIKE HIGH SCHOOL ALGEBRA ALL OVER AGAIN.

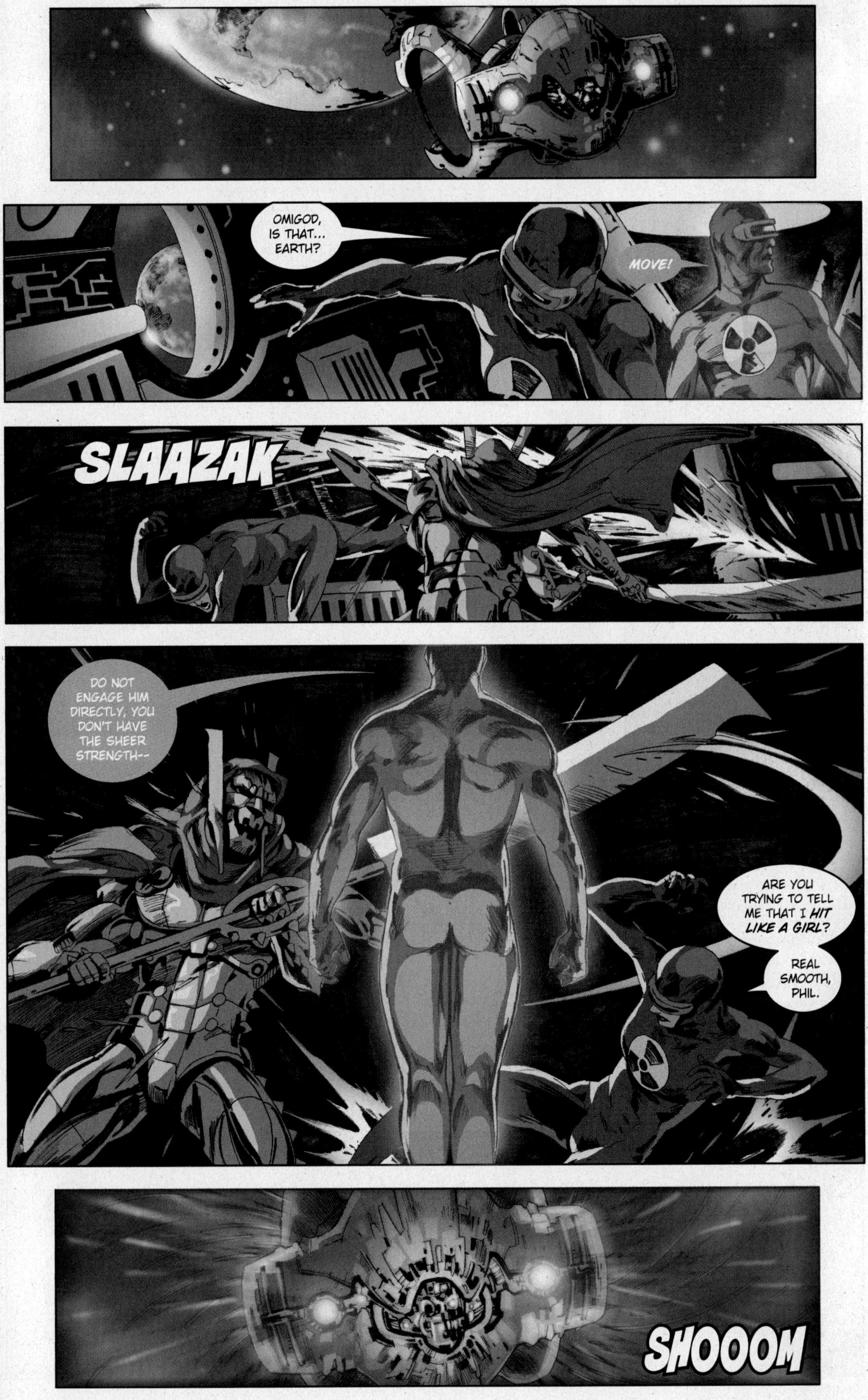
OMIGOD, IS THAT... EARTH?
MOVE!
SLAAZAK
DO NOT ENGAGE HIM DIRECTLY, YOU DON'T HAVE THE SHEER STRENGTH--
ARE YOU TRYING TO TELL ME THAT I *HIT LIKE A GIRL*?
REAL SMOOTH, PHIL.
SHOOOM

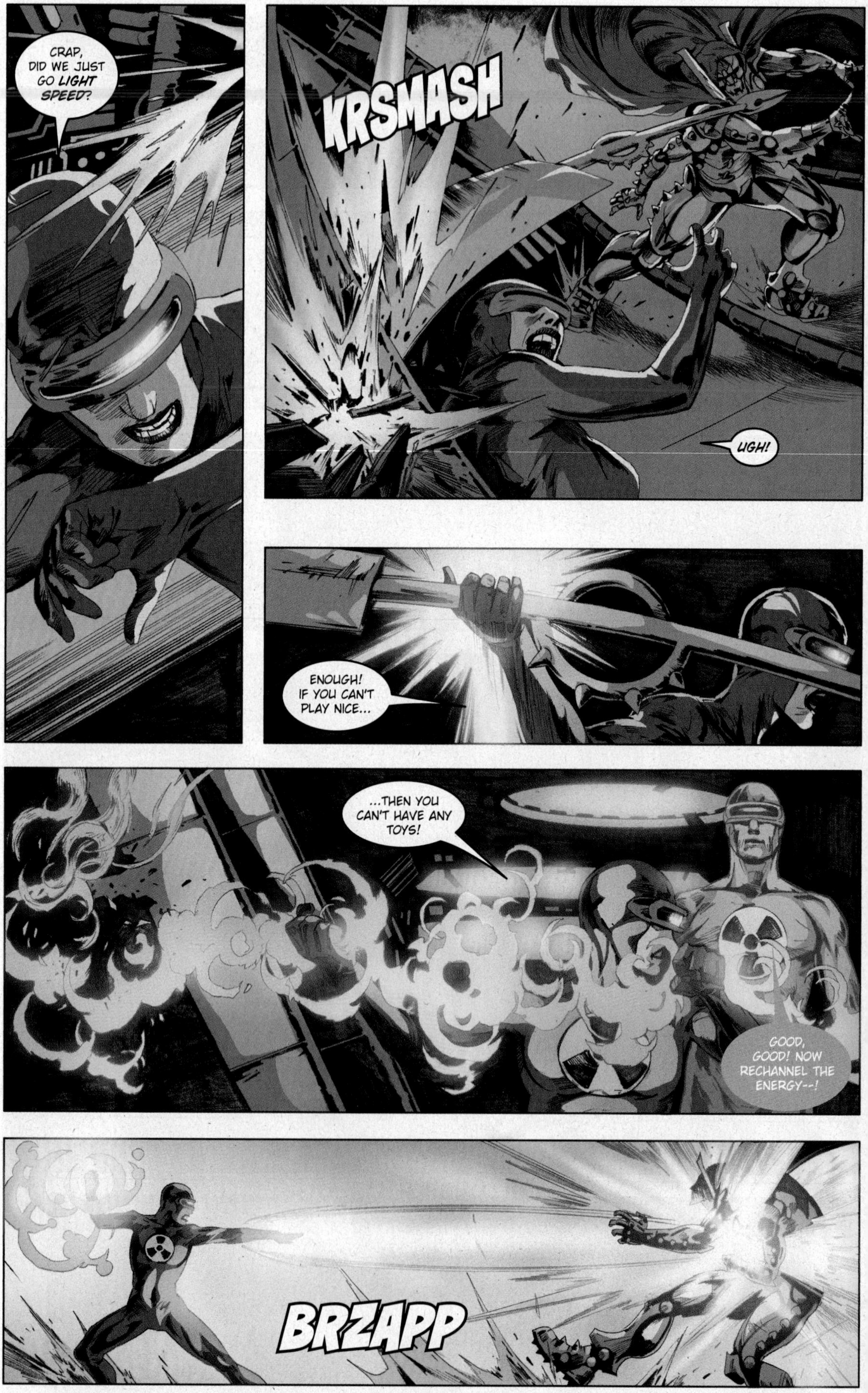
CRAP, DID WE JUST GO LIGHT SPEED?
KRSMASH
UGH!
ENOUGH! IF YOU CAN'T PLAY NICE...
...THEN YOU CAN'T HAVE ANY TOYS!
GOOD, GOOD! NOW RECHANNEL THE ENERGY--!
BRZAPP

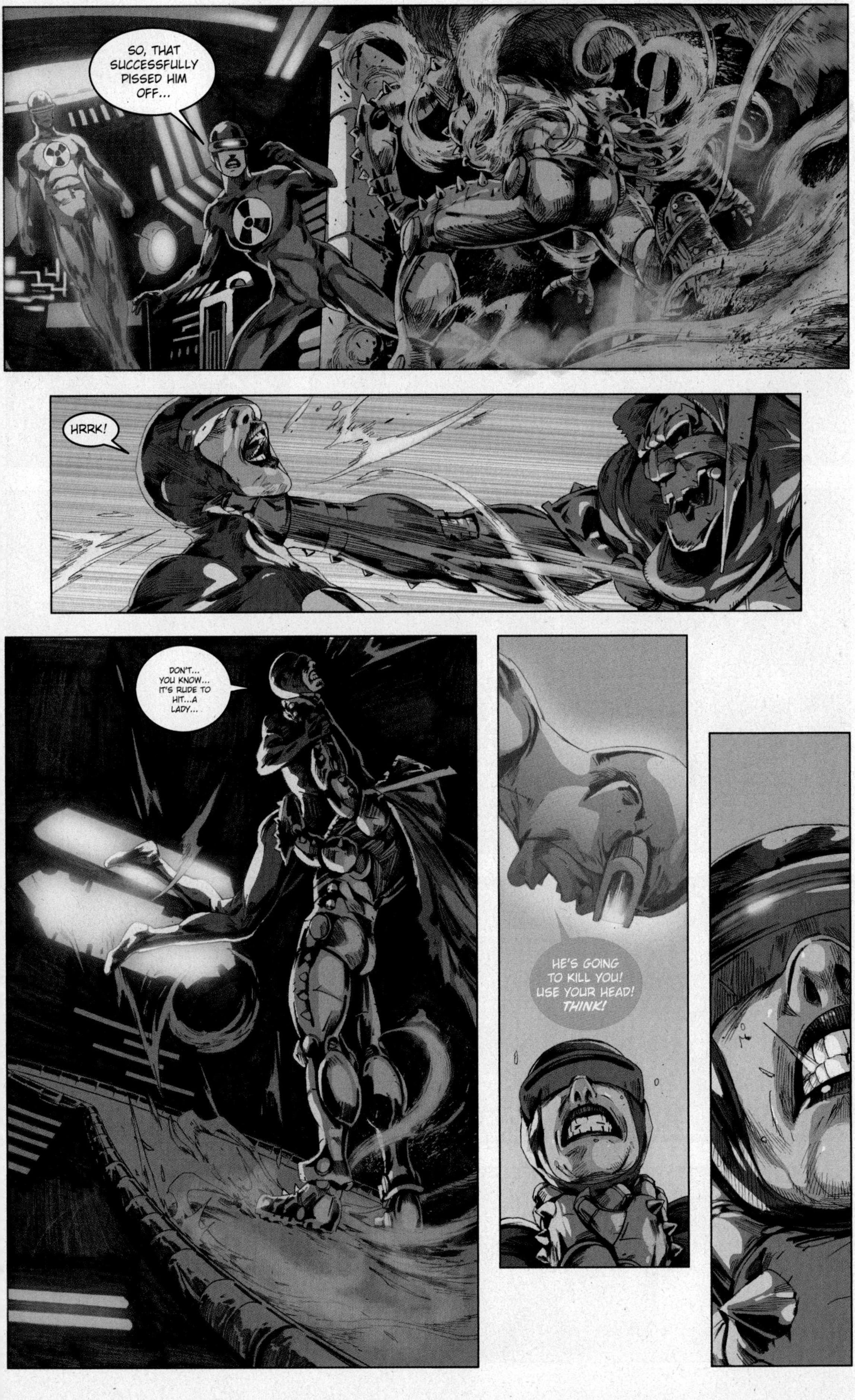
SO, THAT SUCCESSFULLY PISSED HIM OFF...
HRRK!
DON'T... YOU KNOW... IT'S RUDE TO HIT...A LADY...
HE'S GOING TO KILL YOU! USE YOUR HEAD! THINK!

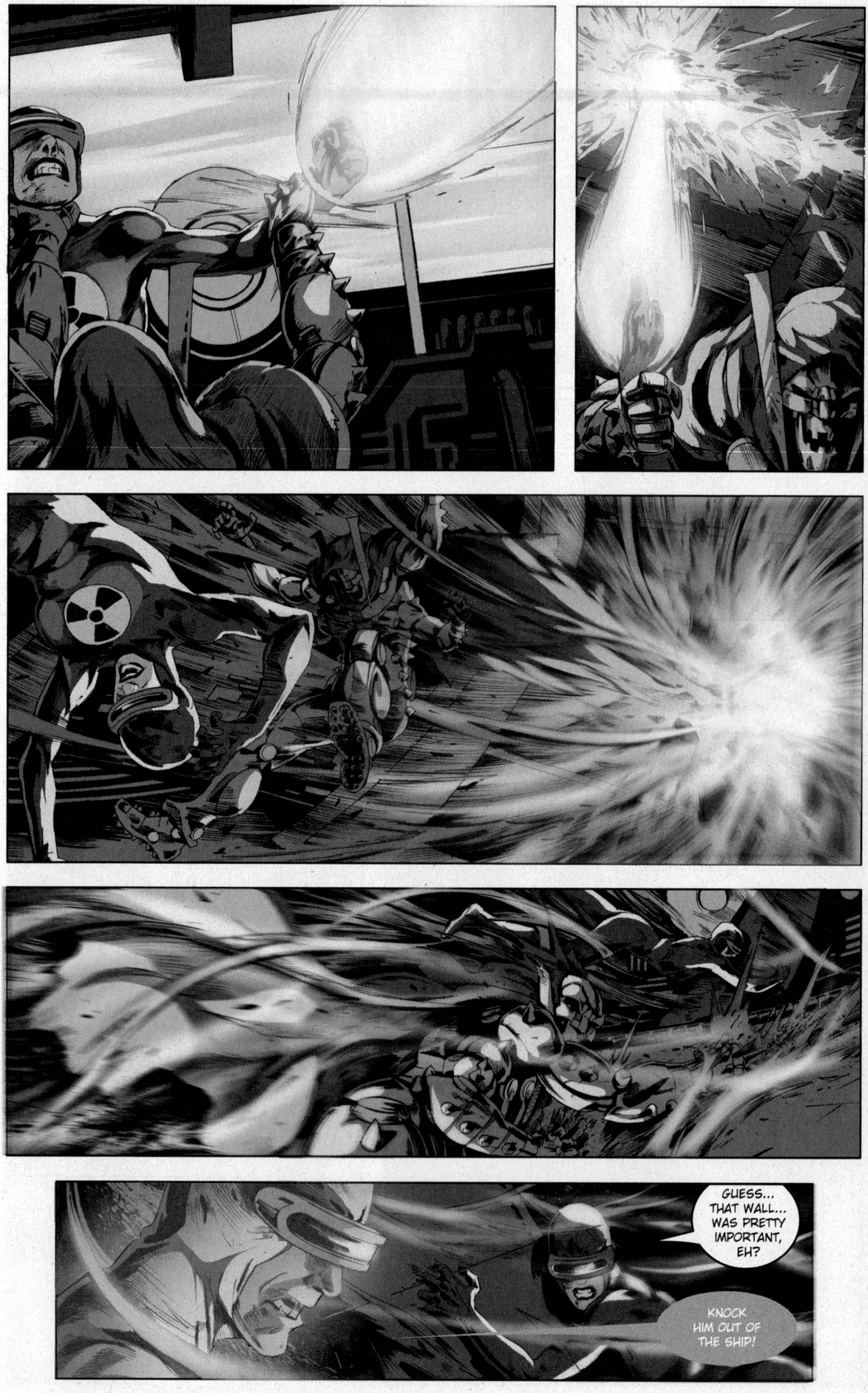
GUESS... THAT WALL... WAS PRETTY IMPORTANT, EH?
KNOCK HIM OUT OF THE SHIP!

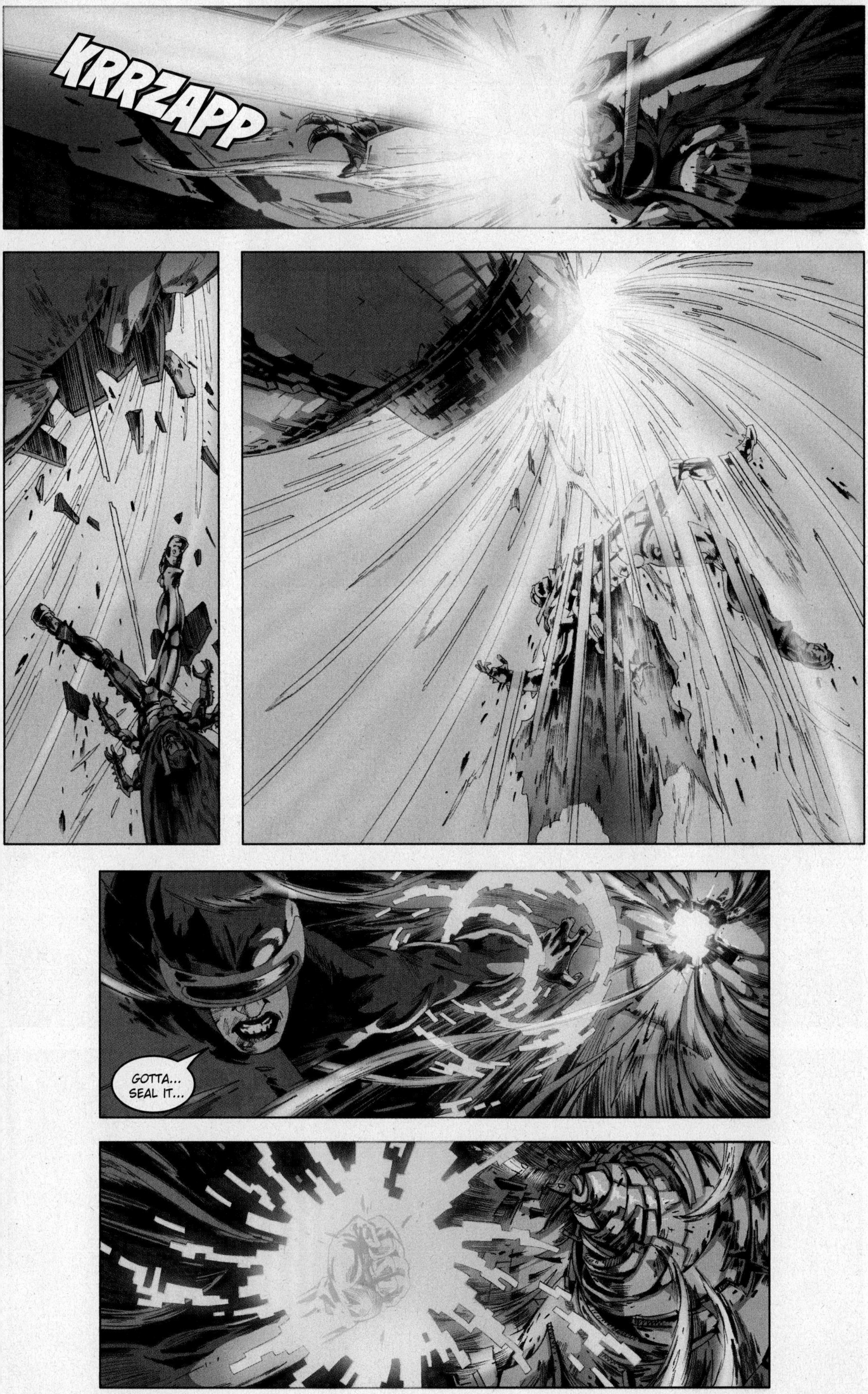
KRRZAPP
GOTTA... SEAL IT...

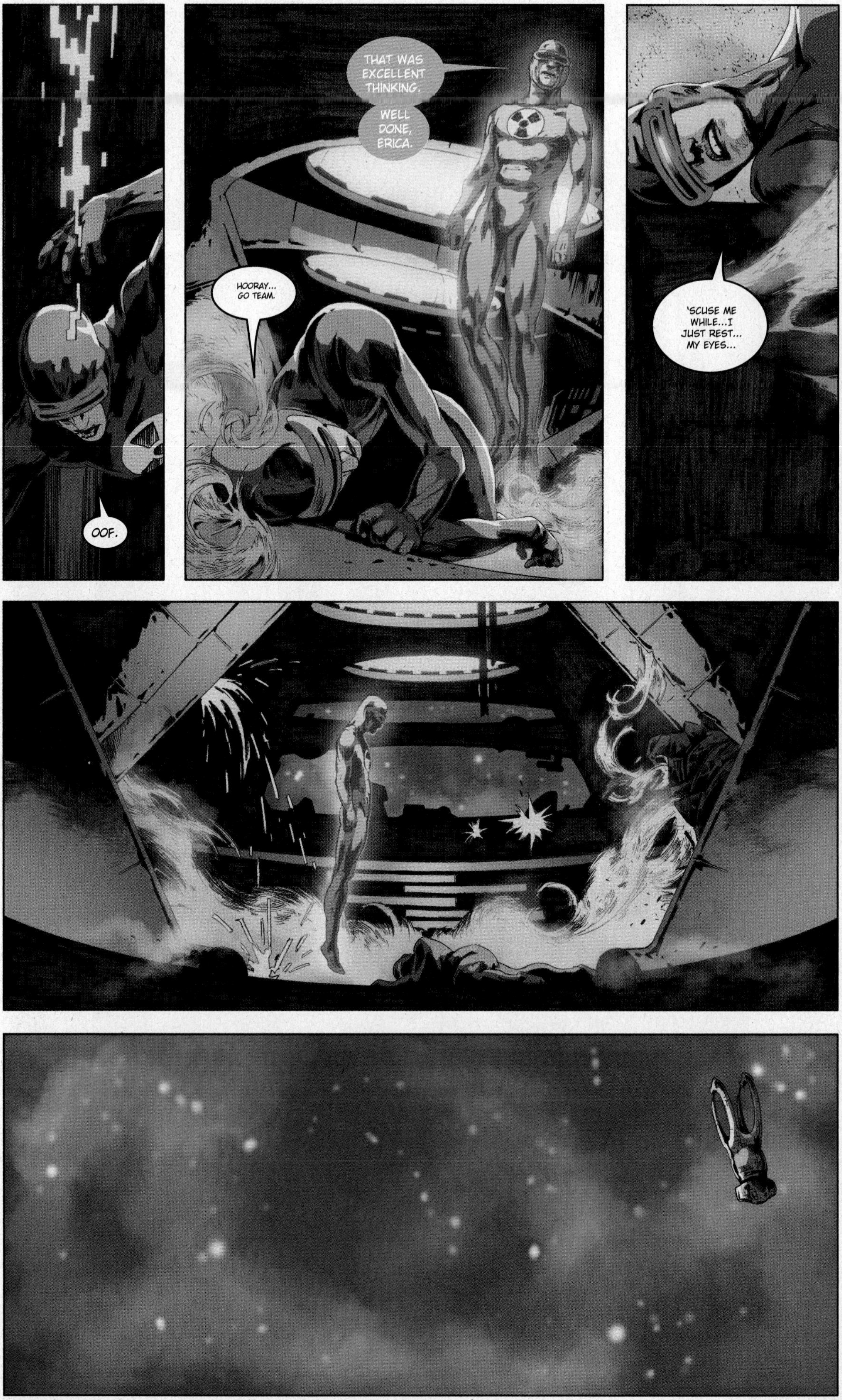
OOF.
THAT WAS EXCELLENT THINKING.
WELL DONE, ERICA.
HOORAY... GO TEAM.
'SCUSE ME WHILE...I JUST REST... MY EYES...

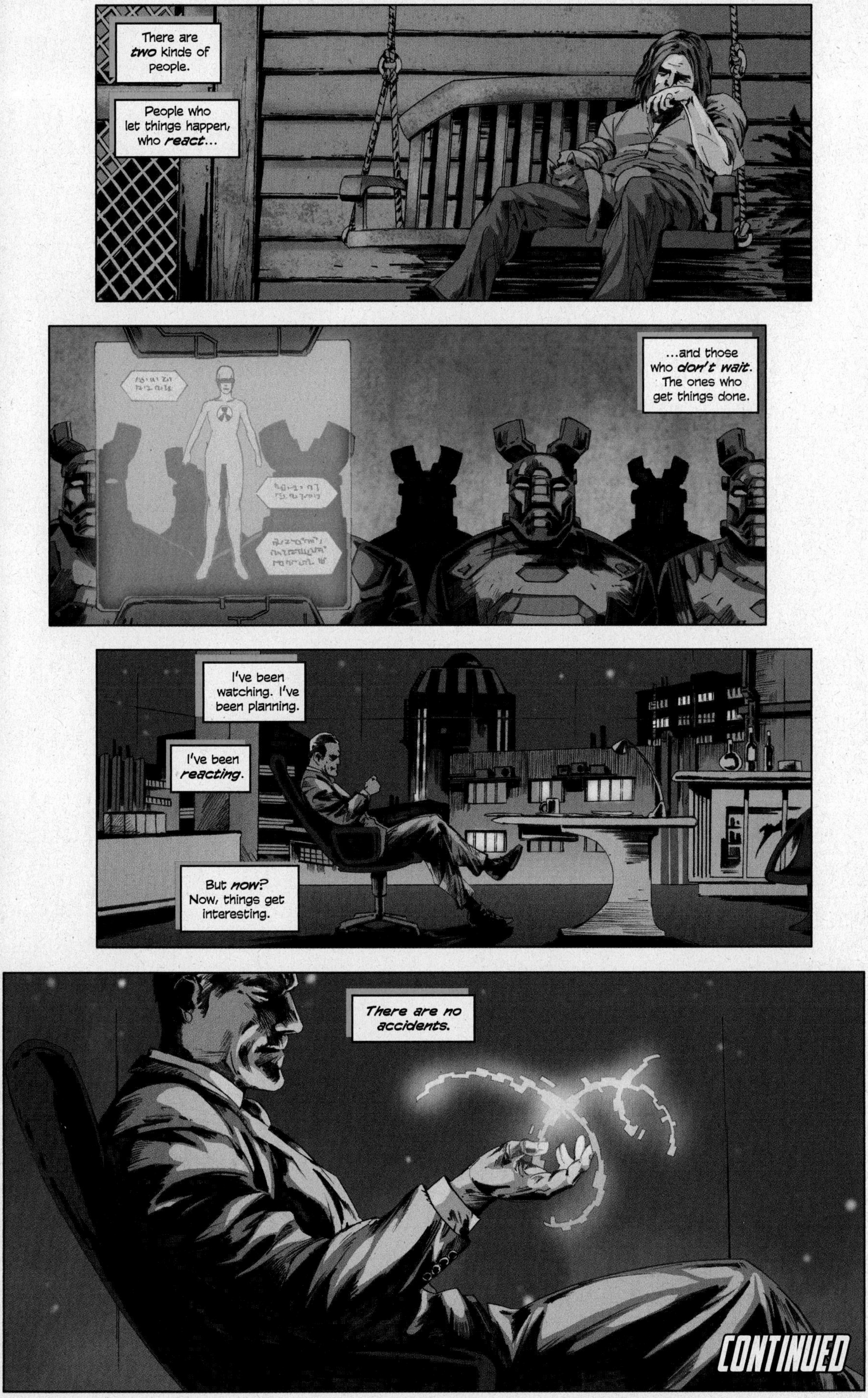
There are two kinds of people.
People who let things happen, who react...
...and those who don't wait. The ones who get things done.
I've been watching. I've been planning.
I've been reacting.
But now? Now, things get interesting.
There are no accidents.
CONTINUED

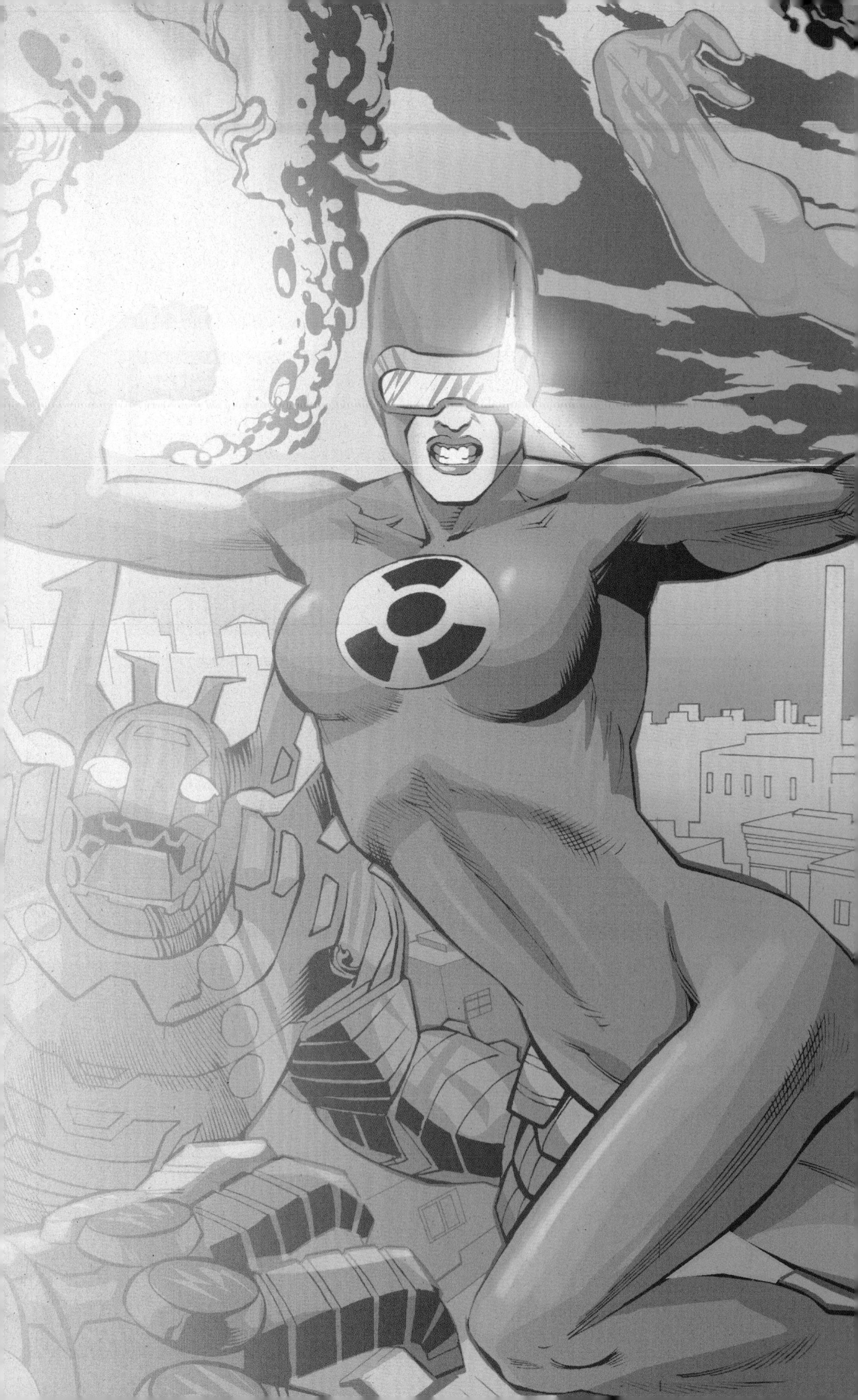

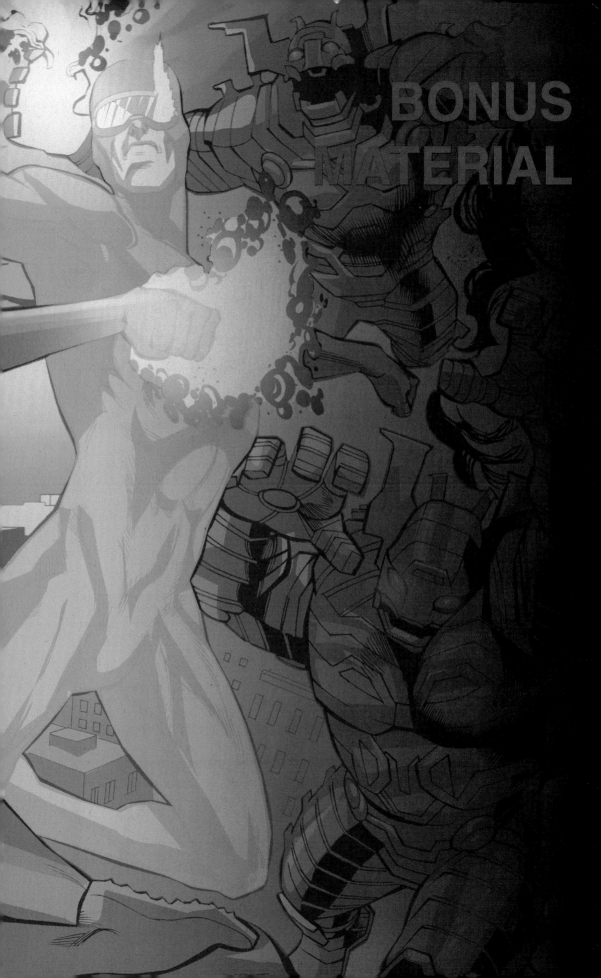

BONUS MATERIAL

Solar: Man of the Atom
Issue One: "CONSTANTS"
Written by Frank Barbiere
Edited by Nate Cosby

PAGE ZERO – BLACK, STARRY PAGE

1 TEXT: This all started with an accident.

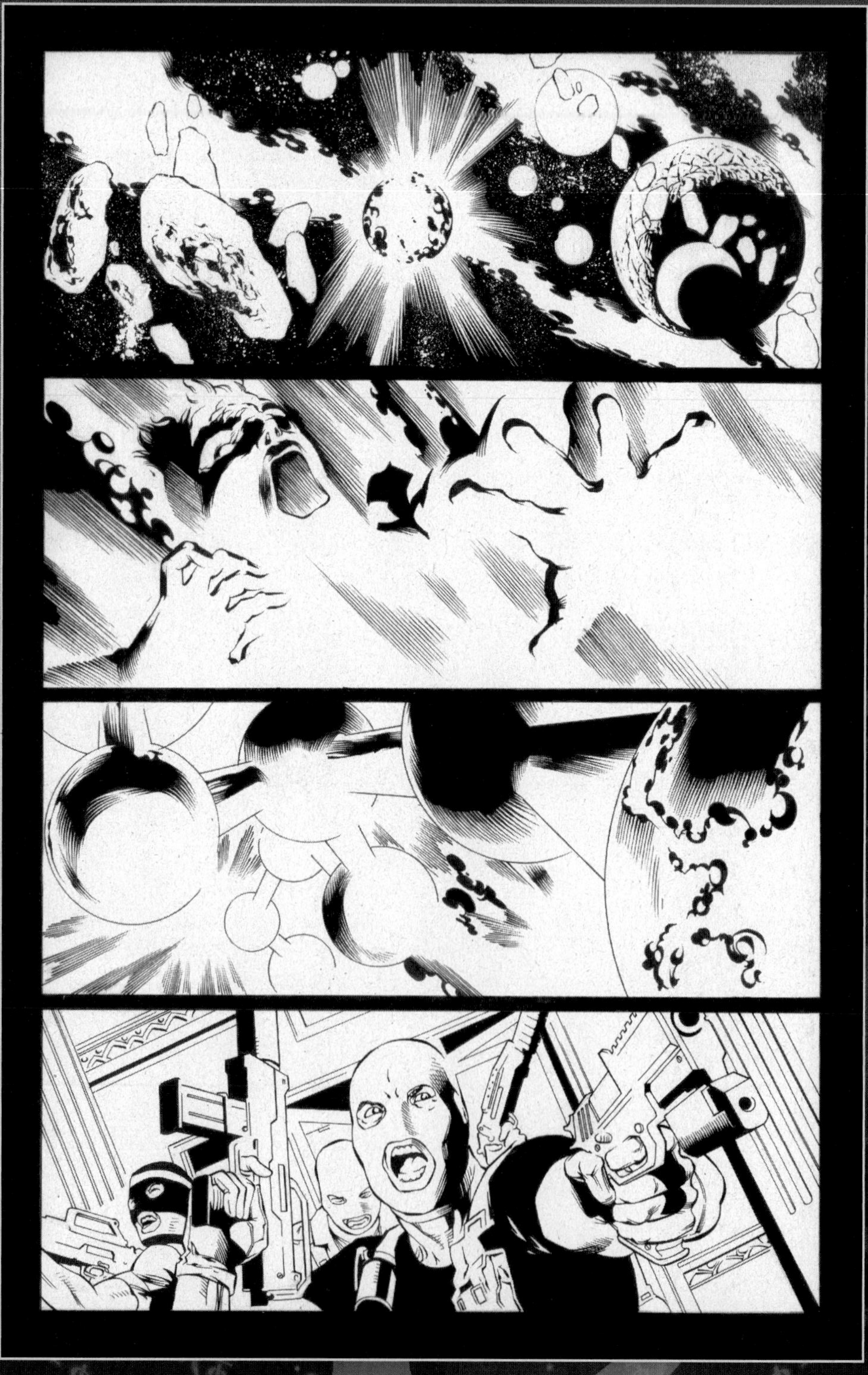

PAGE ONE

A series of four wide panels with black gutters in between.

Panel 1:
A wide shot of deep space. We aren't establishing Earth, so it can be various stars and colorful radiation, burning suns, etc.

1 CAP: *A spark.*

Panel 2:
Close on PHIL SELESKI being doused in radiation. He should have his hands up and be screaming in pain.

2 CAP: Chaos is our only *constant*--it propels us forward, makes us...something more.

Panel 3:
Close on ATOMS and various particles changing in the radiation--presumably Phil's own molecules being irradiated, split apart.

3 CAP: Something *greater*.

Panel 4:
Close on a bank robber, face covered in a ski-mask, holding up a machine gun. He screams out orders, a menacing scowl on his face.

4 ROBBER: Everyone on the floor!

4 CAP: The only certainty is the uncertain.

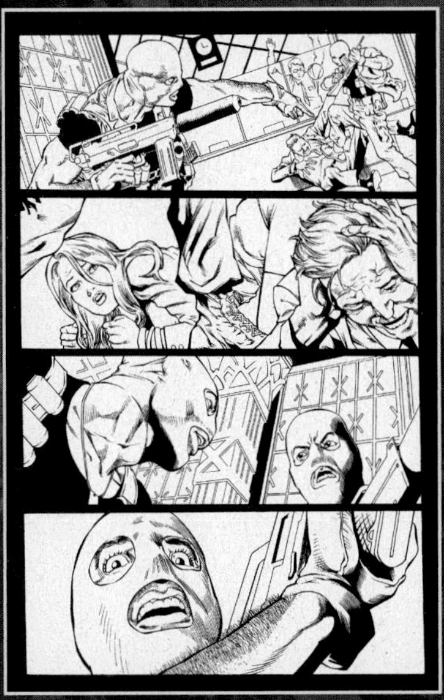

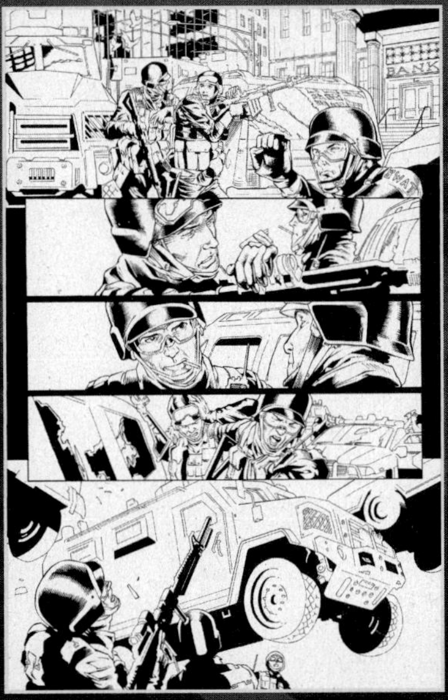
BANK

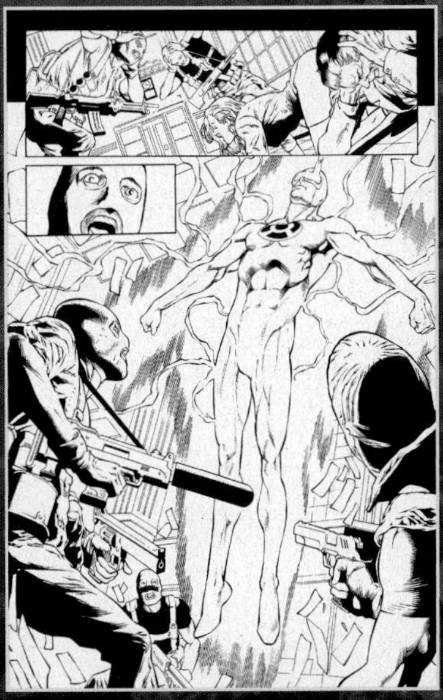

PAGE TWO

Panel 1:
Wide shot of the inside of a bank, a robbery currently in progress.
Our screaming robber clubs a man with the butt of his machine gun, barking out orders. Two other men hold some hostages at bay. The hostages cower and generally look miserable.

1 ROBBER: No funny stuff! Y'hear me?!

Panel 2:
Close on the faces of the hostages, cowering.

2 ROBBER (O.P.): Anyone who tries any *hero* crap will get real dead real fast!

1 CAP SOLAR: But there are *constants*.

Panel 3:
One of the robbers turns to our main robber, inquisitive.

3 ROBBER 2: Hey, you feel that?

Panel 4:
Close on one of the robber's hands: all the hairs on it are standing straight up, crackling. We see his puzzled face in the back of his shot, though his hand takes up the foreground.

4 ROBBER: What the f--

2 CAP SOLAR: Familiar equations.
(interrupting Robber)

PAGE THREE

Panel 1:
A wide shot of outside the bank. It is midday and police cars are lined up. Cops have surrounded the bank.

1 CAP SOLAR: Pre-determined outcomes.

Panel 2:
Two S.W.A.T.-looking guys stand around. One is taking a cigarette out of a fresh pack.

1 GUY 1: How long you think this is gonna last?

2 GUY 2: I'd get comfy--these idiots have a list of *demands*.

Panel 3:
The guy not smoking stretches, annoyed.

3 GUY 1: Are you kidding? I'm missing my kid's birthday for this garbage.

4 GUY 2: Well soon enou--

4 SFX: EEEEEEEEE

Panel 4:
The two S.W.A.T. guys look alarmed at hearing the sound; they search frantically and one of the guys yells into a radio.

5 GUY 1: What the hell is that?! A bomb?!

6 GUY 2 (into radio): We've got a situation here! There's some--

Panel 5:
The two guys look on in awe; the cigarette drops out of the one guy's mouth.
The cop cars are FLOATING. Energy crackles around the whole scene.

PAGE FOUR

Mostly a splash page with a smaller panel across the top and a small inset panel.

Panel 1:
Wide panel across the top of the page.
The robbers cover their ears, the hostages all look as if they are in pain.

1 ROBBER: IS IT AN ALARM?! SOMEONE TELL ME--

2 SFX: EEEEEEEEEEEE

Panel 2:
Small inset panel. Extreme close-up on one of the robbers. His eyes are wide in disbelief, his mouth agape.

1 CAP SOLAR: But even the most *simple* equation can change radically…

Panel 3:
SPLASH.
SOLAR appears in the middle of the bank, floating--energy crackles all around him and he should look extremely iconic. Solar's face has a slight green hue to it--throughout the scene it will gradually become MORE GREEN.
The robbers all look up in disbelief; the hostages continue to cower.

2 CAP SOLAR: With the introduction of the right *variable*.

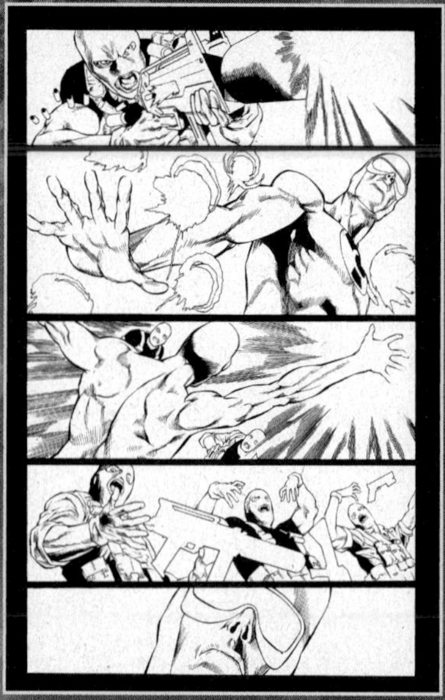

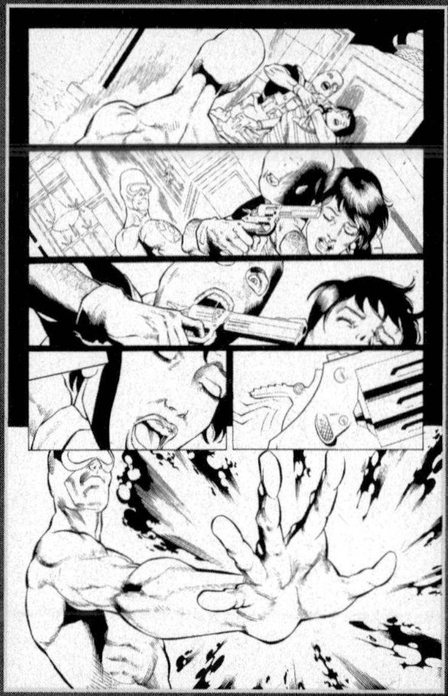

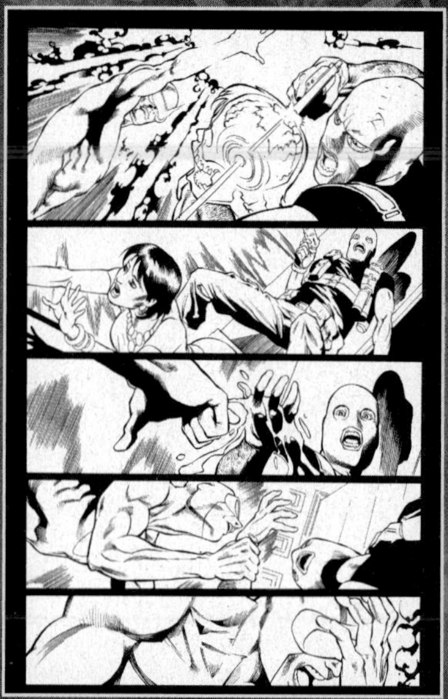

PAGE FIVE

<u>Panel 1:</u>
One of the robbers fires his machine gun at Solar erratically.

SFX: BAM BA BLAM BAM BAMM

<u>Panel 2:</u>
We see Solar from his waist up, his hands outstretched towards us. Solar's face (what we can see of it) is distant and unamused.
Bullets are flying towards him and energy crackles around him. The bullets closing in transform into a STEAMY HAZE.

1 CAP SOLAR: (Equation)

<u>Panel 3:</u>
Solar reaches out one arm, energy still crackling.

2 CAP SOLAR: Matter cannot be created or destroyed--but it can be *transformed*.

<u>Panel 4:</u>
The robbers scream, dropping their machine guns--the guns have turned BRIGHT RED and are BURNING HOT.

3 CAP SOLAR: (Equation)

1 ROBBER: Gah!

<u>Panel 5:</u>
Close on Solar, smirking.

2 ROBBER (O.P.): HEY! FREAK!

PAGE SIX

Panel 1:
Wide panel. We see Solar towards the left side, turning to look across the room where a robber holds a young woman at gunpoint.
In the background we see the hostages fleeing, scurrying about.

1 ROBBER: Let us outta here or she gets it!

Panel 2:
Solar peers at the robber with a quizzical look on his face. He looks distant and strange, as if he is observing an oddity.

1 CAP SOLAR: (Equation)?

2 CAP SOLAR: No, no...hmmm...

2 ROBBER: Don't look at me like that!

Panel 3:
The robber chokes the hostage woman a bit tighter, pressing the gun into her temple.

3 ROBBER: YOU ASKED FOR THIS!

Panel 4:
Close on the woman's mouth as she screams silently.

Panel 5:
Close on the trigger of the gun as the robber PULLS it.

Panel 6:
Solar reaches his hand out, energy crackling around it.

3 CAP SOLAR: (Equation)!!!

PAGE SEVEN

Panel 1:
We see Solar's outstretched hand in the corner of the panel, indicating he is doing something to the woman with his energy powers.
The robber shoots his gun into the hostage's temple, but she has turned strangely transparent. We see the path of the bullet as it phases through the woman's skull. Maybe we can draw her insides almost x-rayed? Her skin totally transparent?

Panel 2:
The robber throws the woman (who now has reverted back to normal) down, frightened.

1 ROBBER: What the hell did you do?!

Panel 3:
Solar points his finger towards the robber's gun and it TURNS TO LIQUID AND MELTS AWAY INTO THE AIR.
The robber looks at the gun and exclaims.

2 ROBBER: UNGH! What...what are you...?! How are you doing this, you god damn--

Panel 4:
Solar grabs him by the wrists, looking intense.

3 SOLAR: *Science.*

1 CAP SOLAR: (Equation begins but trails off)--

Panel 5:
Solar suddenly recoils, shocking with energy.

4 SOLAR: NNNARGHHH!

2 CAP SOLAR: (***)

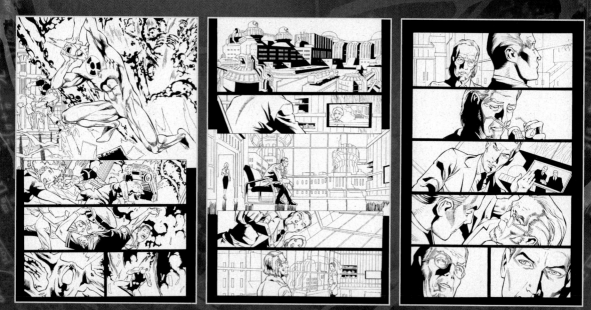

PAGE EIGHT

Panel 1:
Large panel taking up half of the page.
Solar squats down, reaching at his head in immense pain. He shocks with energy, weird distortions in space all around him. The robber next to him is ATOMIZED-- this should look almost like he is turning to liquid (which we will color in a strange, psychedelic Technicolor hue).

In the background we see the hostages fleeing out of the entrance of the bank, along with some of the robbers.

1 CAP SOLAR: (***)

2 CAP SOLAR: The *math*...was...--

Panel 2:
Outside the bank the floating cop cars EXPLODE and CRACKLE WITH ENERGY! We see the hostages fleeing out of the bank in the background.

3 CAP SOLAR: (Another broken equation)

Panel 3:
One of the cops shoos people out.

1 COP: EVERYONE OUT! EVACUATE THE AREA!

Panel 4:
Profile shot of Solar, kneeling in pain, a little bit of energy still crackling around him.

2 SOLAR: ...*nonono*...

4 CAP SOLAR: (****)

5 CAP SOLAR: (****)

Panel 5:
Pull out and we see the inside of the bank is destroyed, small fires burning, papers strewn about.
Solar is on his hands and knees.

3 CAP: This is the story of SOLAR: MAN OF THE ATOM.

1 TV SFX: ...and for those just joining us, we are continuing coverage of the catastrophic incident at First Union bank downtown earlier today.

PAGE NINE

Panel 1:
Establishing shot of SOLARUS INDUSTRIES, the huge power/chemical complex that Phil founded.

1 TV SFX: A radiological team is currently being dispatched after the discovery of radioactive materials in the area.

2 TV SFX: Police are now concerned that the robbers detonated a dirty bomb--

1 CAP COLIN: *Jesus.*

Panel 2:
Wide shot. We see the bank on a television in an executive looking office. The bank is ruined, smoking, and the cop cars are all burnt and totaled.
The TV is on the far right of the panel and we can see most of the office in the panel: it is very neat and modern, with some degrees and awards up on the wall. A figure looms on the left side, but we can only see the slightest suggestion of his torso in a suit.

3 TV SFX: Could this be an act of terrorism? We'll continue to report as the investigation continues--

Panel 3:
We're looking in through a huge glass window and see COLIN SELESKI--Phil's son and head of Solarus Industries looking off pensively, listening to the news report.
A secretary is in a doorway behind him as Colin stares out.

4 SECRETARY: Mr. Seleski? Your 3p.m. is here...

Panel 4:
Colin turns and clicks off the TV.

4 COLIN: Send him in.

Panel 5:
From behind we see a man in a lab coat entering the office. Colin stares out the window in the background, waiting for the man.

We are playing with the ambiguity of identity here: our readers really don't know who Solar is going to be, hence we want the "doctor" (who is in fact Phil/Solar's assistant, Dr. Preston) to remain ambiguous as he enters.

5 COLIN: Ah...*Doctor.*

PAGE TEN

Panel 1:
Dr. Preston is a dorky looking older scientist. This panel serves as his "reveal" (and clearly shows the reader it's NOT Solar that Colin is talking to). He stands nervously as Colin faces away, still gazing out the window.

1 DR. PRESTON: You wanted to see me, sir?

2 COLIN: Preston, we've known each other for, what? Ten years now? You've always been a little shy, but for the last two weeks you haven't taken *any* of my calls down in Beta lab--what gives?

Panel 2:
Dr. Preston cleans his glasses nervously, trying to deflect the question.

3 DR. PRESTON: We...we've hit an integral phase in our research, y-you see...we...*he*...can't be bothered...

1 CAP COLIN: *Excuses.*

Panel 3:
Colin picks up a photo of PHIL AND HIMSELF SHAKING HANDS. A nice portrait..

4 COLIN: We started this company to do some good, and I fully intend to use Dad's research for *something*--not let him squander it away on experiments and selfish musings.

5 COLIN: Why hasn't my *father* been taking my calls?

Panel 4:
Colin turns to face Preston, who is sweating.

6 PRESTON: He...he *disconnected* his phone weeks ago, Mr. Seleski...

Panel 5:
Close on Colin who looks hurt and a bit confused.
Meanwhile, in the corner of the panel, Preston looks like he's about to crack and can't find his words.

7 DR. PRESTON: Didn't he tell you? I...I...--

2 CAP COLIN: ...*disconnected*?

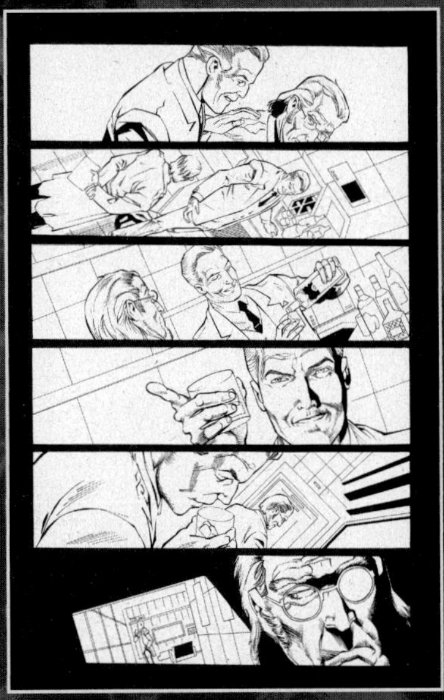

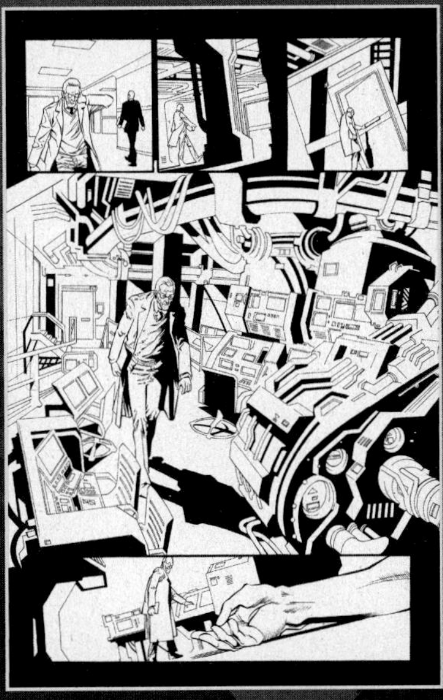

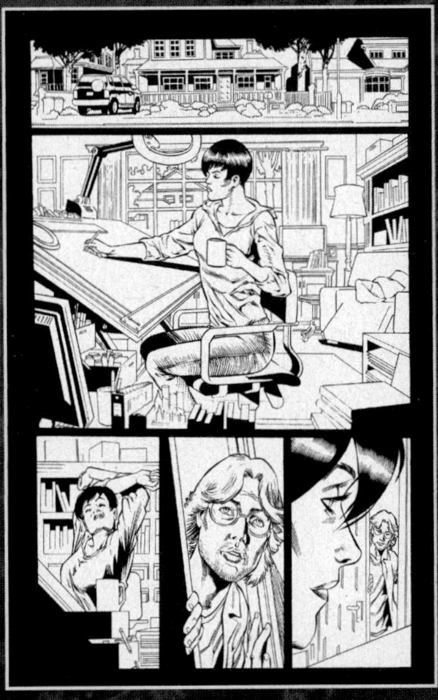

Panel 1:
Colin is next to Preston and slaps him on the back with a smile.

1 COLIN: Jeez, Preston, calm down. I'm not some evil tyrant.

1 CAP COLIN: *Is he trying to cut me out? After everything I've done for the company?*

Panel 2:
Preston exhales and Colin grabs a bottle of bourbon from a small bar in the corner.

2 COLIN: I really just want to help.

3 PRESTON: Yes, it's just that your father is a very...*complicated* man.

4 COLIN: Don't I know it.

Panel 3:
Colin lounges up on the bar casually, pours a drink.

5 COLIN: But I've got a shareholder's meeting at the end of the month and they need to see concrete results. We have to give them *something*.

Panel 4:
Close on Colin as he gestures to Preston with his drink, smiling wryly.

5 COLIN: So being as he can't be *bothered* with my calls, be a good little bird and give him my message directly, won't you?

Panel 5:
Preston turns to leave, Colin sips his drink.

6 PRESTON: Thank you, sir. I'll let him know immediately.

Panel 6:
Preston walks out the door in the background, Colin stares out, sipping his drink.

2 CAP COLIN: *What are you up to, Dad?*

PAGE TWELVE

Panel 1:
Preston walks through the halls of Solarus industries, moving briskly with a nervous look.

1 PRESTON (small): Philip, Philip--what are we going to do?

Panel 2:
Preston walks into an area that looks industrial and more laboratory-esque.

Panel 3:
Preston pushes open a door labeled BETA LABS.

Panel 4:
Large panel. Preston enters a large laboratory that is state of the art. It is a little barren as there is no one there, but it is super high-tech and has all kinds of strange science equipment.

2 PRESTON: Phil! Where are you? We have to talk!

3 SOLAR (weak, O.P.): Eri...

Panel 5:
Wide panel across the bottom of the page.
Preston looks behind him, far off in the panel, and in the foreground we see a RED HAND lying on the ground (towards the right edge of the panel).
The reader can't see, but it's SOLAR.

4 SOLAR (weak): *Erica...Erica...*

PAGE THIRTEEN

Panel 1:
Establishing shot. A nice, suburban ranch-style house.

1 CAP ERICA: Windows? What about windows...

Panel 2:
Large panel.
We see ERICA SELESKI sitting at a drafting table. She's working on a sketch of a building and we see her office: it is artsy but neat, with various paintings and degrees on the wall. We definitely want to establish a much more "free" style vs. Colin's office--maybe some plants, crumbled papers on the floor, etc.
There is a cat curled up on the top of her chair as she works. A radio is also on in the corner and is playing softly. The radio plays SEARCH & DESTROY by the Stooges.

RADIO:
I'm a street walking cheetah
with a heart full of napalm

2 CAP ERICA: No, but the archway should be a little larger...

3 CAP ERICA: Still looks funny...maybe if I--

2 MAN'S VOICE (O.P.): Erica!

4 CAP ERICA: But seriously--who doesn't love windows?

Panel 3:
Erica stretches, and the cat jumps off the chair.

3 MAN'S VOICE (O.P.): Erica! Can you hear me?! There's--

RADIO: I'm a runaway son of the nuclear A-bomb

3 ERICA: Dammit, Dave--how many times do I have to tell you not to yell for me when I'm working?

5 CAP ERICA: Windows. Lots and lots of windows.

Panel 4:
Dave, Erica's husband, pops his head in the door. He is a John Lennon-looking type, a Philosophy professor who slants towards "hippy" in style. He has large, thin-rimmed circular glasses.

RADIO:
I am a world's forgotten boy
The one who searches and destroys

4 DAVE: Honey, there's someone at the door for you. He insists it's important.

Panel 5:
Erica sets her drafting pen behind her ear and stands.

RADIO:
Soul radiation in the dead of night
Love in the middle of a fire fight
Honey gotta strike me blind
Somebody gotta save my soul

5 ERICA: David, they *always* say it's important. Probably wants to sell us knives or something.

PAGE FOURTEEN

Panel 1:
Erica is at her front door and we see Dr. Preston outside, looking anxious.

1 ERICA: Whatever it is, I assure you--I don't want it.

2 PRESTON: Are you...*Erica Seleski*?

1 CAP ERICA: What about an elevator? Forget the windows...

Panel 2:
Close on Erica, looking sassy and holding up her wedding ring.

3 ERICA: I go by Erica Roberson these days, but yeah--that's me.

Panel 3:
Preston looks desperate and Erica looks surprised as he speaks.

4 PRESTON: Erica...I'm here on behalf of your father. He's been trying to reach you--

Panel 4:
Erica looks away, her hand in the doorframe. Preston looks dire and straightens his glasses.

5 ERICA: Oh, I'm well aware. He's been calling for the last two weeks--

6 PRESTON: Please...my name is Doctor Preston and I am Philip's lab assistant. Your father...

7 ERICA: My *father* should forget my number before I get a restraining order!

Panel 5:
Erica turns to face Preston, visibly annoyed.

8 ERICA: And you'd think he'd have the courtesy to come see me face to face, it's not like he's...

Panel 6:
Erica looks across the panel at Preston, who looks extremely serious with some sadness in his eyes. Erica stares surprised, suddenly realizing the urgency.

1 CAP: Science is governed by principles, not laws.

PAGE FIFTEEN

Panel 1:
We see the earth from space, small and with a lot of space visible.

1 CAP: Things are always shifting, always changing.

Panel 2:
We pull out a little further and see a small SPACE SHIP.

CAP: But there are constants...

Panel 3:
We see inside the ship It should be techno-organic--definitely have the semblance of being a living vessel while looking high-tech.
A huge commanders chair of sorts faces a HOLGRAPHIC SCREEN that prominently displays SOLAR. We don't see who is in the chair quite yet, but maybe arms from the side? If so--the arms are ARMORED and STEEL--almost like DESTROYER or NIMROD from Marvel comics.

3 CAP: Certainties. We know that for every action...

Panel 4:
A steel, robotic alien hand presses a strange button on a weird, almost biological console.

Panel 5:
We see something rocketing off of the ship and headed towards earth.

4 CAP: ...there is a *reaction.*

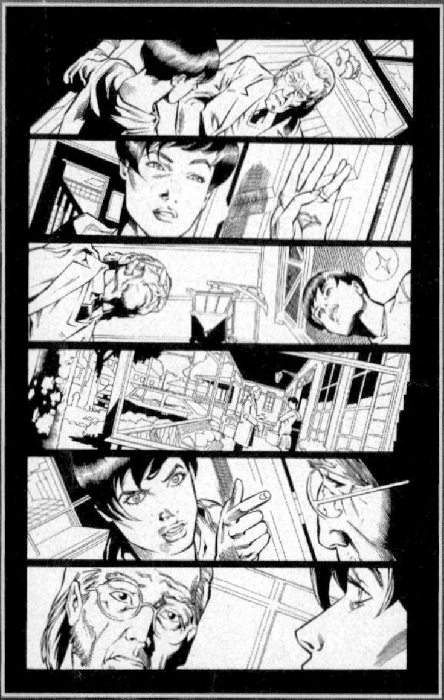

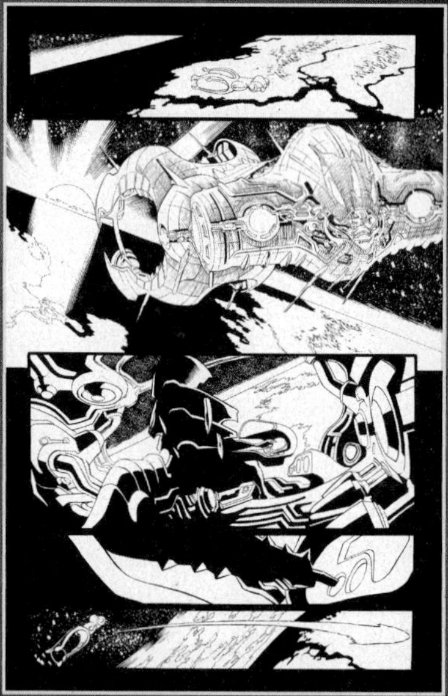

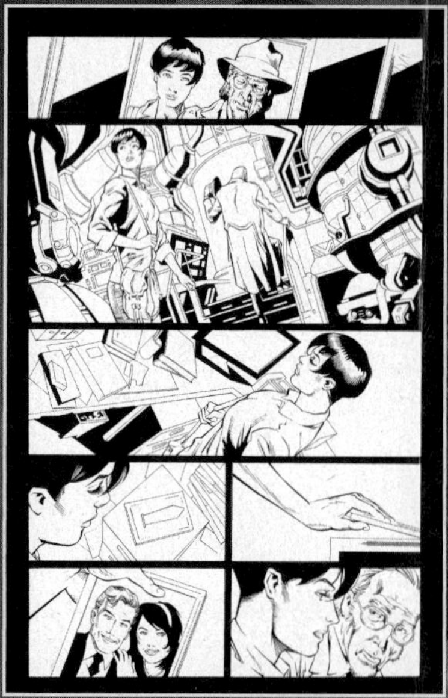

PAGE SIXTEEN

Panel 1:
We're inside the lab and see two figures through the glass doorway--it's Preston and Erica. Preston is unlocking the door.

1 PRESTON: ...it took me a while to figure out where you were. Fifteen years I've worked with your father, and he's never mentioned you until--

2 ERICA: I'd rather not talk about it, thanks.

Panel 2:
Big panel. Preston and Erica enter the lab. Erica is pretty astonished by all the

equipment and surroundings, Preston leads her along.

1 CAP ERICA: Jesus. This place looks like a sci-fi movie.

4 PRESTON: We've been conducting very serious research here, but I won't bore you with the specifics...

Panel 3:
Erica has wandered over to Phil's desk--there are notes scattered all over and it in general disarray.

2 CAP ERICA: Definitely Dad's desk...

Panel 4:
Erica looks puzzled as she reaches towards a photograph facing FACE DOWN ON THE DESK.

Panel 5:
Erica turns the framed photo up and sees PHIL AND HIS WIFE, A BEAUTIFUL YOUNG WOMAN. Erica looks at the photo with a sad, longing gaze.

3 CAP ERICA: *I shouldn't be here.*

Panel 6:
Wide panel across the bottom of the page.
Erica gazes at the photo in reverie, while Preston puts his hand on her shoulder, calmly and kindly getting her attention.

7 PRESTON: I...I think it's time to *see your father*.

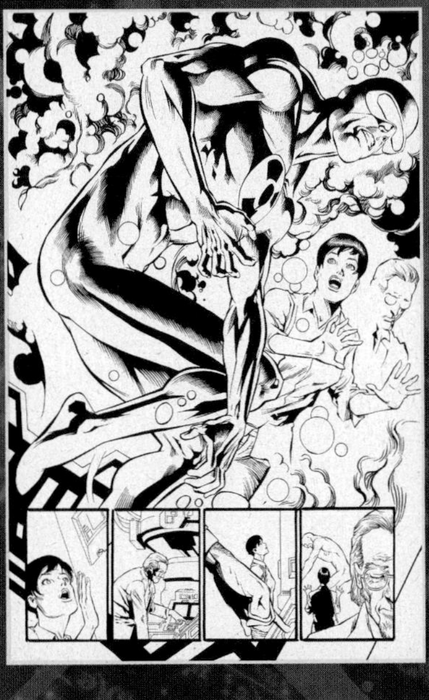
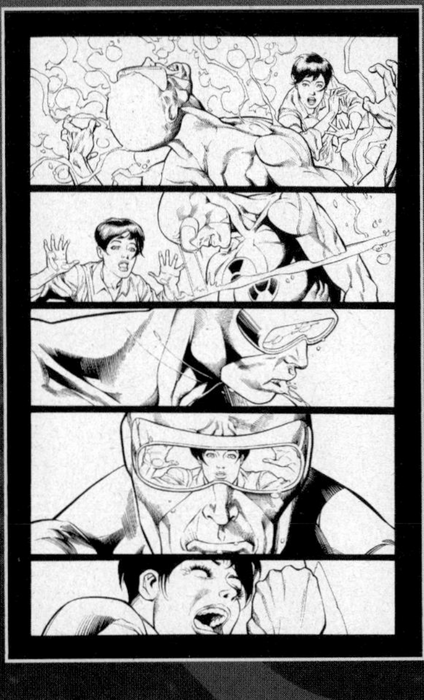
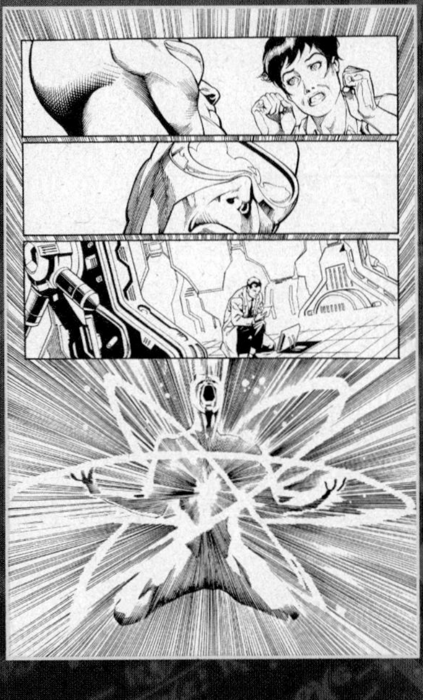

PAGE SEVENTEEN

Panel 1:
Half-splash.
Erica recoils, next to Dr. Preston. Phil's containment tube is prominent in the foreground and we are witnessing Erica's reaction. She looks frightened and surprised. Preston looks somber, adjusts his glasses.

1 ERICA: Omigod. *Dad...?*

Panel 2:
Erica puts her hand up on the tube and gazes at it with a regretful look in her eyes.

1 CAP ERICA: What the hell is he *wearing...?*

Panel 3:
Preston is back at his terminal. We see him from the side.

3 PRESTON: His body is in an extremely unstable state. He's *changing--* transforming into pure energy.

4 PRESTON: The containment suit I designed is all that is holding him together, along with the ionization chamber.

Panel 4:
Preston hits a key and Erica (who still has her hands on the ionization tank) looks over at him.

5 PRESTON: But perhaps it's best if he explained *himself.* I'll leave you two to...*catch up.*

Panel 5:
Dr. Preston walks off, and Erica turns her head towards him.

6 ERICA: Hey! You can't just leave me--

PAGE EIGHTEEN

A series of three tall panels across the top of the page as Phil is REVIVED in the tank.

Panel 1:
The containment tank shocks with electricity.

1 CAP PHIL: Physics is full of uncertainty.

Panel 2:
The liquid is draining from the tank--it's about level with Phil's chest.

2 CAP PHIL: Probability, chance, *chaos*--a meeting of two foreign entities that defies all logic.

Panel 3:
Phil coughs inside the tube.

3 CAP PHIL: This is how life begins and ends--creation fumbled in such *clumsy* hands.

1 PHIL: *cough* What...where...*cough*

Panel 4:
A wide panel. Erica looks up into Phil's eyes and he looks down at her. A dramatic moment.

2 PHIL: (Equation)...(Equation)...this is--

3 PHIL: Who...*Erica*?

Panel 5:
Erica bangs on the outside of the tank with balled fists, tears in her eyes.

3 ERICA: What...*what have you done*?

PAGE NINETEEN

Panel 1:
Let's have the profile shot again, but perhaps change sides?
Phil talks to Erica from inside the tank as she leans her head against it.

1 PHIL: The math...it was all...(Equation)...it's...

Panel 2:
Close on Phil's face. He looks confused and disoriented; Phil's face begins to turn green.
2 PHIL: I can solve this. I can...

Panel 3:
Flashback panel.
We see Phil as a scientist meddling with a strange, glowing reactor.

3 PHIL: *There was an accident.*

Panel 4:
We see Phil in tattered, ripped clothes post-explosion, looking at his glowing hands.

4 PHIL: I found...(equation)...something new. Something *more.*

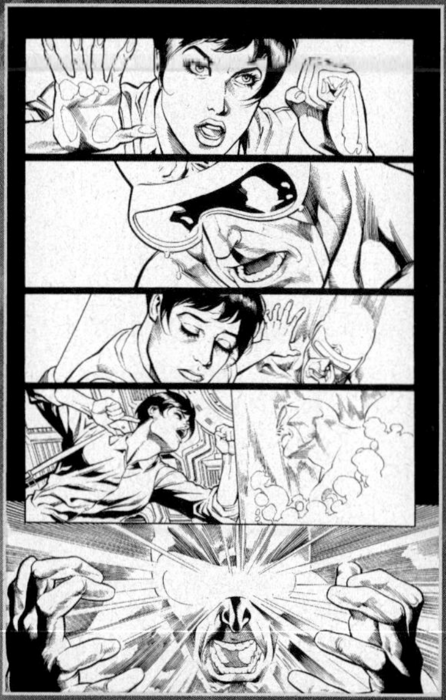

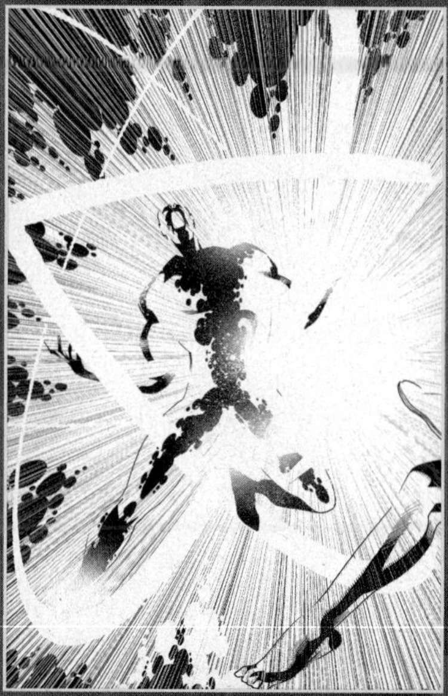

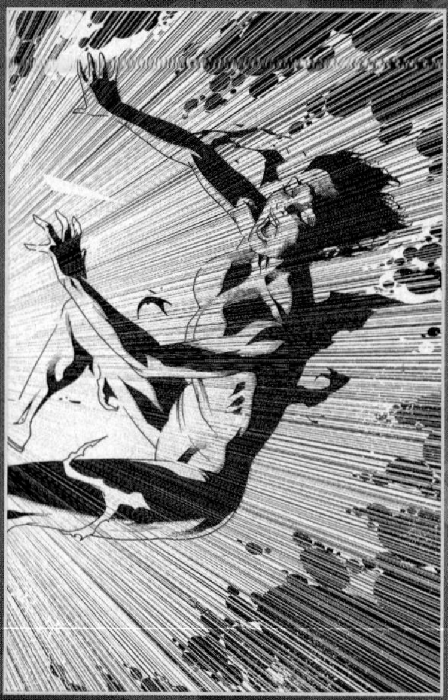

PAGE TWENTY

<u>Panel 1:</u>
Erica looks very concerned, the tank glowing on her face.

1 ERICA: Dad, I think you need help...you have to get out of here and get to a hospital or--

<u>Panel 2:</u>
Close on Phil in the tank, now glowing a bit. His face has turned green.

2 PHIL: You have to listen to me! I know what I'm doing! (Equation)!

<u>Panel 3:</u>
Erica turns back towards Phil with tears in her eyes.

3 ERICA: I don't know what that means! I haven't seen you in years...and now you're here and I don't know what to do!

<u>Panel 4:</u>
Erica points angrily at Phil, who is now glowing strongly.

4 ERICA: You left, Dad! *You left.* And now I have no idea--

<u>Panel 5:</u>
Phil closes his eyes in pain, glowing.

6 PHIL: No...I...argghhh!

1 CAP: It *always* starts with an accident.

PAGE TWENTY- ONE, TWENTY-TWO

This is a splash with a small, wide insert panel on top.

Panel 1:
Small, wide panel--close on Erica's eyes--sad, intent and confused.

1 ERICA: *...Dad...?*

1 CAP: Change is our only *constant*--it propels us forward, makes us...something more. Something *greater*.

Panel 2:
The containment tank is centered in the panel and Phil goes NUCLEAR inside. He should mostly be a glowing shadow, energy exploding and pouring out of him (maybe we can use Kirby dots for a fun, retro effect?).
Erica is shielding herself, but being blown back in the crazy blast. Her mouth is open letting loose a silent scream.

2 CAP: This is the story of SOLAR: MAN OF THE ATOM...

3 CAP: *...and how he died.*

TO BE CONTINUED.

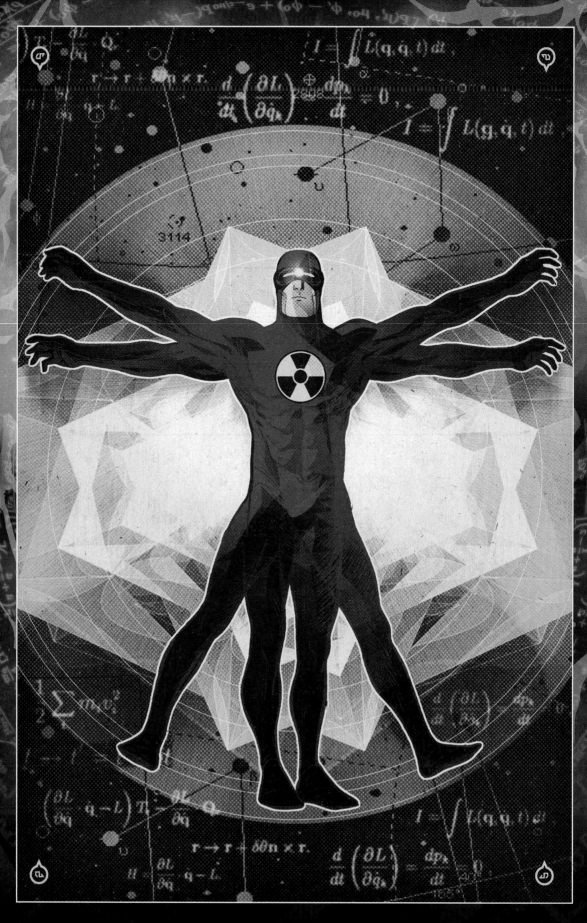

issue #1 cover by JUAN DOE

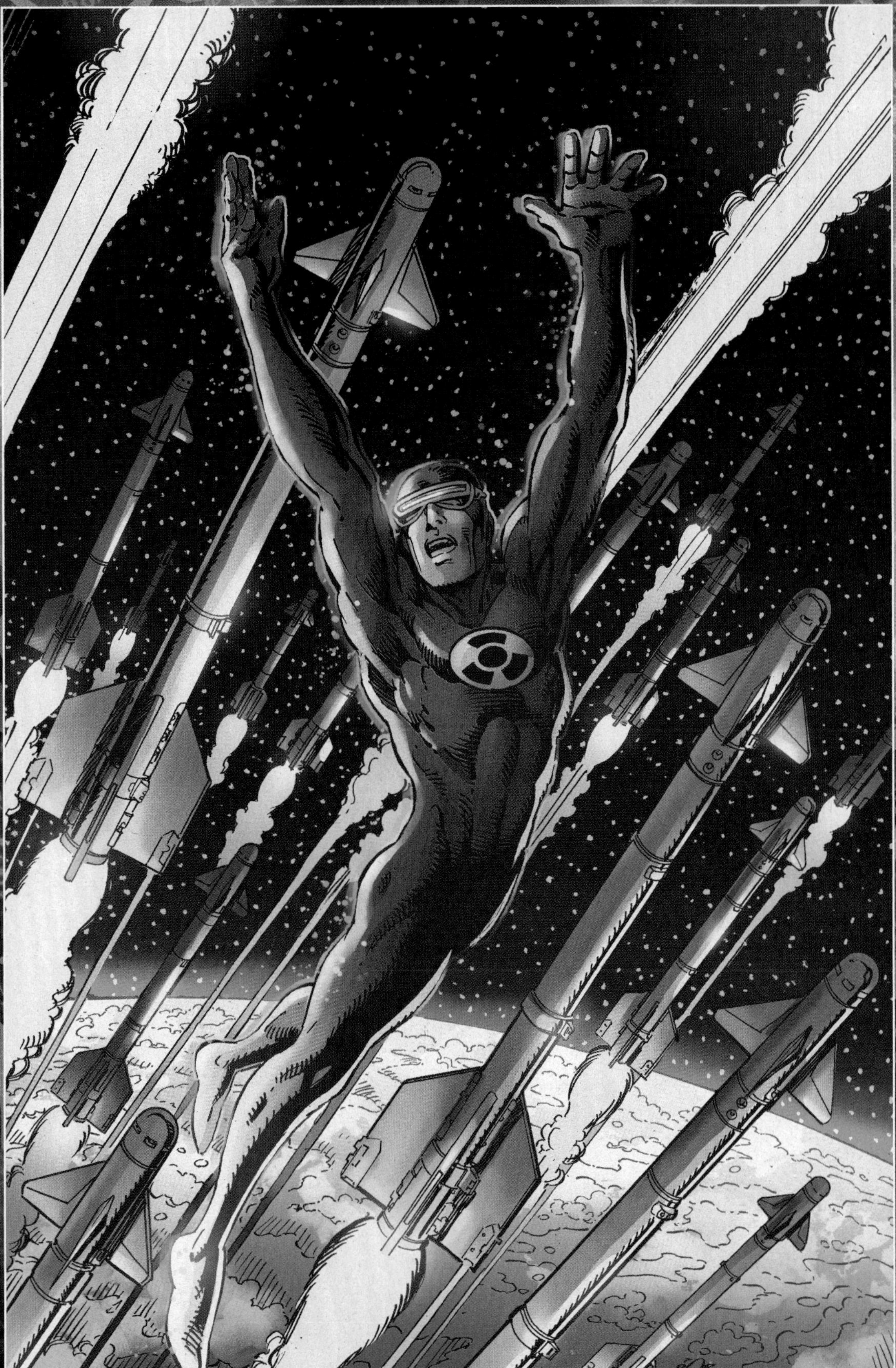

issue #1 cover by BOB LAYTON
colors by MIKE CAVALLARO

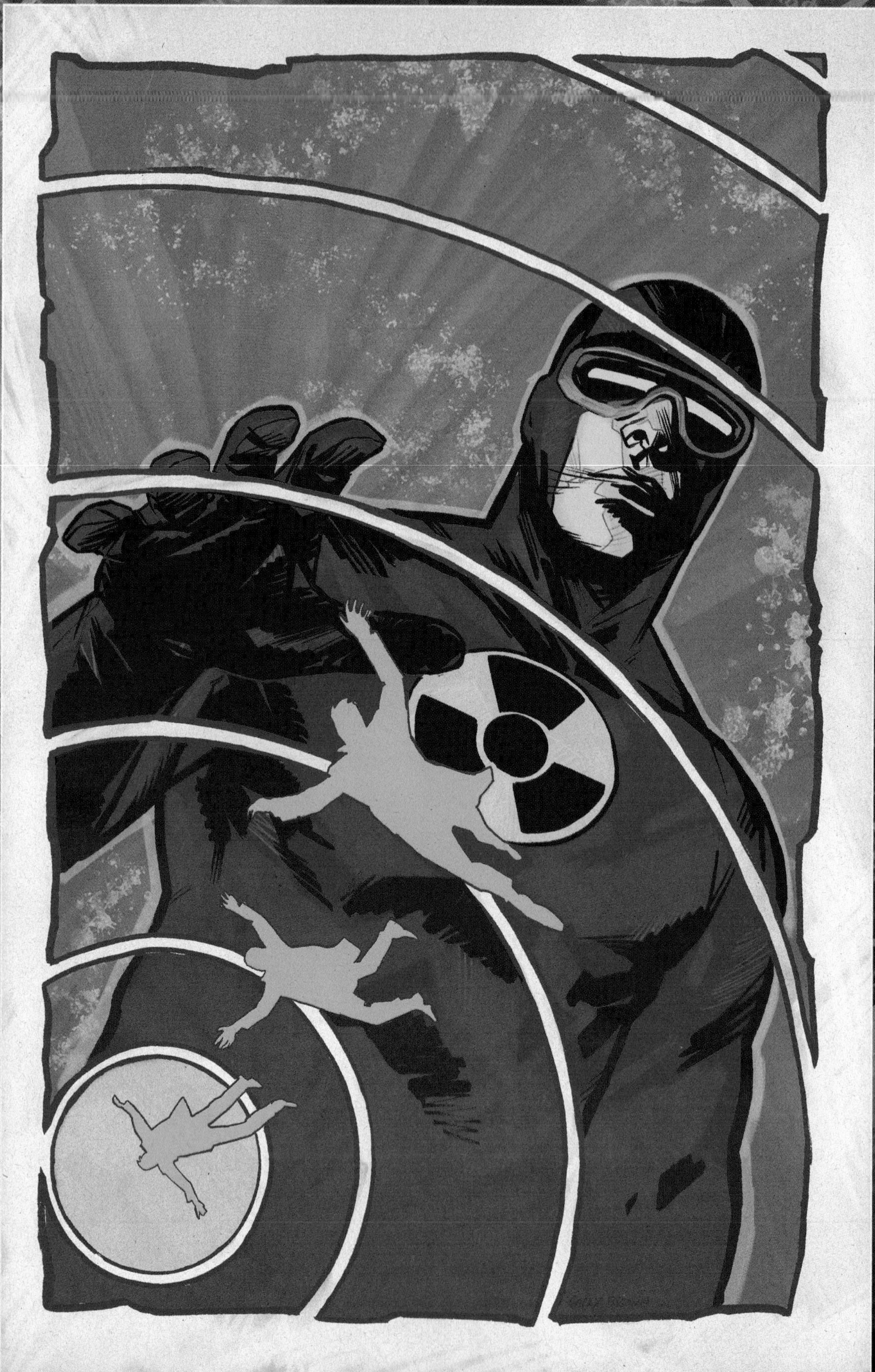

issue #1 cover by GARRY BROWN

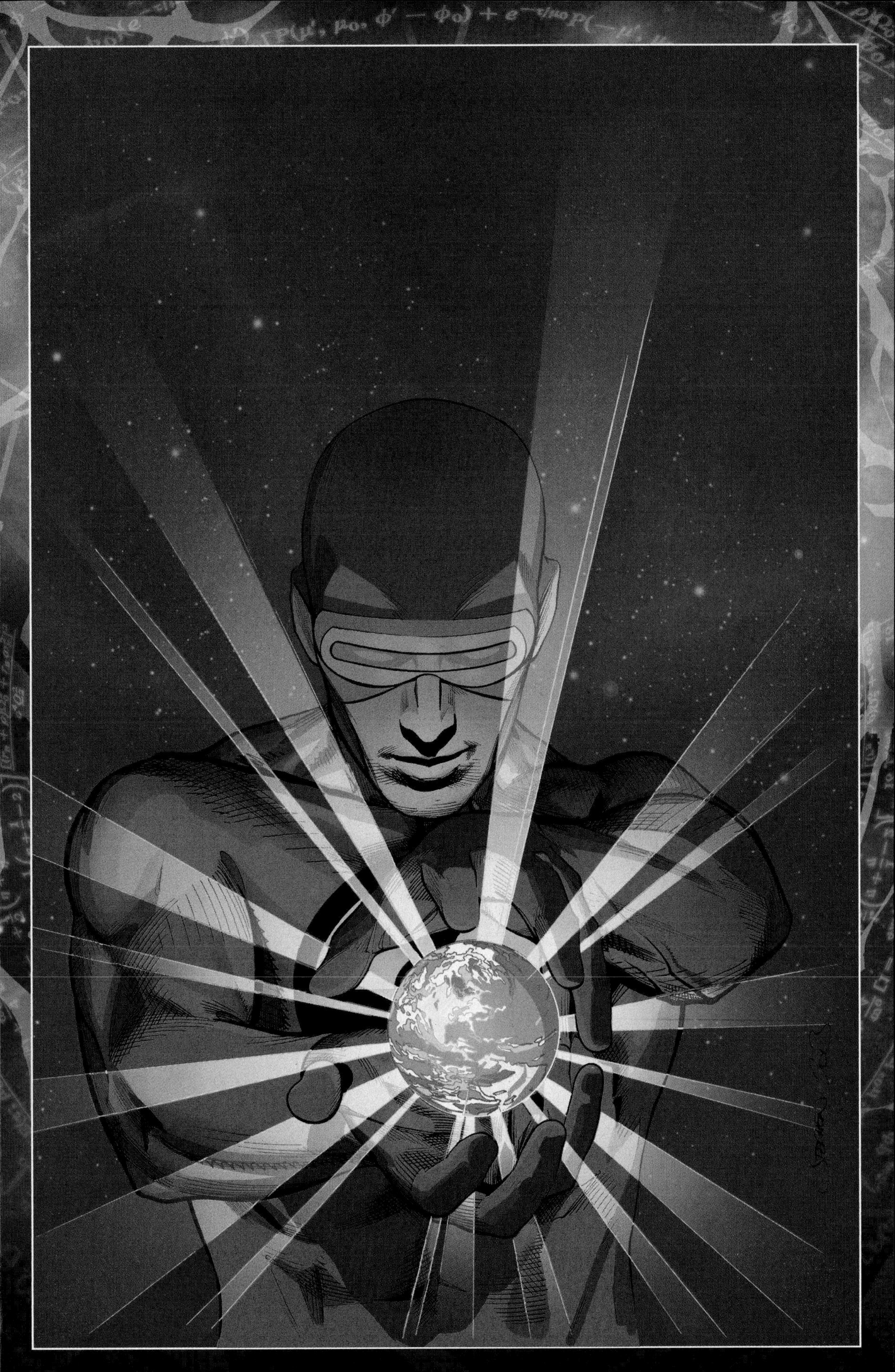

issue #1 cover by STEPHEN MOONEY

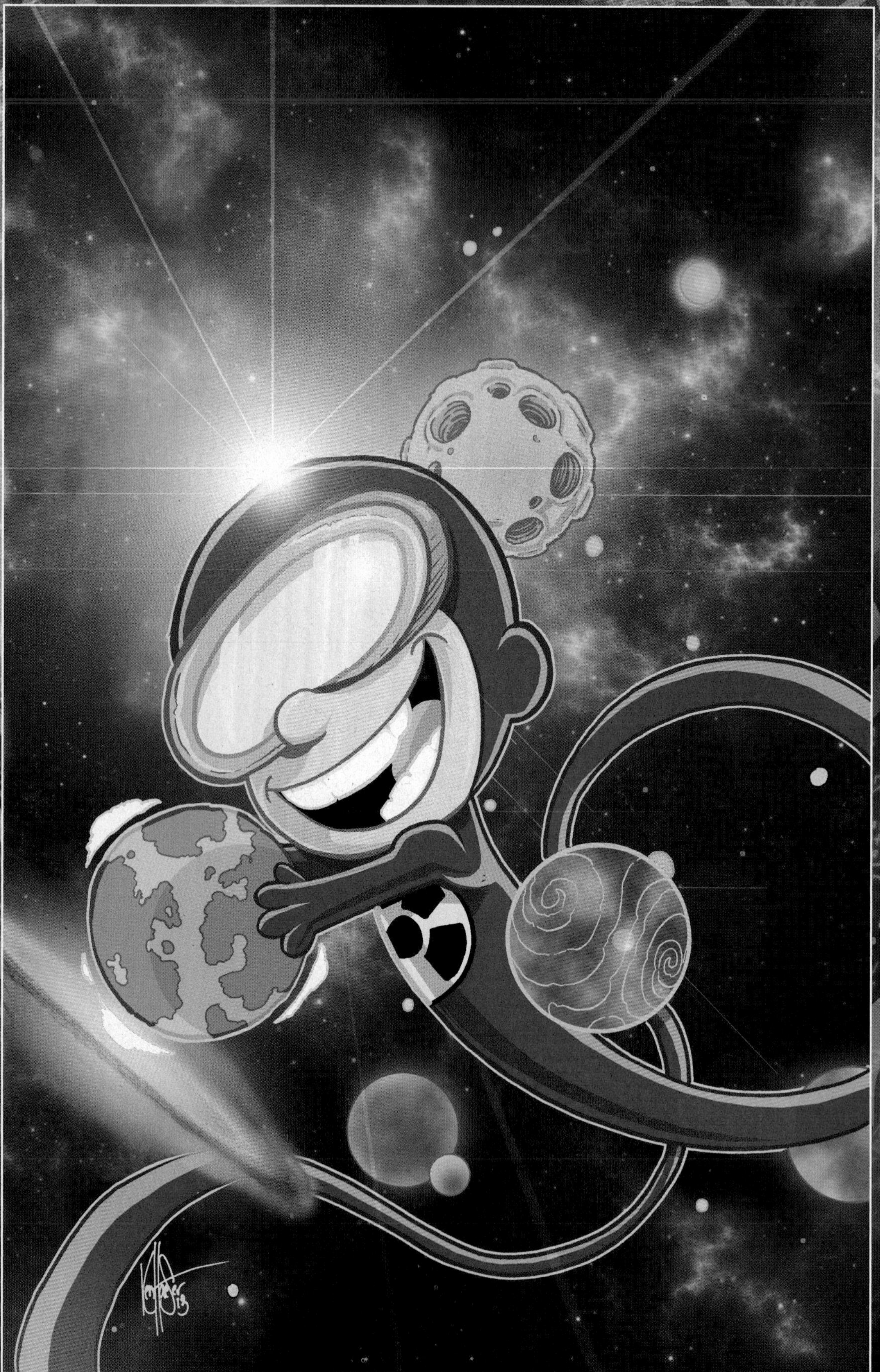

issue #1 cover by KEN HAESER
colors by BLAIR SMITH

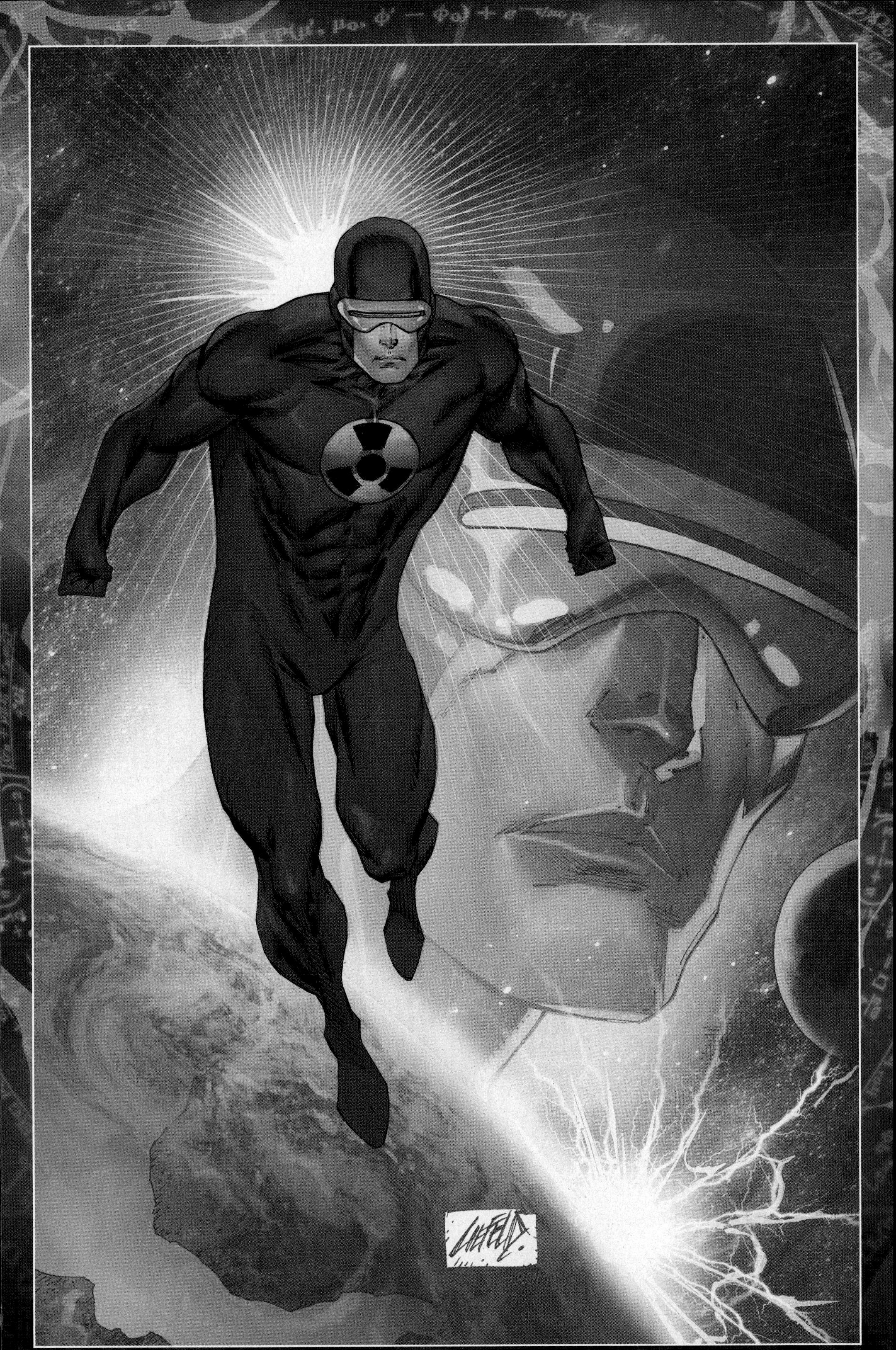

issue #1 cover by ROB LIEFELD
colors by ANDY TROY

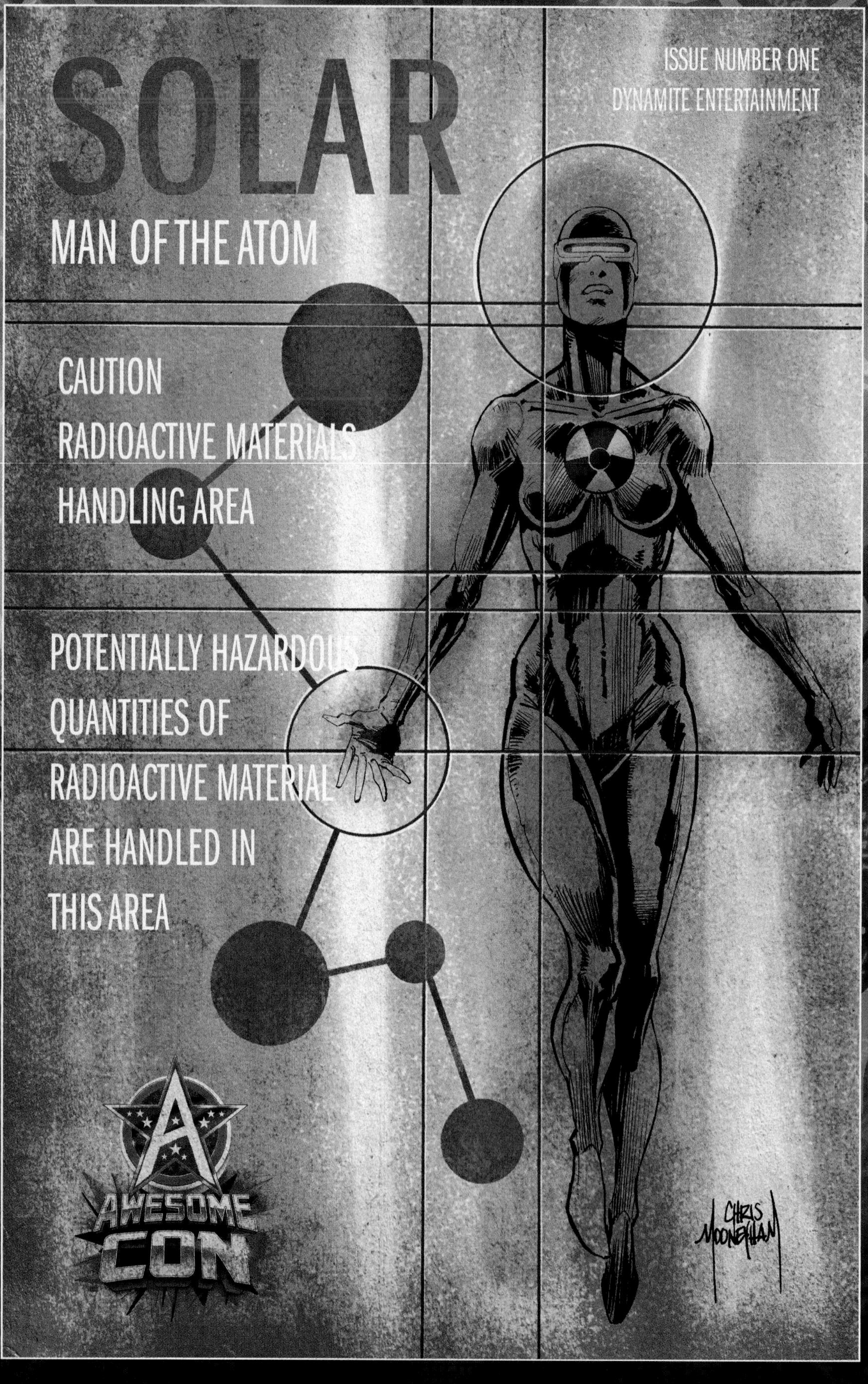
SOLAR
MAN OF THE ATOM
ISSUE NUMBER ONE
DYNAMITE ENTERTAINMENT
CAUTION
RADIOACTIVE MATERIALS
HANDLING AREA
POTENTIALLY HAZARDOUS
QUANTITIES OF
RADIOACTIVE MATERIAL
ARE HANDLED IN
THIS AREA
AWESOME CON
CHRIS MOONEYHAM

issue #1 awesomecon exclusive cover by CHRIS MOONEYHAM

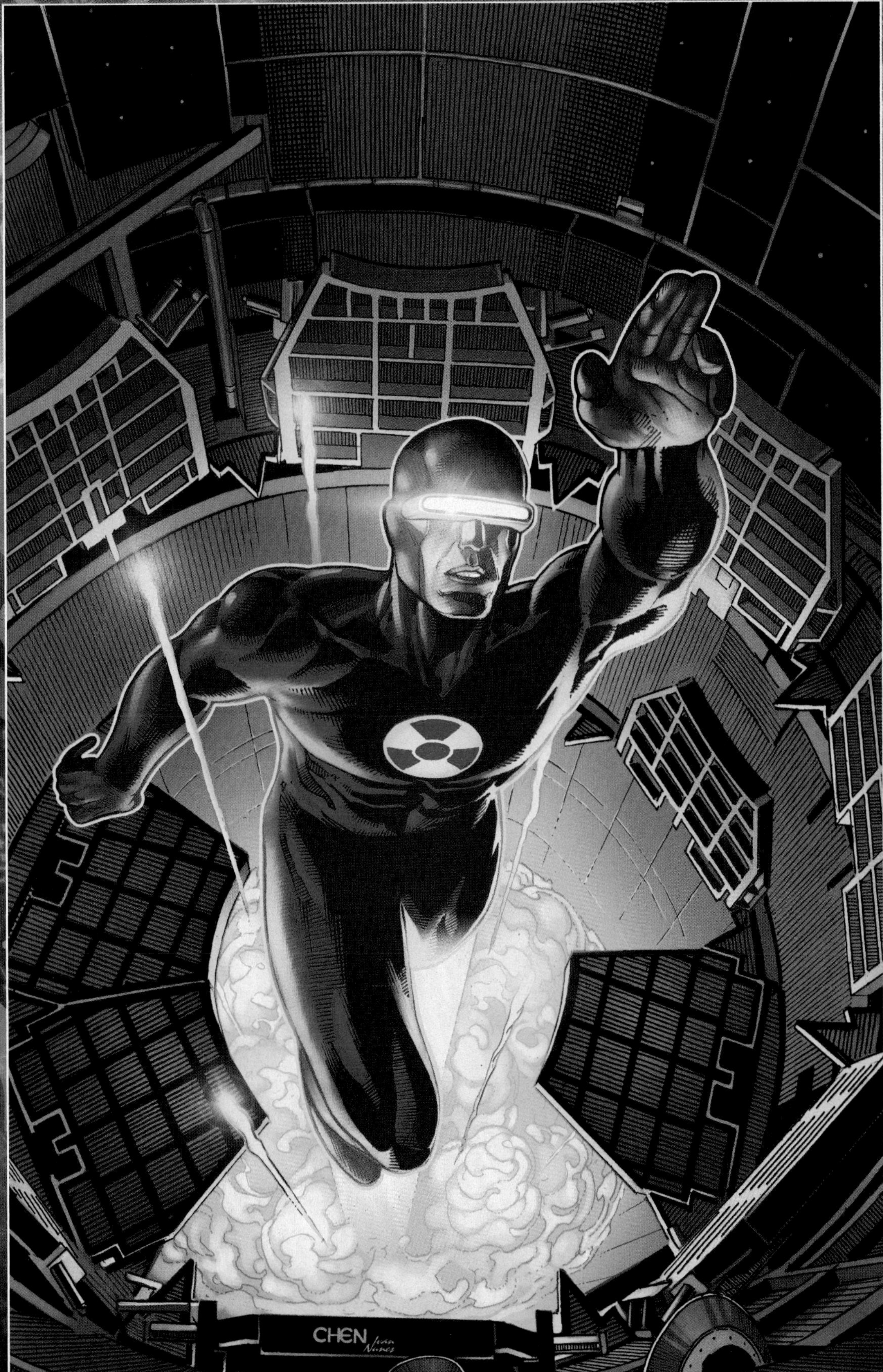
CHEN

issue #1 cards, comics, and collectibles exclusive cover by SEAN CHEN
colors by IVAN NUNES

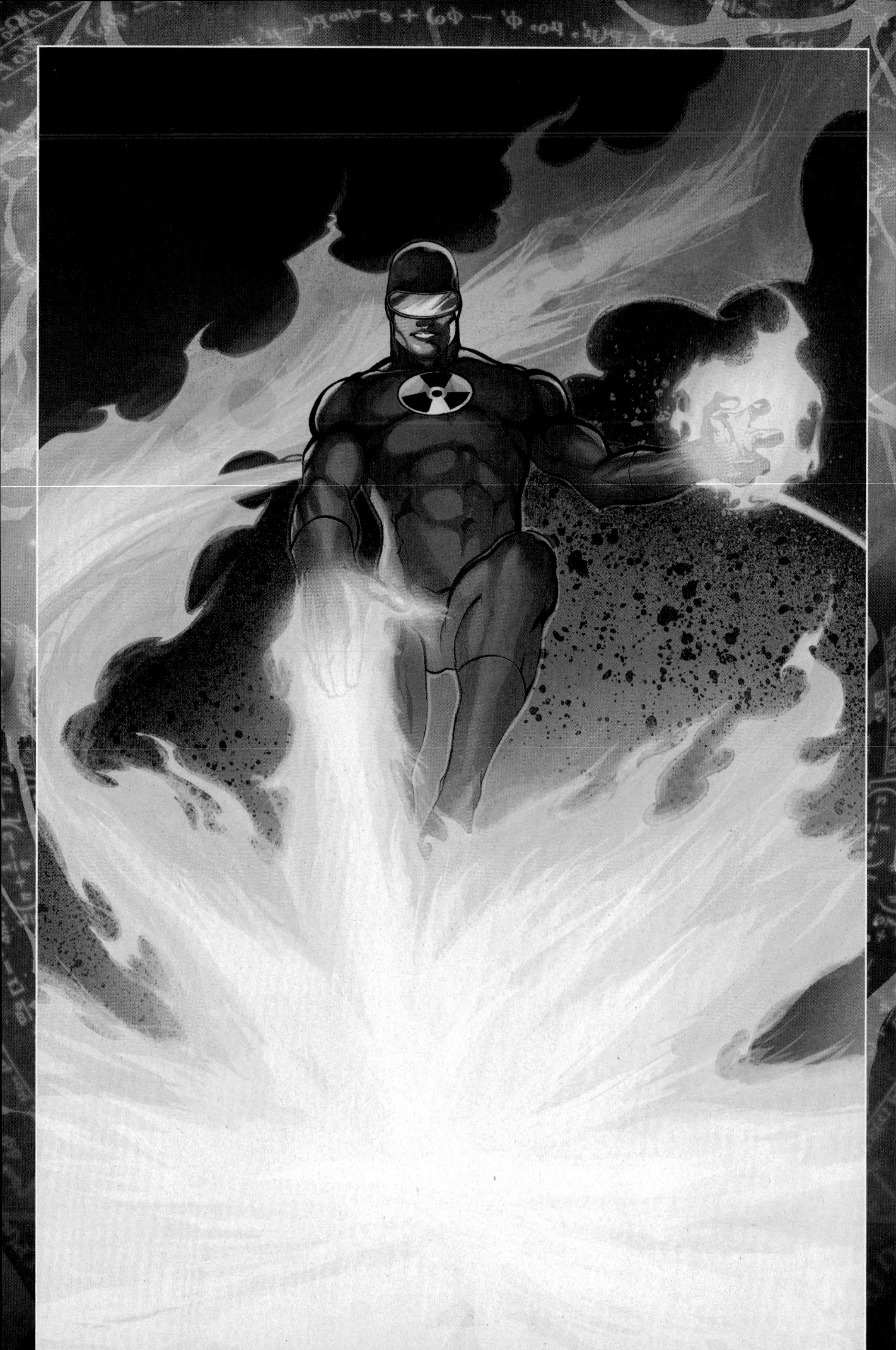

issue #1 "retailer heroic exclusive" cover by ROBERTO CASTRO
colors by ADRIANO LUCAS

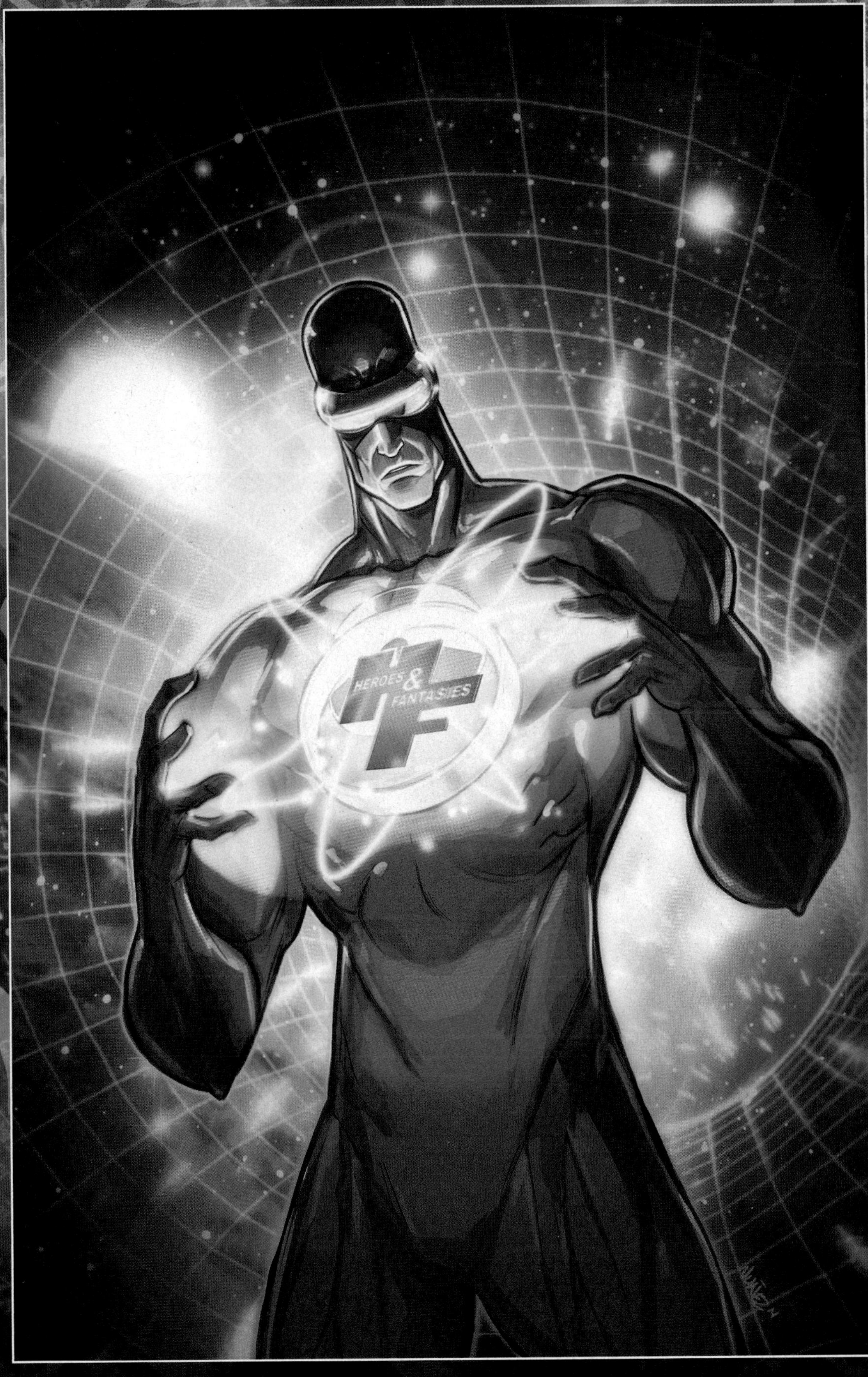
HEROES & FANTASIES

issue #1 heroes and fantasies exclusive cover by EDDIE NUNEZ

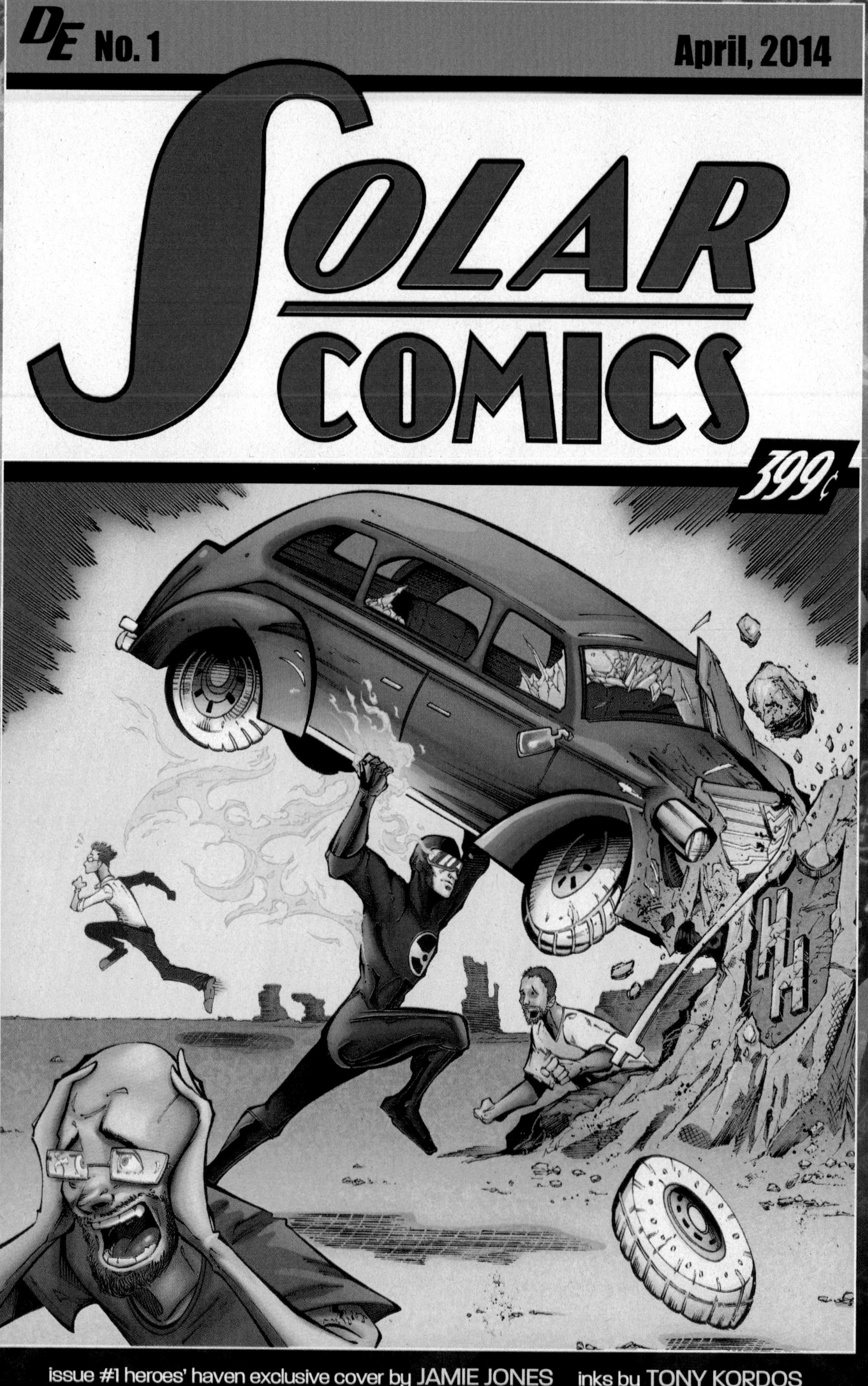
DE No. 1
April, 2014
SOLAR
COMICS
399¢

issue #1 heroes' haven exclusive cover by JAMIE JONES inks by TONY KORDOS
colors by MORRY MOLLOWELL

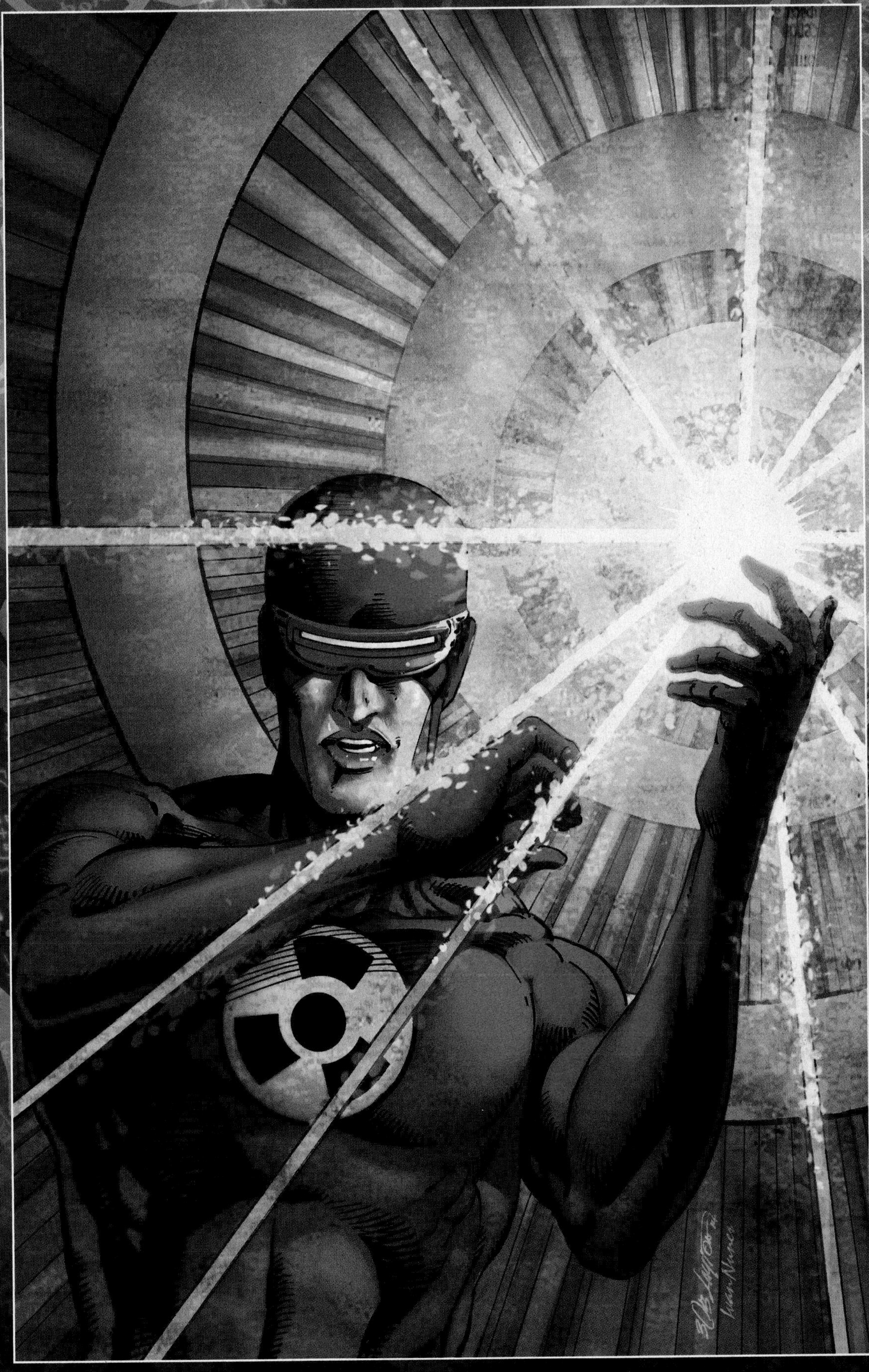

issue #1 larry's comics exclusive cover by BOB LAYTON
colors by IVAN NUNES

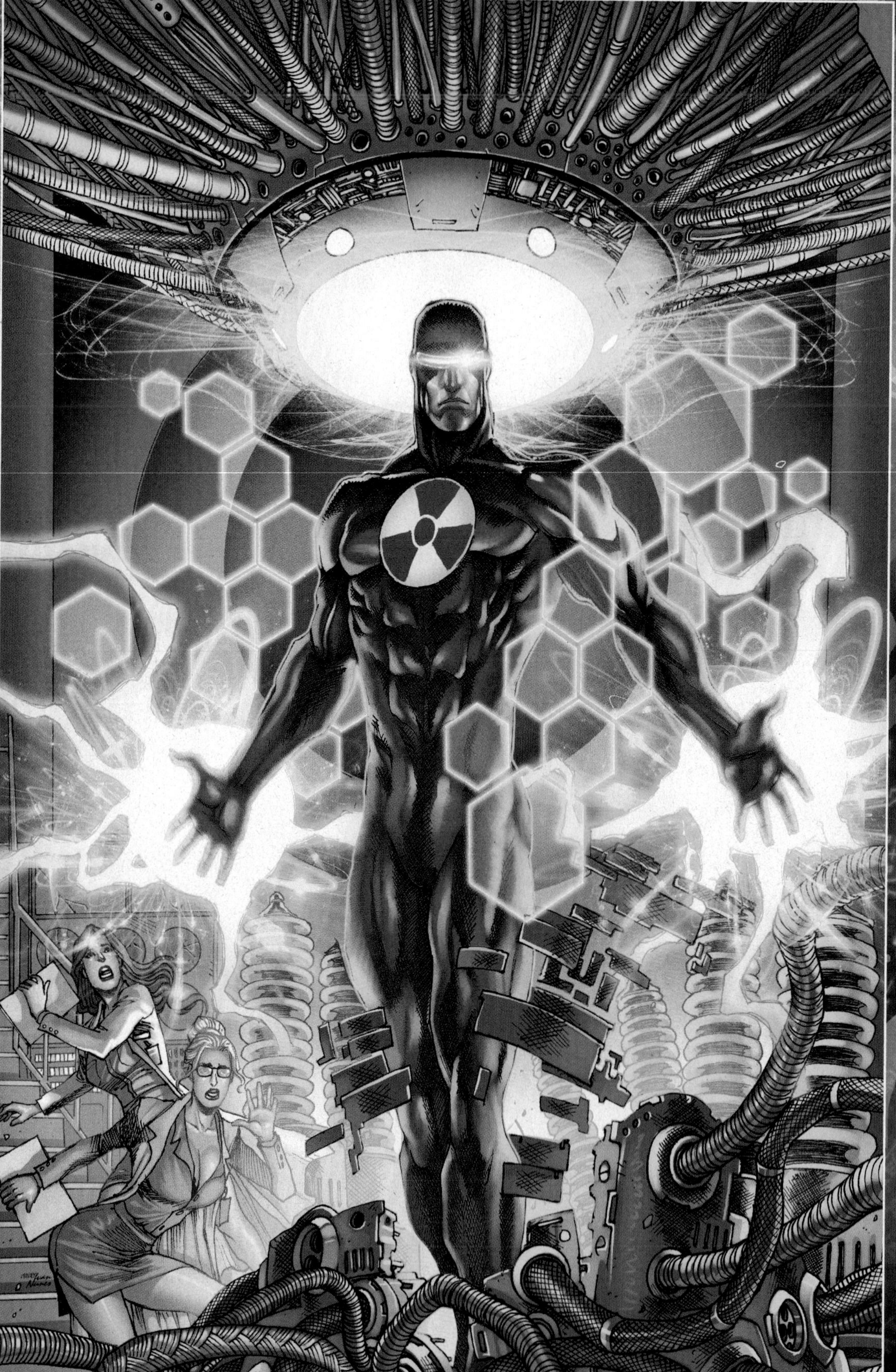

issue #1 mile high comics exclusive cover by LUI ANTONIO
colors by IVAN NUNES

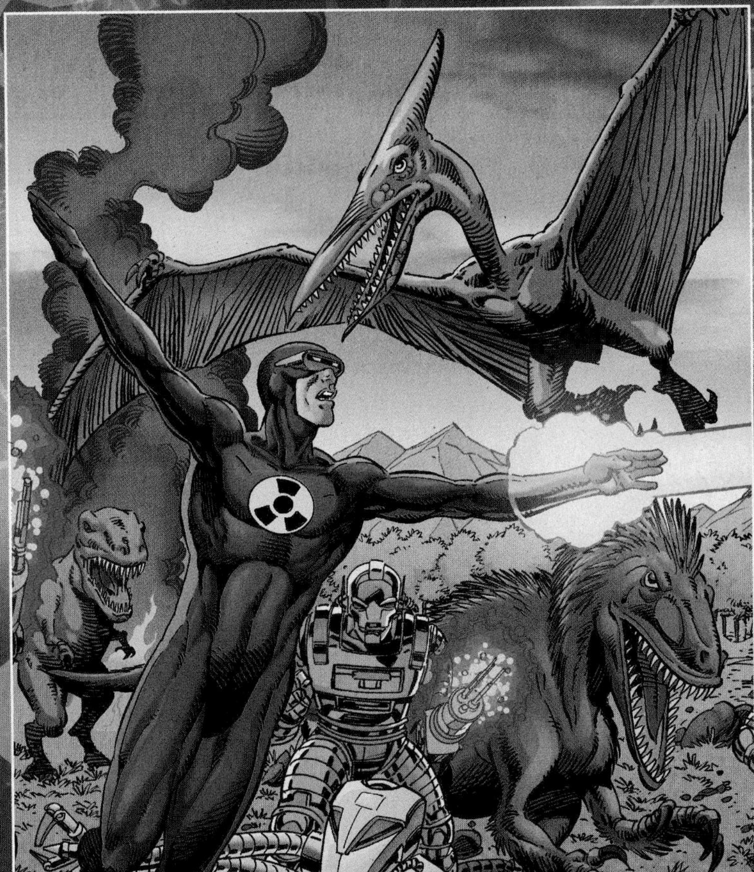

issue #1 sharps comics exclusive cover by BOB LAYTON
colors by MIKE CAVALLARO

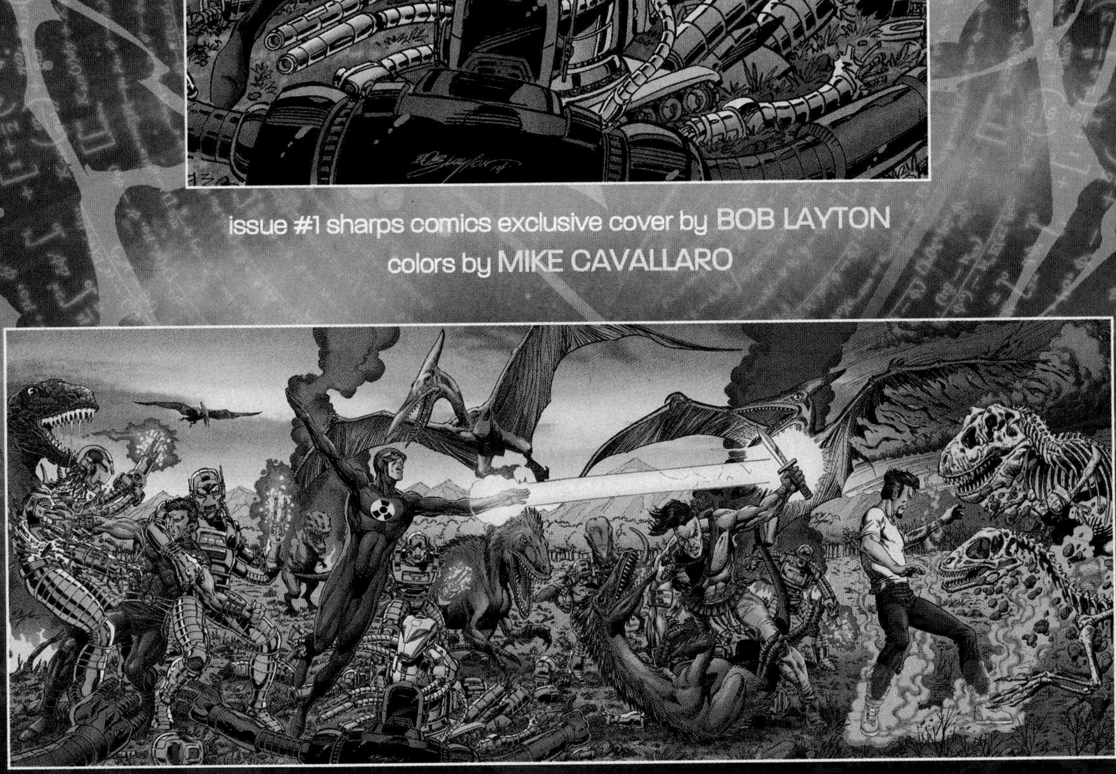

connects MAGNUS #1, TUROK #1, and DOCTOR SPEKTOR #1

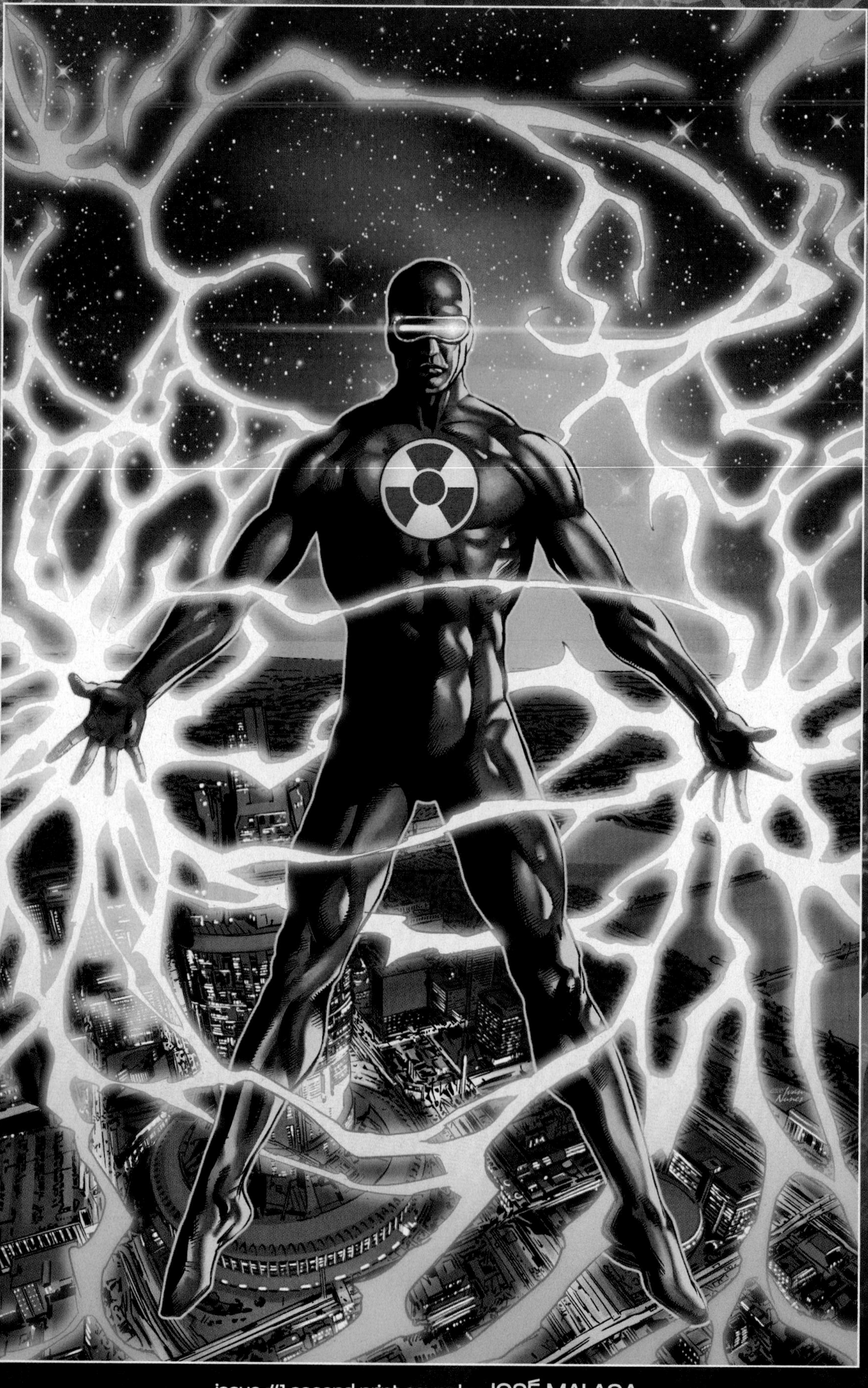

issue #1 second print cover by JOSÉ MALAGA
colors by IVAN NUNES

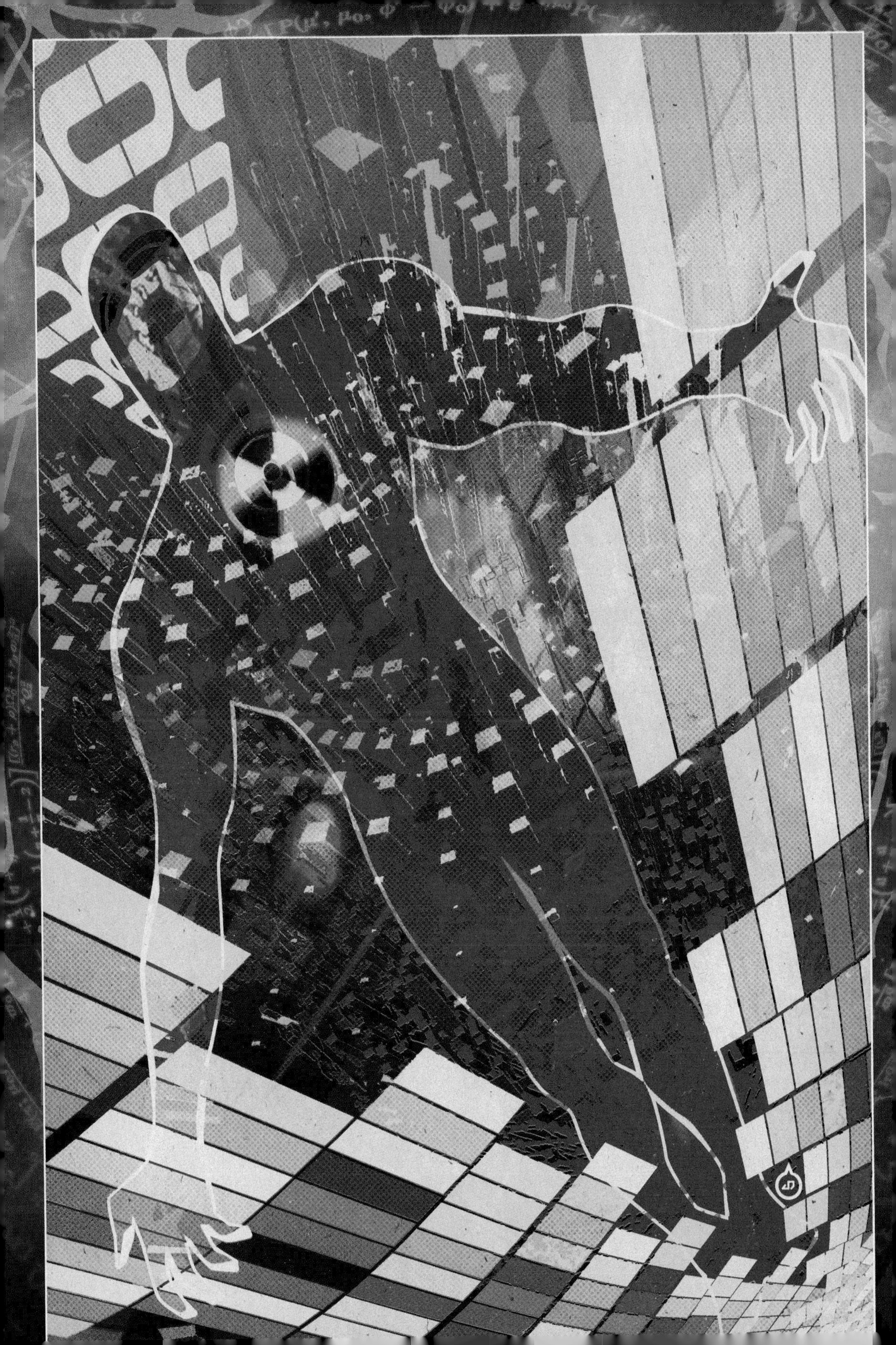

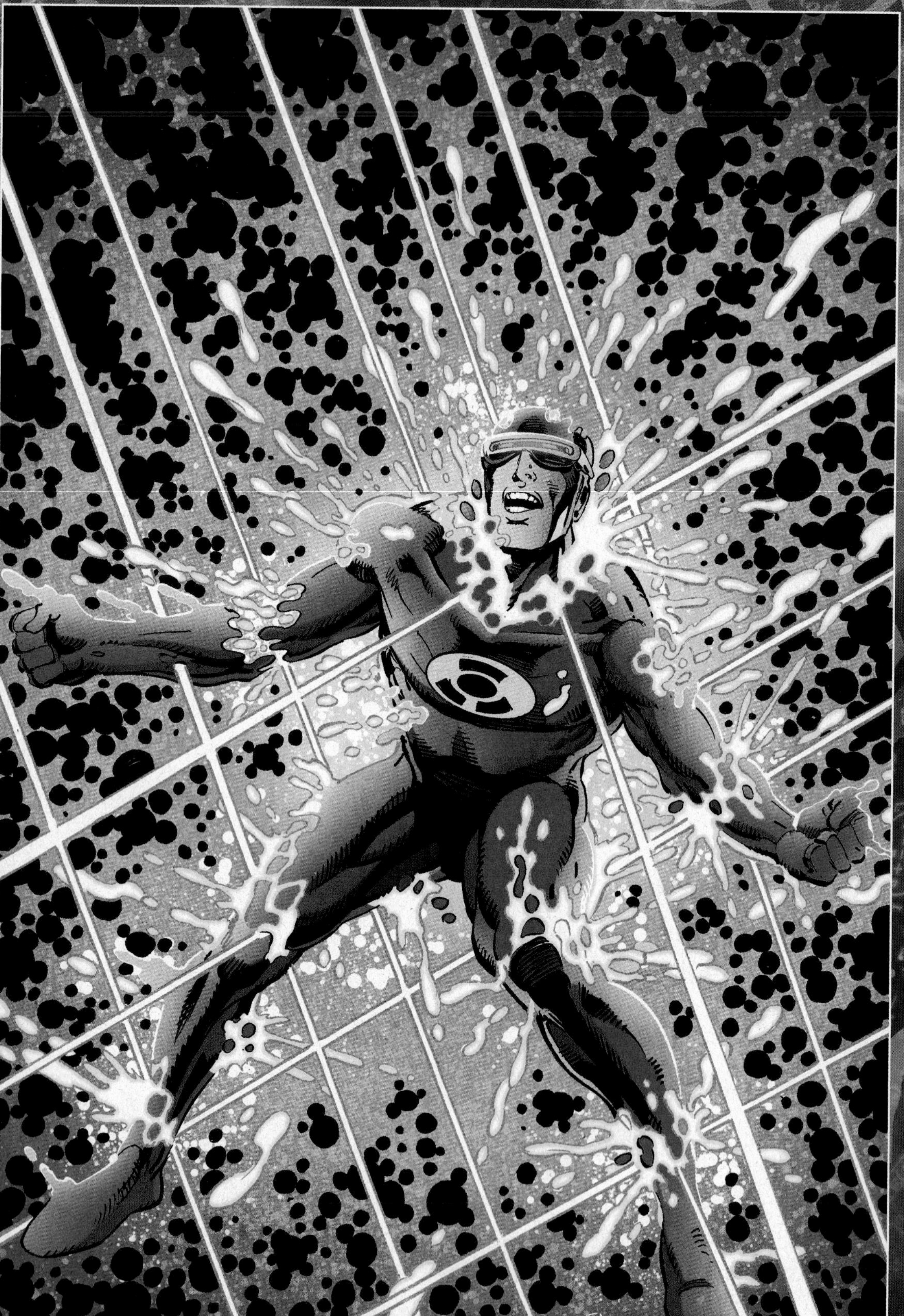

issue #2 cover by BOB LAYTON
colors by MIKE CAVALLARO

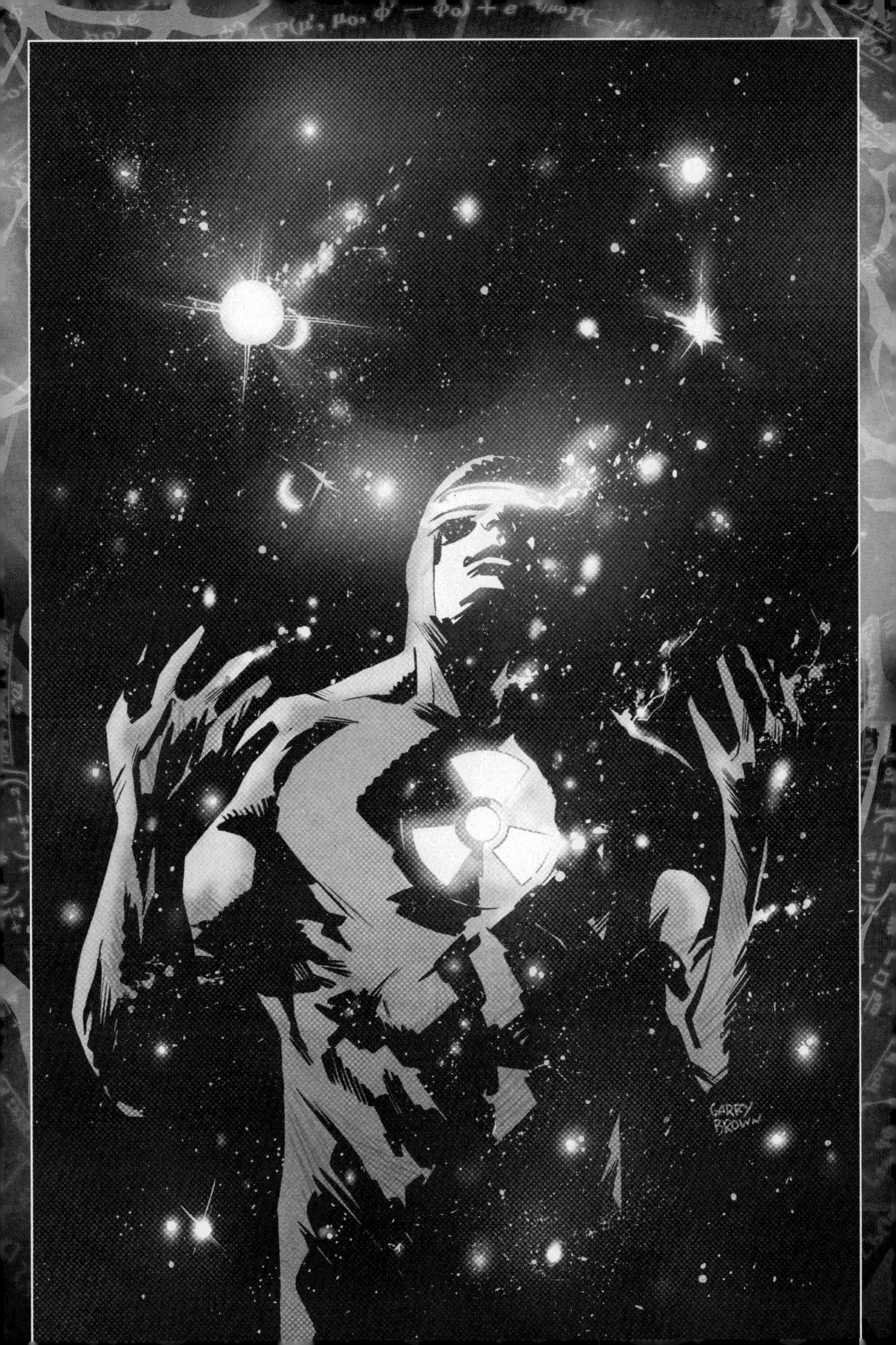
GARRY
BROWN

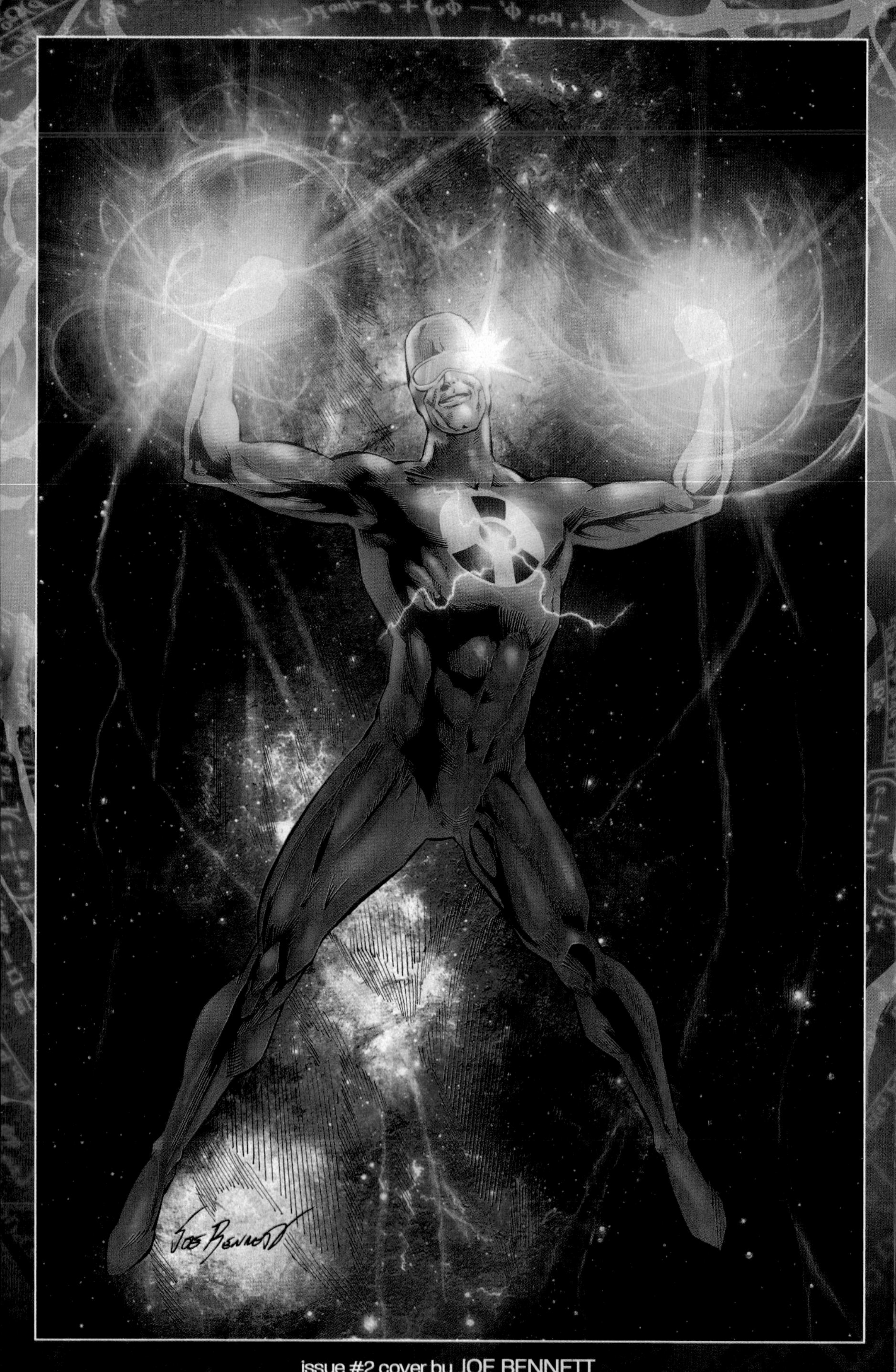

issue #2 cover by JOE BENNETT
colors by MAURÎCIO WALLACE

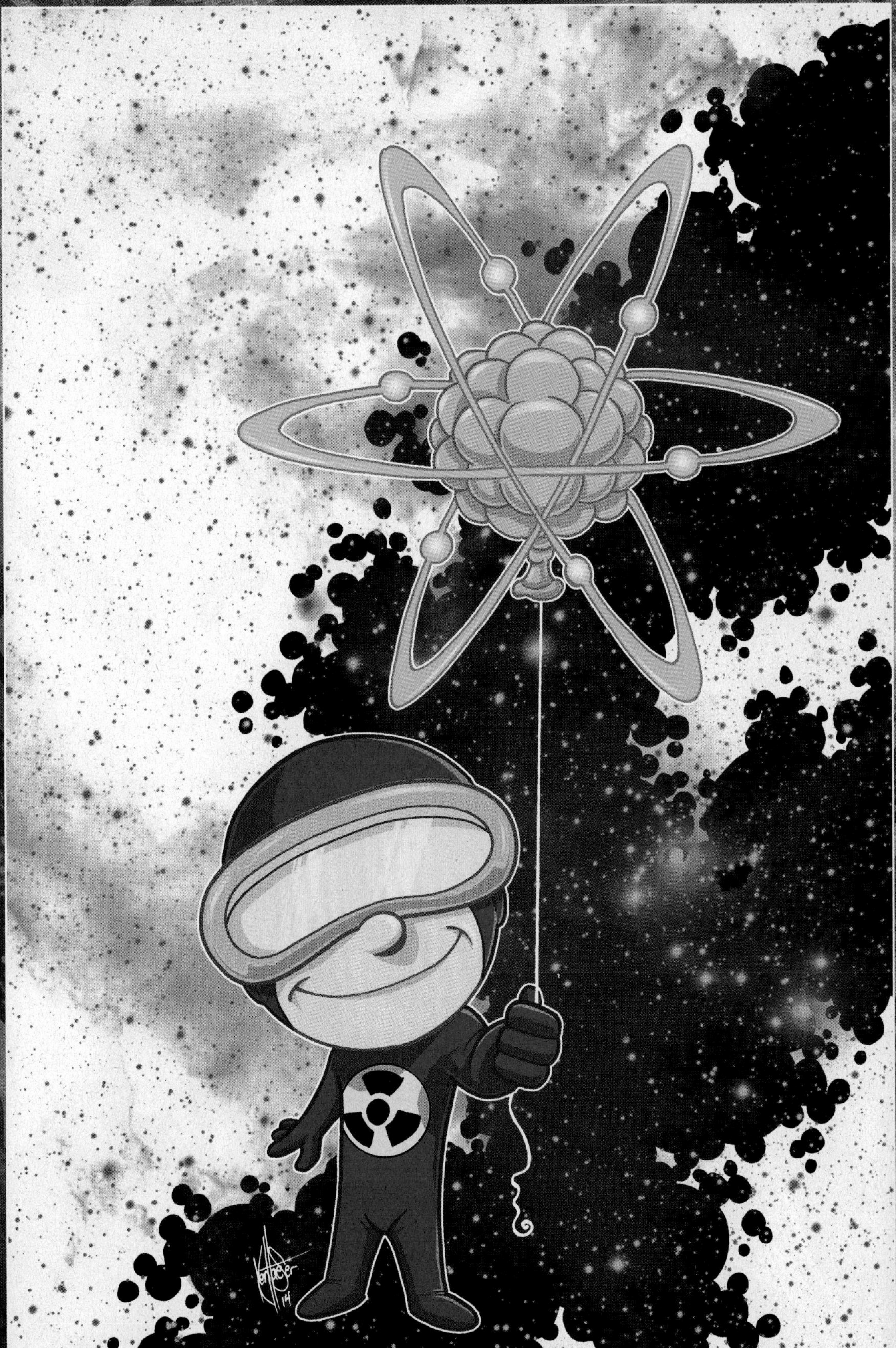

issue #2 cover by KEN HAESER

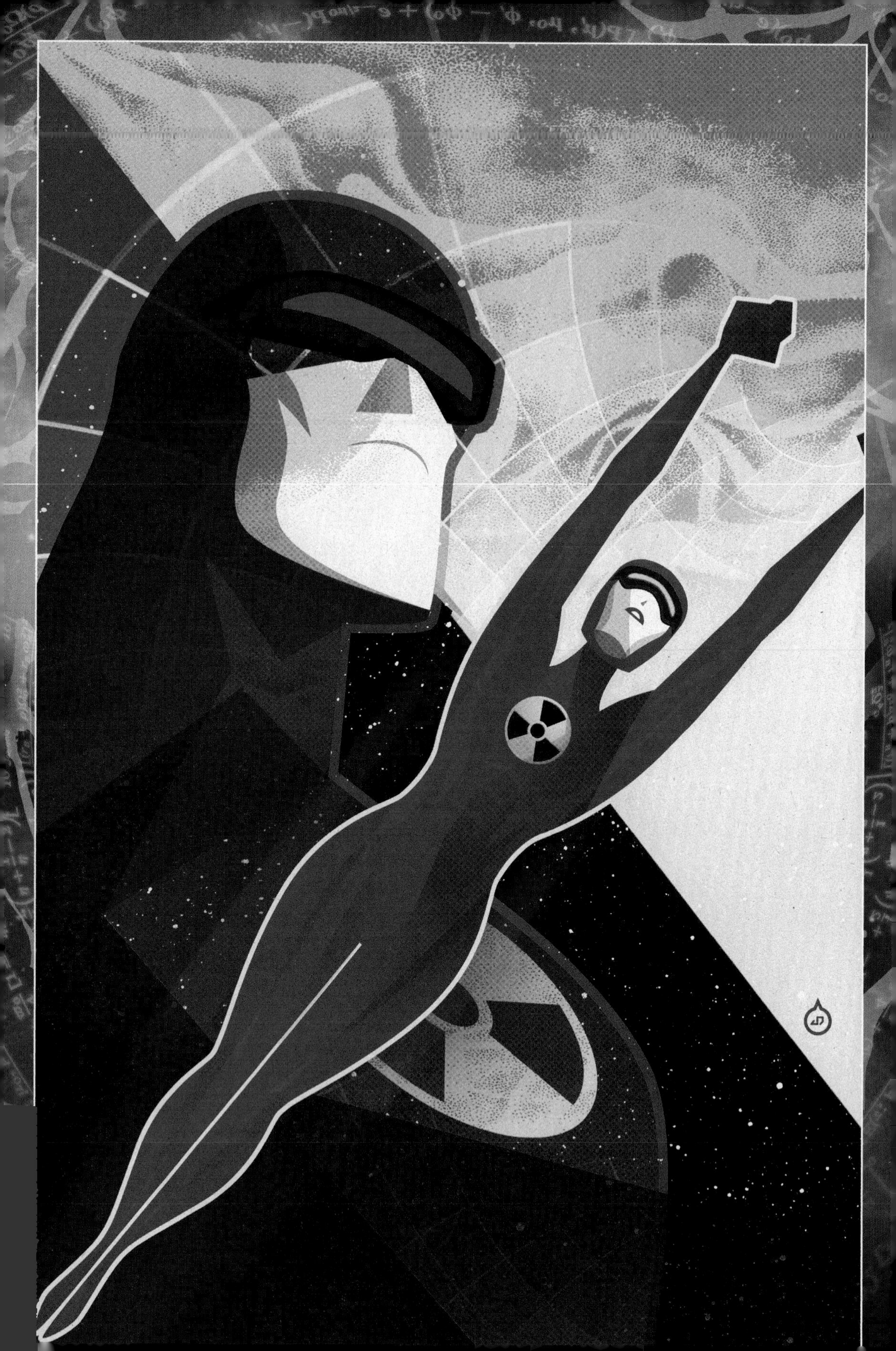

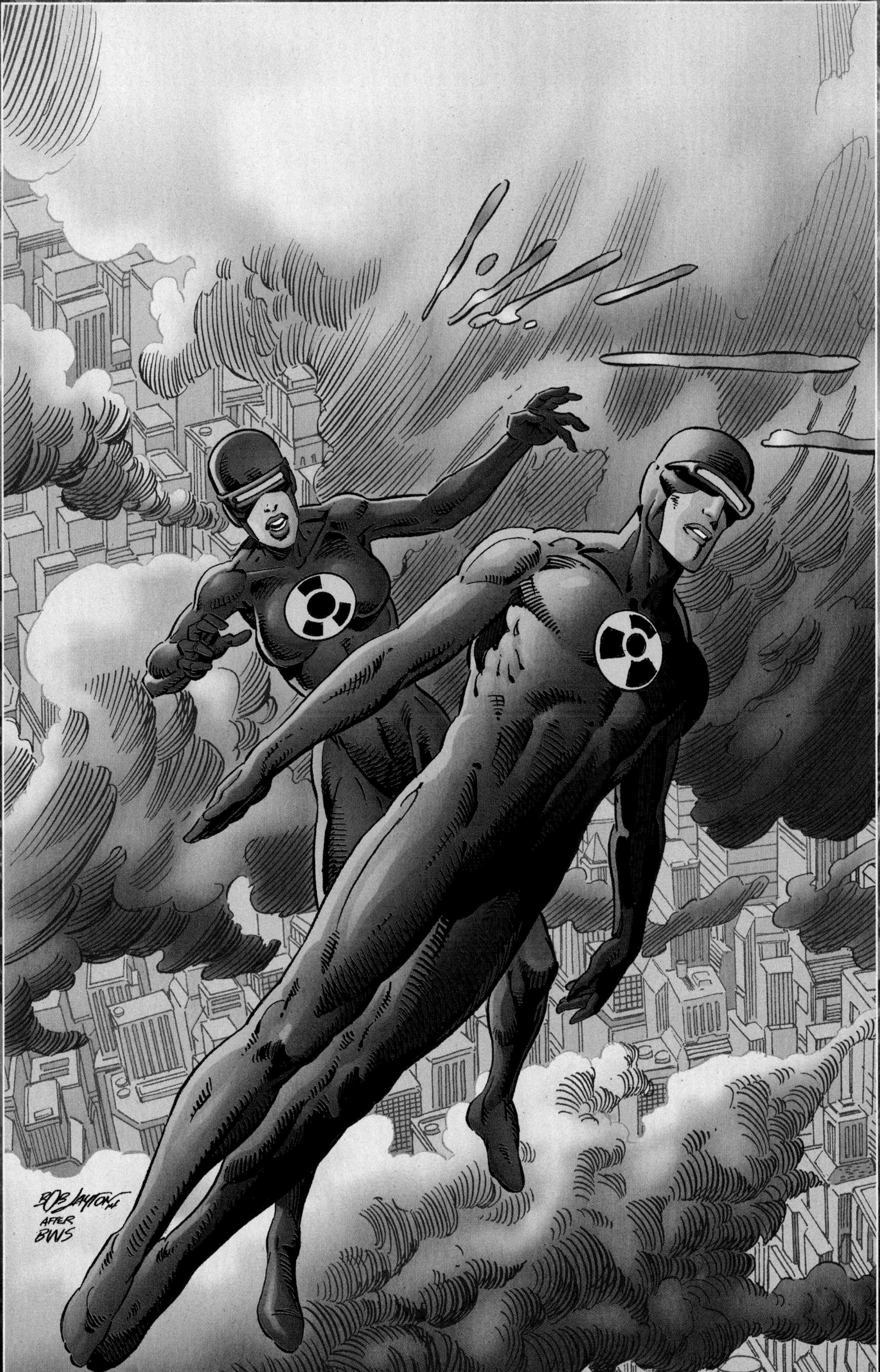
BOB LAYTON
AFTER
BWS

issue #3 cover by BOB LAYTON
colors by MIKE CAVALLARO

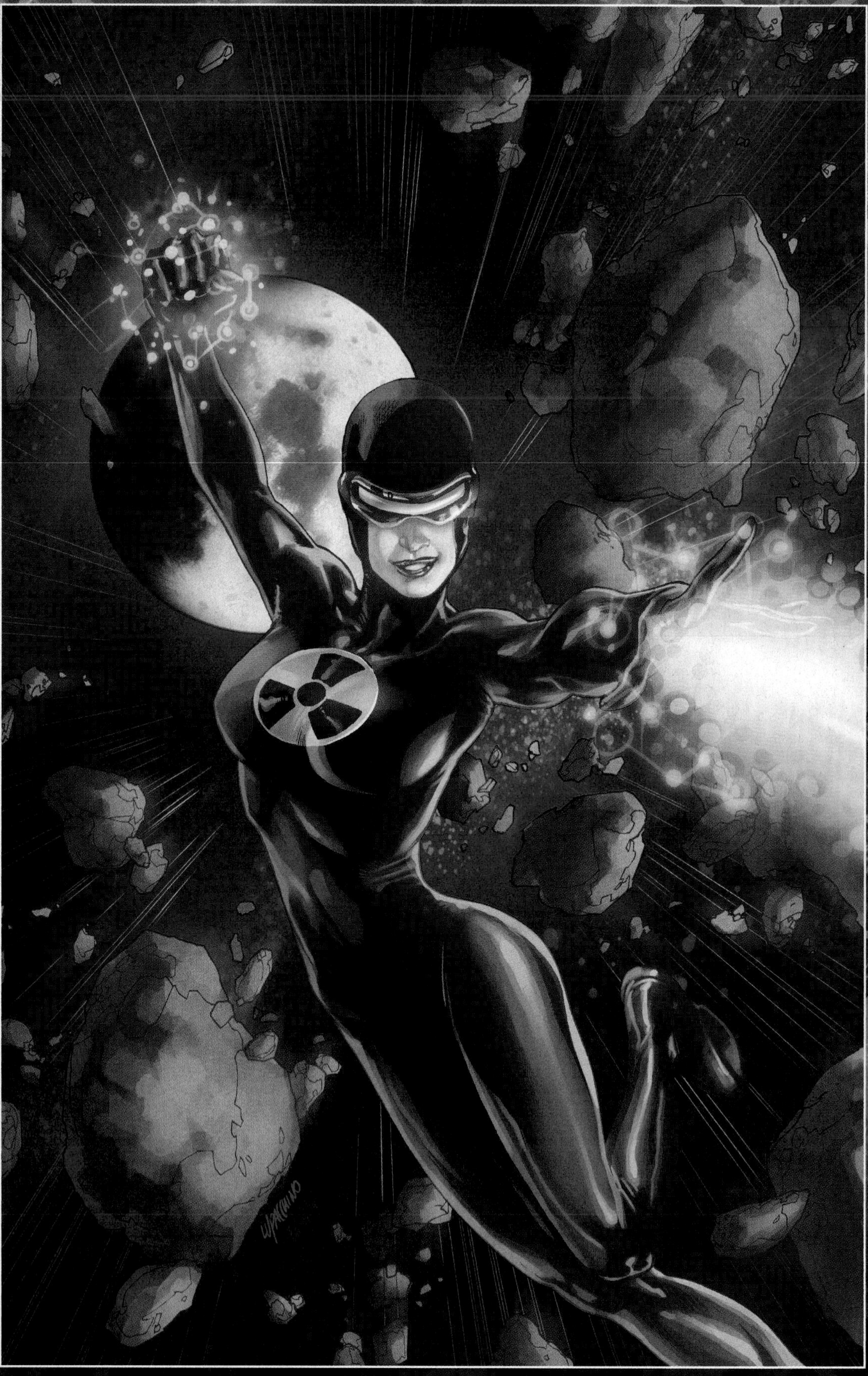

issue #3 cover by EMANUELA LUPACCHINO
colors by ELMER SANTOS

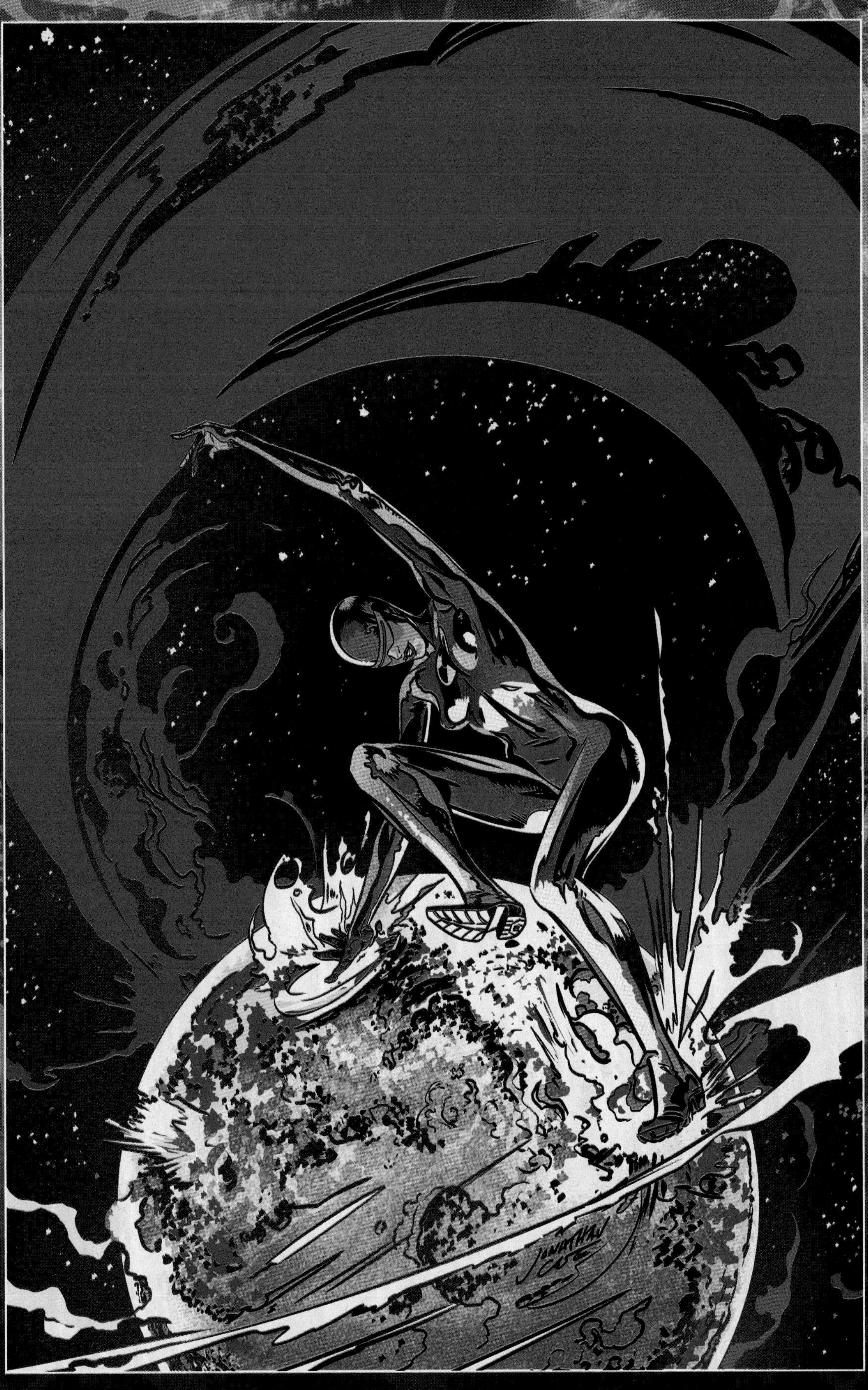
JONATHAN CASE

issue #3 cover by JONATHAN CASE

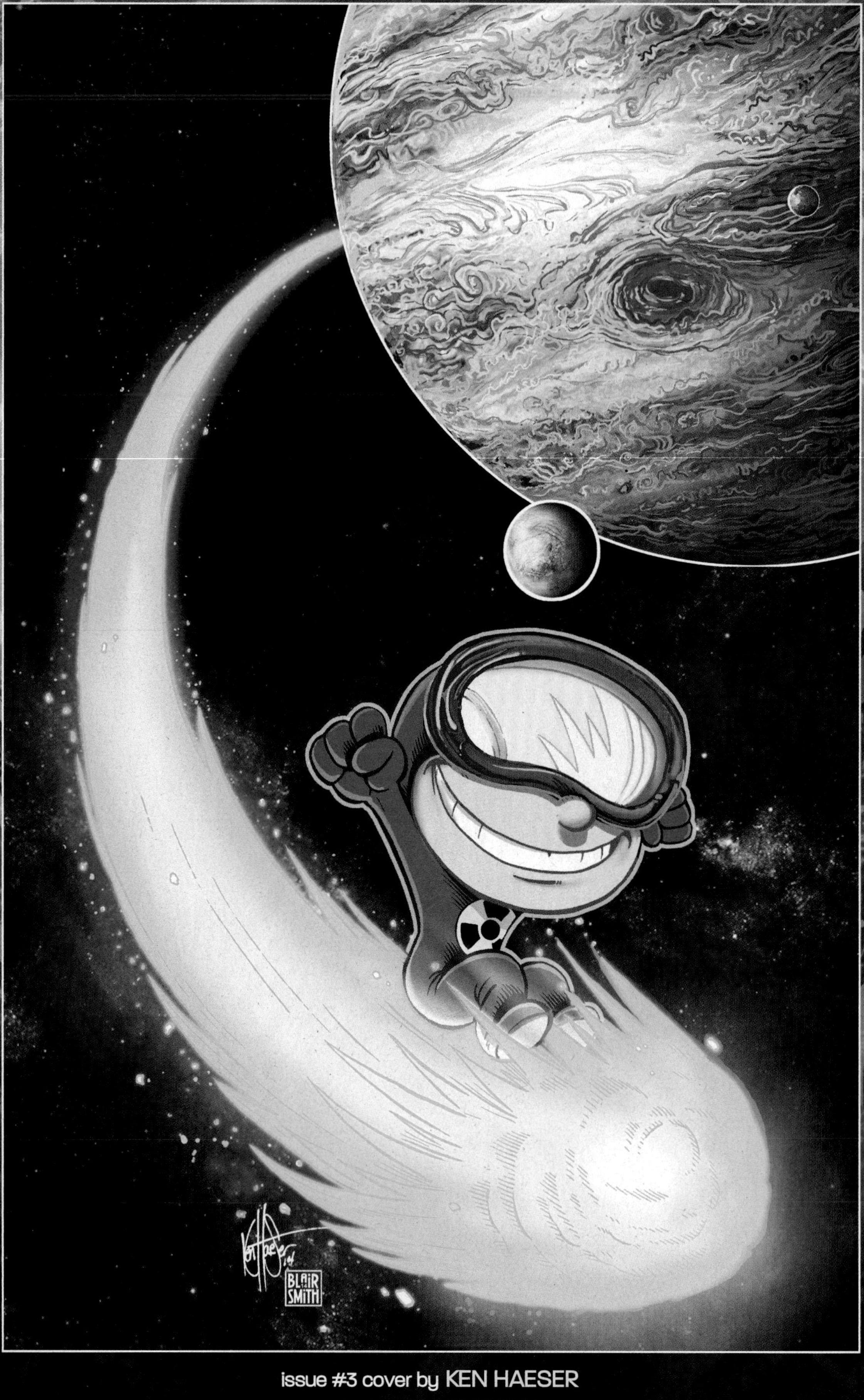
BLAIR SMITH

issue #3 cover by KEN HAESER
colors by BLAIR SMITH

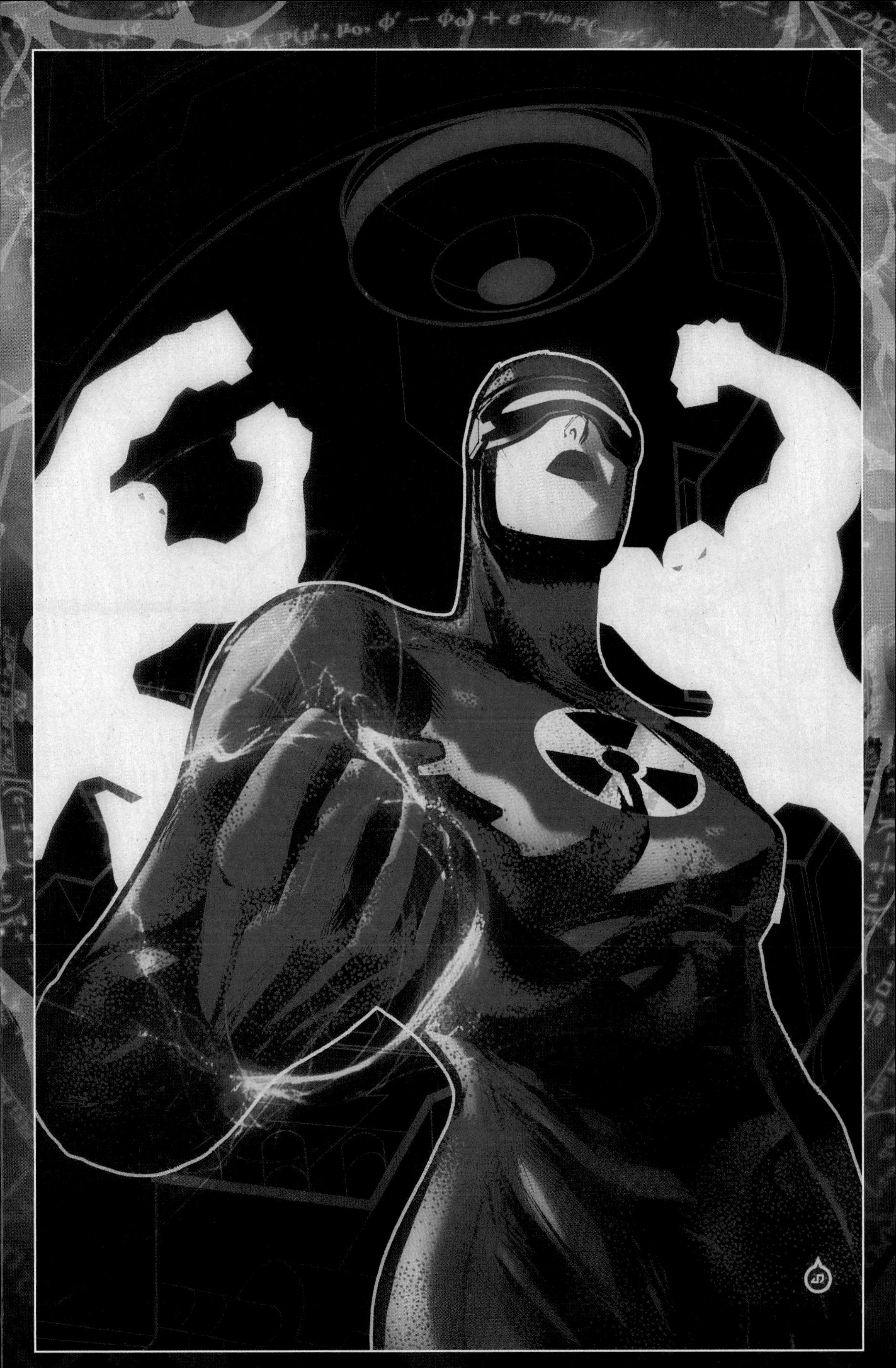

issue #4 cover by JUAN DOE

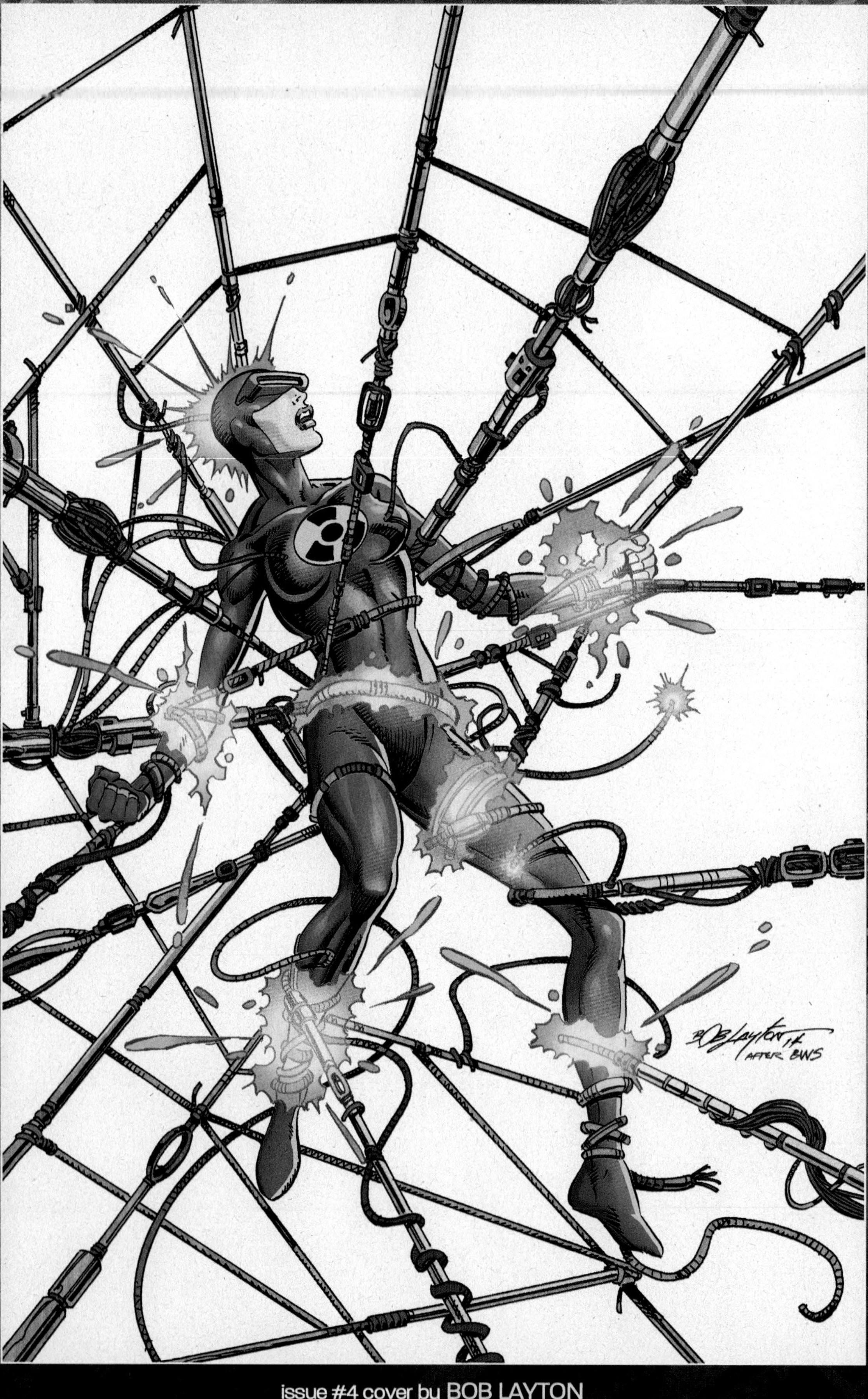
BOB LAYTON '14
AFTER BWS

issue #4 cover by BOB LAYTON
colors by MIKE CAVALLARO

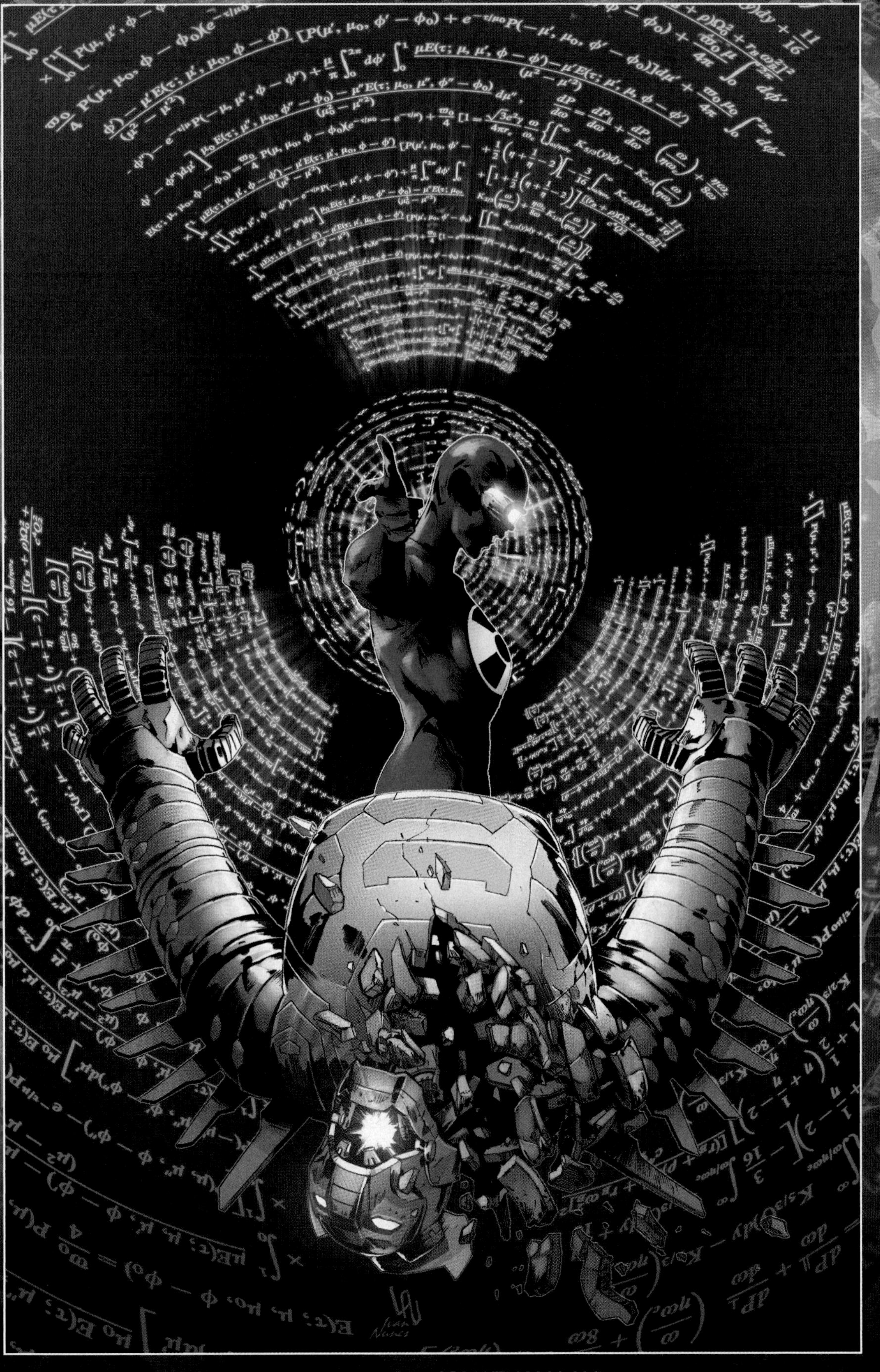

issue #4 cover by JONATHAN LAU
colors by IVAN NUNES

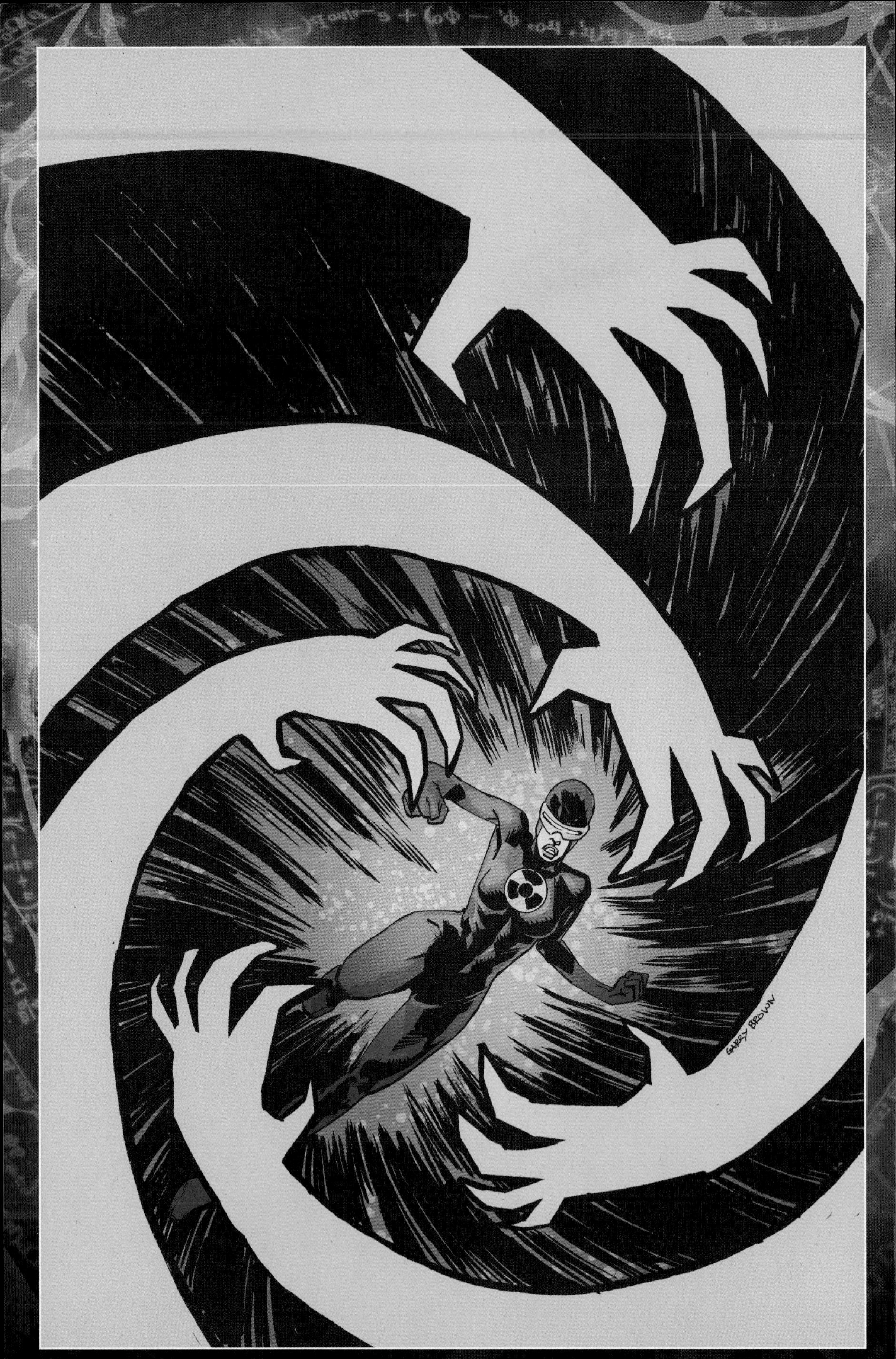
GARRY BROWN
issue #4 cover by GARRY BROWN

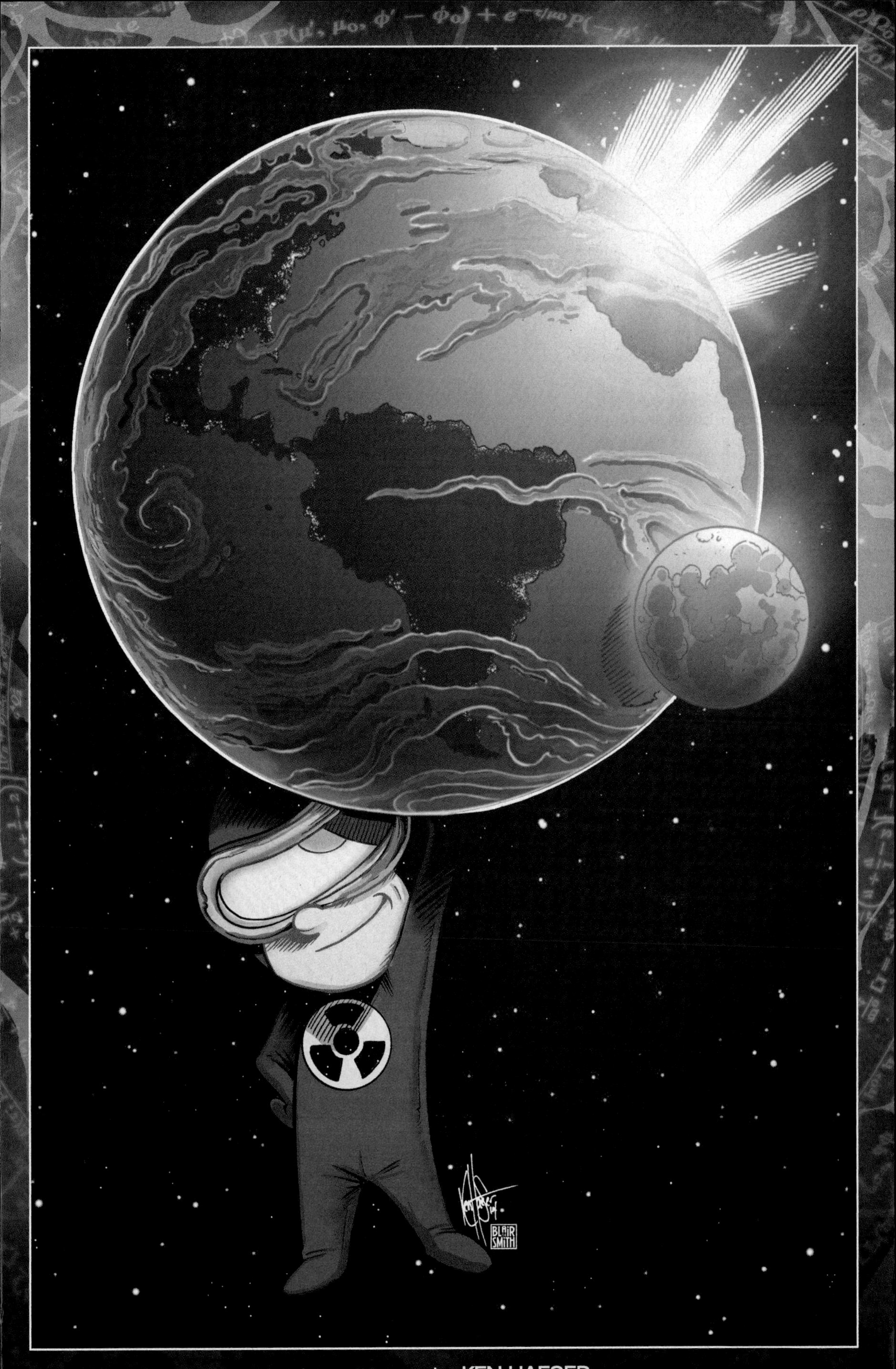
BLAIR SMITH

issue #4 cover by KEN HAESER
colors by BLAIR SMITH